Homer Simpson
Goes to
Washington

Homer Simpson Goes to Washington

American Politics through Popular Culture

Updated Edition

EDITED BY JOSEPH J. FOY

With a Foreword by Stanley K. Schultz

THE UNIVERSITY PRESS OF KENTUCKY

Copyright © 2008 by The University Press of Kentucky
Paperback edition 2010

Scholarly publisher for the Commonwealth,
serving Bellarmine University, Berea College, Centre College of Kentucky,
Eastern Kentucky University, The Filson Historical Society, Georgetown College,
Kentucky Historical Society, Kentucky State University, Morehead State
University, Murray State University, Northern Kentucky University,
Transylvania University, University of Kentucky, University of Louisville,
and Western Kentucky University.
All rights reserved.

Editorial and Sales Offices: The University Press of Kentucky
663 South Limestone Street, Lexington, Kentucky 40508–4008
www.kentuckypress.com

14 13 12 11 10   5 4 3 2

The Library of Congress has cataloged the hardcover edition as follows:

Homer Simpson goes to Washington : American politics through popular
    culture / edited by Joseph J. Foy ; with a foreword by Stanley K. Schultz.
        p. cm.
    Includes bibliographical references and index.
    ISBN 978-0-8131-2512-1 (hardcover : alk. paper)
    1. United States—Politics and government—Miscellanea. I. Foy, Joseph J.
    JK31.H85 2008
    320.973—dc22   2008016854
    ISBN 978-0-8131-9254-3 (pbk. : alk. paper)

This book is printed on acid-free recycled paper meeting
the requirements of the American National Standard
for Permanence in Paper for Printed Library Materials.
♾ ❀

Manufactured in the United States of America.

Member of the Association of
American University Presses

CONTENTS

Part 3. Lights, Camera, Politics: Contemporary Issues in American Government

FOREWORD

Let's not begin by debating the relevance of various popular culture materials to our understanding of theory and practices in the supposedly democratic arena of American politics. Let's also refuse to dicker over the merits of "high culture" (enduring classics in art, architecture, literature, poetry, and music in both Western and non-Western traditions) versus "low culture" (the entertainment mediums of the masses, both past and present). Let's not become proverbial dogs chasing our own tails with "logic" such as: *Shakespeare and opera were entertainment vehicles for the common folks until they became, in more modern times, the cultural preserves of elitist snobs.* We need not follow these pathways. The authors of this book's essays present thorough disquisitions about the seemingly endless debates, dickering, and tail chasings among academics and other self-proclaimed cultural gurus over such issues.

Instead, let's agree, as an even cursory review of the nation's past reveals, that in the American experience at least, political practices, institution building, and reform campaigns have stood at the core of, have been shaped by, and in turn have reshaped our popular cultural expressions. Let's concur that, more often than not, the mediums of popular culture at given moments in the past have both reflected current political practices and redirected those practices for present and following generations.

No less an intellectual gadfly than Ralph Waldo Emerson once landed on the assertion that "the education of the general mind never stops. . . . What the tender poetic youth dreams, and prays, and paints today . . . shall presently be the resolutions of public bodies; then shall be carried as grievance and bill of rights through conflict and war, and then shall be triumphant law and establishment for a hundred years, until it gives place in turn to new prayers and pictures." Emerson concluded that "the history of the State sketches in coarse outline the progress of thought, and follows at a distance the delicacy of culture and of aspiration." Although Emerson always was ready to pontificate on any subject and therefore uttered more than his rightful share of nonsense, this observation strikes me as a particularly apt analysis of the inevitable interplay between popular culture and politics in America. Americans are a people who, from their national birth pangs onward, have told themselves as well as the rest of the world that they have built a classless society based on human equality, freedom of boundless opportunity, and reward for individual initiative. How could such a people's politics and political institutions ever stand separate from their everyday cultural activities and aspirations?

Emerson hardly occupied a solitary position in showing the interplay of politics and popular culture in the American past. In colonial New England towns, for example, where citizens lacked other forms of public engagement and entertainment, church sermons served as the social glue that held communities together. They functioned as instruction, edification, and drama and were nearly the sole form of public cultural discourse. Law required everyone's attendance at the two sermons on the Sabbath, at the customary Thursday lecture-sermon, and at the many days appointed for fasting and thanksgiving throughout the year, while the election-day sermon was the vehicle that drove political events and public participation in politics prior to the American Revolution. What happened in religion happened elsewhere in society. If we gather together the usual crop of historical personages (*usual* to American historians, at least) and review their observations, we find that Emerson was in the mainstream.

In his classic (always quoted by historians of the American colonies) *Letters from an American Farmer* (1782), French émigré J. Hector St. John Crèvecoeur answered his own question of "What is an American?" by emphasizing the fluid intermingling of cultural practices and attitudes with political activity:

> As citizens it is easy to imagine, that they will carefully read the newspapers, enter into every political disquisition, freely blame or censure governors and others. As farmers they will be careful and anxious to get as much as they can, because what they get is their own. As northern men they will love the cheerful cup. As Christians, religion curbs them not in their opinions; the general indulgence leaves every one to think for themselves in spiritual matters; the laws inspect our actions, our thoughts are left to God. Industry, good living, selfishness, litigiousness, country politics, the pride of freemen, religious indifference, are their characteristics.

Another Frenchman, Alexis de Tocqueville, published in 1835 the comprehensive study *Democracy in America.* For most historians, the work remains one of the two definitive explications of the American social order by an outside observer. For Tocqueville, whatever Europeans meant by "culture" was, in the United States, by definition a commonly shared set of attitudes, beliefs, and practices, in short, a *popular* culture: "A middling standard has been established in America for all human knowledge. . . . As a result one finds a vast multitude of people with roughly the same ideas about religion, history, science, political economy, legislation, and government." These social commonalities underlay Americans' faith in the sovereignty of *the people* and inevitably shaped the nation's politics. "It is easy," Tocqueville affirmed, "to deduce the political consequences of such a social state. By no possibility could equality ultimately fail to penetrate into the sphere of politics as everywhere else."

The other literary crutch on which many historians lean to explain the so-called American national character is a tome by English historian Lord James Bryce, *The American Commonwealth*, first published in 1888 and then revised by Bryce several times when he served as British ambassador to the United States from 1907 to 1913. Bryce detailed intimate connections between popular culture and the politics of governing in the United States. He asserted that here, more than anywhere else in the world, differing segments of the public mostly agreed with one another and, in their agreement, were ready to believe that for every problem there was a practical solution for those who acted with (and the phrase is telling) "common sense."

Bryce said of the Americans that since "each man likes to feel that his ideas raise in other minds the same emotions as in his own, a sentiment or impulse is rapidly propagated and quickly conscious of its strength. Add to this the aptitude for organization which their history and institutions have educed [developed], and one sees how the tendency to form and the talent to work combinations for a political or any other object has become one of the great features of the country." The Englishman declared that public opinion formed the bedrock of American popular sovereignty. He concluded that "in the United States public opinion is the opinion of the whole nation, . . . the resultant of the views, not of a number of classes, but of a multitude of individuals, diverse, no doubt, from one another, but, for the purposes of politics far less diverse than if they were members of groups defined by social rank or by property." In short, Americans shared a common culture that molded their governing; their ways of governing, in turn, both reflected and refracted American cultural values.

Crèvecoeur, Tocqueville, and Bryce form a Holy Trinity of analysts and authorities for most historians who profile American culture and society. All three men of course primarily presented their insights *before* the advent of the forms of popular culture dissected by this book's authors—radio, television, motion pictures, nationally available newspapers and magazines, and recorded and widely distributed music. These, and other vehicles of mass entertainment and personal engagement, resulted from what Pulitzer Prize–winning historian Daniel J. Boorstin labeled the "Graphic Revolution" of the nineteenth and especially the twentieth centuries: "Man's ability to make, preserve, transmit, and disseminate precise images—images of print, of men and landscapes and events, of the voices of men and mobs." In an extraordinarily important book, originally published in 1962 as *The Image; or, What Happened to the American Dream* (reissued and better known today as *The Image: A Guide to Pseudo-Events in America*), Boorstin provided the history behind, the context of, and the present American social, cultural, and political order illuminated by the authors of *Homer Simpson Goes to Washington*.

Setting the tone for Boorstin's arguments in *The Image* is a provocative epigraph drawn from the writings of Max Frisch, a post–World War II author of prize-winning, politically themed novels about crises of personal identity in the modern world: "Technology . . . the knack of so arranging the world that we don't have to experience it." For Boorstin, the most significant outcome of the Graphic Revolution was "how we have used our wealth, our literacy, our technology, and our progress, to create the thicket of unreality which stands between us and the facts of life." He looked at a variety of American popular cultural phenomena—news reporting through radio, television, and newspapers; product advertising for a consumer culture society; entertainment complexes such as Disney-like theme parks; motion pictures, both fluffy and "serious," as examinations of social and personal problems; elevation of so-called celebrities to the status of at least minor gods; local and especially national politics; even the formation and selling of our foreign policy to ourselves and to the world at large. Boorstin contended that increasingly the messages within those phenomena consisted not of what was true in reality but rather of illusions manufactured to create favorable images that might or might not be true.

Denoting these images as "pseudo-events," as opposed to the spontaneous events that historically defined the lives of individuals, Boorstin explained that pseudo-events are (1) usually more dramatic, (2) planned for public exposure and therefore "newsworthy," (3) infinitely repeatable and therefore reinforced in their alleged importance, (4) advertised in advance and rerun to maximize profit, (5) consciously intended to simplify complex situations so that people can regard themselves as informed or knowledgeable, although in reality they probably are neither. As a clinical example of a pseudo–event bridge between popular culture and American politics, Boorstin pointed to the application of the television quiz show format in 1960 to the first televised debates between presidential candidates. The four programs, according to Boorstin, "were remarkably successful in reducing great national issues to trivial dimensions." This manufactured event led to an emphasis on pseudo-qualifications for the highest political office in the nation: "If we test Presidential candidates by their talents on TV quiz performances, we will, of course, choose presidents for precisely those qualifications. In a democracy, reality tends to conform to the pseudo-event. Nature imitates art."

Now, I don't ask you to believe Boorstin without reading and pondering his insights any more than I expect you to accept on my word alone that the connections between our popular culture and our politics are well documented by Ralph Waldo Emerson, J. Hector St. John Crèvecoeur, Alexis de Tocqueville, Lord James Bryce, and other commentators in the nation's past. I also do not anticipate that you will read through the many thought-provoking essays in *Homer Simpson Goes to Washington* and unquestioningly agree with every point made by each and every author. What I hope is that, having read and considered carefully what these authors have to say, you will view in a different manner than when you picked up this book the engines of popular culture that generate the rhythms of your life. Such reading is likely to change the ways you think about American society, and about yourself.

Stanley K. Schultz
Professor Emeritus
Department of History
University of Wisconsin–Madison

INTRODUCTION

American Idle: Politics and Popular Culture

Joseph J. Foy

In 2005, George Clooney received an Academy Award for Best Supporting Actor for his portrayal of CIA agent Bob Barnes in the political thriller *Syriana*. No less controversial than the film were Clooney's remarks upon receiving the Oscar: "We are a little bit out of touch in Hollywood every once in a while. I think it's probably a good thing. We're the ones who [talked] about AIDS when it was just being whispered, and we talked about civil rights when it wasn't really popular. And we, you know, we bring up subjects." Clooney was chastised and mocked by people ranging from director Spike Lee to the writers of *South Park* for his comments, who claimed that he was both smug and overstating the progressiveness of Hollywood. However, his underlying message linking popular culture and American politics seemed to be simply reinforced by these criticisms and discussions. Hollywood has been, is, and will continue to be an avenue for "bringing up subjects."

Not everyone is necessarily excited by the prospect of politics and popular culture being inextricably entwined. Critics on the right see Hollywood and other manufacturers of popular culture as attacking traditional values and destroying the foundations of what make this country so great and powerful. For example, former President George H. W. Bush once claimed that America needed a lot more families like the Waltons and a lot less like the Simpsons, and his vice president, Dan Quayle, famously attacked the television series *Murphy Brown* because the lead character was going to have a baby out of wedlock. Conservatives on the right have echoed similar sentiments about popular culture countless times. Critics on the left, however, also have their arguments against the influence of popular culture on American politics and society. Leftist critics like Noam Chomsky claim that the entertainment industry is used to pacify and distract Americans from

Although often lampooning icons of popular culture who attempt to influence politics, the citizens of *South Park* teach valuable lessons about American politics and government. (Photofest)

engaging in the political. It is, for these critics, a tool manufactured by elites to distract, placate, and control the masses. Ironically, pop culture itself has offered similarly self-critical arguments along these lines, like that developed in the hip-hop song "Television, the Drug of a Nation" by the Disposable Heroes of Hiphoprisy, which blames television for uniting us into a "United States of unconsciousness."

While both sides have their arsenal of weapons prepared to lob at the entertainment industry, what they overlook is the truly valuable democratic role that the manufacturers of popular culture play when their medium begins a broader social dialogue on issues. People may embrace messages displayed on a movie screen, or pumped through the earphones of their iPods, and become mobilized to stand up and speak out. Activism is democracy. People may disagree with a movie or television show or song lyrics and openly criticize the medium and message. Disagreement is democracy. People may become introduced to ideas and concepts that they never thought about before because of a concert or graphic novel. Information is democracy. Thus, some may applaud while others boo, but in both the cheers and jeers is a vibrant expression of democracy in action.

There is another role popular culture plays in advancing the political, and that is the role of education. People often become familiar with concepts and issues when they see them in a movie, watch them on TV, read about them in a book or comic, or listen to them on the radio. As this book will show, many people first learn about important governmental offices, such as the presidency, Congress, the courts, and the public bureaucracy, and organizations such as interest groups and political parties not from a textbook or political science class, but from a TV show, a movie, or a song. Likewise, exposure to concepts such as civil rights and liberties, terrorism and torture, domestic and foreign policy, and even political philosophy and culture is often delivered through entertainment and that which is "pop." The familiarization of such complex and heady concepts through popular culture is often scoffed at, but, as this book argues, entertainment media can help bring politics to life for those people who have always felt it a distant machine that has nothing to do with them. It can help them discover that the politics they think they are avoiding when they try to escape from the world around them are still there and always will be.

Finally, popular culture offers a way of connecting the apathetically disinterested to a political system that very much needs them. Democracy is a government "of the people, by the people, and for the people," and, yet, with some notable exceptions, declining trends in voter turnout and engagement in the United States lead many to ask, "Where are *the people*?" This problem is compounded by the fact that once people have turned away from politics, then public officials, leaders, politicians, and interest groups no longer have a way to reach them. However, as the contributors to this volume show, popular culture can work to counterbalance that negative effect resulting from apathy. An example of this was the October 1, 2000, airing of the *King of the Hill* episode "The Perils of Polling." Broadcast a month prior to the actual start of the show's fifth season, this episode was released as a public service announcement to all who watched, especially the youth audience who tends not to vote. The show itself was an argument in favor of voting and political participation. Hank Hill even comes on with Bobby during the credits to tell viewers that they should fill out their voter registration cards to be "eligible to win these valuable prizes—freedom, civic pride, and a brand new president." Here, popular culture is pushing people back toward political participation, rather than allowing them to turn from it.

The purpose of this book, therefore, is to help people decode some of pop culture's countless ventures into the realm of the political. By taking concepts and controversies within American government and politics and explaining them through the lens of popular culture, it is my hope to break down the artificial barriers that keep people detached from their government. If politics is more familiar, and we begin to routinely see it played out around us, then we may begin to see in it the causes and solutions to problems that we confront. In the end, the goal of this book is to show how popular culture and the entertainment media are not an escape at all, but an awakening into politics and government. Politics, after all, is not a game for "them," but for all of us, and in the immortal words of Pericles, "Just because you do not take an interest in politics does not mean that politics will not take an interest in you."

In order to meet the goals laid out for this volume, the book has been divided into three sections. Part 1 provides a framework for understanding the relationship of politics and popular culture, and provides a context for interpreting American politics and government through founding philosophy, principles, and beliefs. In chapter 1, Greg Ahrenhoerster provides an argument in favor of using popular culture to understand and interpret politics and government, explaining that although some might turn their nose up at such a venture, their view of the ceiling causes them to overlook the valuable ways in which popular culture can enhance democratic citizenship.

Clearly supporting Ahrenhoerster's position, Dean A. Kowalski (chapter 2) uses the movie *V for Vendetta* as a basis for understanding American political thought. Kowalski explains the social contract theories of Thomas Hobbes and John Locke present in the film and demonstrates the influence these philosophers' views on liberty and the state had on Thomas Jefferson when he drafted the Declaration of Independence and set the stage for American political philosophy. Likewise, in chapter 3, J. Michael Bitzer uses *The Simpsons* as a vehicle for identifying American political culture, attitudes, and beliefs all in the context of the mythical "American Dream." As a whole, this section provides the analytical framework for understanding the basis for American democracy and politics.

Part 2 moves away from the "ideas" of America and into its "institutions." Using popular culture to identify, explain, and analyze the institutional components that make up American government, the chapters in this section demonstrate how popular culture brings government to life, making it accessible to people who might otherwise turn away. Chapters 4–6, for example, engage in an analysis of the three branches of American government: the executive, legislative, and judicial. However, rather than merely being a clinical look at the procedures and activities of these institutions, the authors explore critical issues surrounding each and examine the implications for democracy. In chapter 4, John Grummel explores issues of representation in Congress by comparing the idealistic images of *Mr. Smith Goes to Washington* with the cynical attack on representation in the movie *Bulworth*. Next, Jennifer J. Hora introduces in chapter 5 the heroic-president model of executive leadership as embodied in the highly acclaimed television series *The West Wing*. And, in chapter 6, Kristi Nelson Foy and Joseph J. Foy offer a critical analysis of perceived racial and economic inequalities within the judicial branch of government as portrayed by comedian Dave Chappelle in his groundbreaking *Chappelle's Show*.

The second section of the book goes beyond the traditional tripartite approach to institutions and looks also to the institutions that support government in the form of civil society. Joseph J. Foy (chapter 7) examines the institutions of group politics and classical notions of pluralism as portrayed in the film and novel *Thank You for Smoking*, and uses interest group methods and strategies as the basis for evaluating democracy in America. Additionally, Christopher A. Cooper and Mandi Bates Bailey (chapter 8) and Dick Flannery (chapter 9) explore the media, American government's "fourth branch." Cooper and Bates test the impact of entertainment news on the political knowledge of audiences of shows like *The Daily Show, The Colbert Report, The Tonight Show with Jay Leno, Late Show with David Letterman,* and *Real Time with Bill Maher.* Flannery turns an eye toward traditional broadcast news and uses films like *Good Night, and Good Luck, Network,* and *Wag the Dog* to ask whether the "millennial media" is doing right by democracy and the American people.

The final section of the book, Part 3, is devoted to pop culture explorations of contemporary political issues ranging from the global war on terror and U.S. foreign policy, to civil rights and civil liberties, to public forms of protest. Timothy Dunn (chapter 10) uses the award-winning television series *24* to examine political and philosophical questions about the ethics and logic of governmental policy in waging the war on terror, and, turning an eye to domestic issues, Nathan Zook (chapter 11) uses the movie *The Siege* to confront the tensions that are manifest between civil rights and liberties and efforts on the part of the government to promote security. Brett S. Sharp (chapter 12) looks at U.S. foreign policy more broadly through the lens of popular music, while Craig Hurst (chapter 13) uses folk music as the foundation for discussing the "popularization of protest" in American history.

The last chapter is written by Margaret Hankenson and offers your "moment of Zen" for the book as a whole. Using the MTV Films cult classic *Election*, Hankenson evaluates electoral politics in the United States and touches on not only the campaign and election process, but also the promises versus the realities of American democracy.

I would like to thank each of the authors for their time, expertise, and exceptional contributions, and my colleagues Bill Schneider and Dean Kowalski for their insights, reflections, and assistance. Additionally, thanks to my friend Phil Zweifel for enduring my pop culture references while trying to bring me to really know Bob Dylan, and to Scott Silet for his help tracking down elusive articles and materials. I would also like to thank Anne Dean Watkins for her willingness to embrace this project and for her help along the way. Likewise, I wish to extend a similar thanks to Stephen Wrinn and the good people at the University Press of Kentucky. Your support and professionalism are appreciated. Finally, special thanks to Dr. Sue, Jim, and Kristi. I am truly blessed.

Part 1

SETTING THE STAGE

AMERICAN POLITICAL THOUGHT, BELIEFS, AND CULTURE

1

AYE ON SPRINGFIELD

Reasons to Vote "Yes" on Popular Culture

Greg Ahrenhoerster

Late in Walker Percy's novel *The Moviegoer*, Binx Bolling's Aunt Emily chastises Binx about his apathetic attitude and selfish behavior. In their conversation Emily reveals that she had higher hopes for Binx's character, assuming he would have the grace, class, and noblesse oblige of the southern aristocracy that she believed in so strongly and worked so hard to instill in him. Emily concludes her lecture with an interesting question: "What has been going on in your mind during all the years when we listened to music together, read the *Crito*, and spoke together . . . of goodness and truth and beauty and nobility?" Essentially, Aunt Emily is working under the same assumption that many of us in the ivory tower of higher education cling to: that exposing people to "high culture" (e.g., classical music, philosophy, and great works of literature, drama, and fine art) will transform them into "better" people—responsible citizens of high moral character. Furthermore, the implied assumption of Emily's question is that the movies that Binx is drawn to have done nothing to advance his character and, in fact, seem to be destroying it—an accusation, as Michael Berube notes in "The 'Elvis Costello Problem' in Teaching Popular Culture," that has been leveled against popular culture "for three millennia and counting."[1]

The belief that a classical liberal arts education creates better citizens continues to be used by institutions of higher learning to justify their existence today (see, for example, Marshall Gregory's "The Value of a Liberal Arts Education at Butler University" or the University of California, Berkeley's "A Liberal Arts Education," both of which claim attending their institutions will provide students with a stronger moral compass). In particular, the desire to make students into better citizens has long been a stated goal of political science instruction. William Bradshaw's review of the American Political Science Association's 1951 book *Goals for Political Science* explains that "training for citizenship is the predominant interest and emphasis among political scientists." Thus, colleges and universities continue to teach students music appreciation and Plato, as Aunt Emily did for Binx, in the hopes that they will be transformed into educated and responsible citizens.[2]

And, like Aunt Emily, many members of the "intellectual upper class" are concerned about the mental and moral damage being caused by popular culture. For example, there was a considerable amount of eye rolling and gnashing of teeth by academics and sociopolitical commentators throughout the United States after a much-publicized 2006 report by the McCormick Tribune Foundation, which found, among other things, that while 22 percent of Americans can name all five members of the family from the popular television show *The Simpsons*, only 0.1 percent could name all five freedoms guaranteed by the First Amendment to the Constitution. Similarly, while 25 percent of Americans could name all three judges on the television show *American Idol*, only 8 percent could name at least three of the First Amendment protections. This was decried as yet more evidence of the downfall of American society, particularly among the younger generations (among the subgroup of Americans aged 18–34 in the survey, 53 percent were able to name all five Simpson family members, while none among this group could name all five freedoms protected by the First Amendment). Given that the purpose of the McCormick Tribune Foundation is to "advance the ideals of a free democratic society by investing in our children, communities and country," and the fact that they have set up a museum that seeks to promote knowledge of the U.S. Constitution and the freedoms it provides, it seems likely that, through their survey, the McCormick Foundation was seeking evidence that popular culture is getting in the way of their mission.[3]

Of course, molding better citizens is not the only reason that we in the ivory tower teach our students about high culture. As an English professor, I have my students read Shakespeare, in part because it teaches well, which is to say that interesting classroom discussions are the result. *Hamlet, Othello, Macbeth*, etc., all explore important sociopolitical issues and reveal complex aspects of humanity in ways that the students may not have considered before; thus these works help them generate important new ideas. I tend to steer clear of literature that I fear will not lead to such stimulating discus-

Nearly one quarter of Americans can name all five of the ever popular Simpson family (Homer, Marge, Bart, Lisa, and Maggie), whereas only one American in a thousand can name all five protections of the First Amendment (speech, press, religion, assembly, and to petition government for a redress of grievances). (Jerry Ohlinger's Movie Material Store)

sions and will leave me with fifty minutes of "dead air" to fill. I assume I am not alone here. This might, perhaps, be one reason why some professors avoid popular culture in the classroom: they simply fear it will not lead to illuminating conversations of the same depth and substance that high culture does. However, I suspect that for many of us in higher education, resistance to popular culture also comes from an "Aunt Emilyish" snobbishness. "You're damn right we're better," Emily says about people of her class, just as we believe in our hearts that our beloved canonized writers and composers really are better than what is currently on television, in movie theaters, and on the radio and that this inferior art simply does not contribute to the development of responsible citizens in the same way that high culture does.[4]

Yet for the past few decades, the formal study of popular culture (usually seen to include such things as television, movies, popular music, advertising, magazines, comic books, Web sites, and spectator sports) has increased considerably. Certainly, it is no longer uncommon for college instructors to invoke popular culture examples to help students understand a term or concept with which they are unfamiliar. For instance, Jerilyn Marshall reports that college librarians frequently use popular culture references when teaching students research strategies, and Archana Ram writes about a professor at Muhlenberg College in Pennsylvania who uses examples from *Star Trek* to introduce concepts in theology. I do this in my own teaching as well. When introducing the literary term "foil" in an introductory-level literature course, one of the examples I always use is Han Solo from *Star Wars,* who serves as an obvious foil for Luke Skywalker. Certainly I could, instead, cite the example of Hotspur from Shakespeare's *Henry IV, Part One,* but why not use an example that my students are more likely to be familiar with when introducing a concept that it is important for them to understand? I suspect that most professors would acknowledge that using familiar examples to illustrate unfamiliar terms is an intelligent teaching decision. Taking this a step further, entire courses devoted to the study of popular culture are becoming increasingly common. Such courses are usually in either communications or sociology departments (for example, the University of Illinois at Urbana-Champaign's "COMM 320—Popular Culture" and Northwestern University's "Sociology of Popular Culture"). In some cases, such as at Bowling Green State University, graduate-level programs in popular culture studies have emerged. The usual justification for these courses and programs is that studying these artifacts helps us understand "the things that shape and drive American culture." In other words, we can learn something important about people by looking at what they find entertaining.[5]

However, the purpose of this book goes beyond the simple use of popular culture examples to illustrate basic concepts or an examination of what popular culture reveals about Americans or even an analysis of the politics of popular culture, such as the one that John Street provides in *Politics and Popular Culture*. Rather, this text provides an in-depth discussion of American politics through the lens of popular culture. One might question the wisdom of this, fearing that referencing *Chappelle's Show* or *The West Wing* might encourage the students to take the issues less seriously. However, as Aristotle points out in *Nicomachean Ethics, Book I*, "Each man judges well the things he knows, and of these he is a good judge." In other words, it may be wise to allow students to practice their critical thinking skills and political analysis on subject matter they already know, such as television shows and popular films. Aristotle goes on to assert that only "the man who has been educated in a subject is a good judge of that subject, and the man who has received an all-around education is a good judge in general. Hence a young man is not a proper hearer of lectures on political science; for he is inexperienced in the actions that occur in life, but its discussions start from these and are about these." This suggests that by providing students with the critical thinking skills of a liberal arts education, even if they develop these skills by examining popular culture, they will be better able to apply sound judgment to the political issues they will continue to be confronted with as they go through life.

Indeed, my own experience as a literature and composition instructor supports this theory. I have found that popular culture is an excellent tool for getting students to understand and engage with important political and social issues that they might otherwise be reluctant or unprepared to approach. In particular, I have found that popular culture helps students find a pathway into conversations about complex and abstract topics and makes them more comfortable discussing controversial issues.

One abstract topic I frequently try to get my literature students to explore (usually when we move into postmodernism) is the question of "what is art?" I am the first to admit that this is an incredibly complicated question that can lead to perplexing, circular discussions. Regardless, it is a topic that I would like my students to consider. Until recently, I had a miserable time getting otherwise talkative and eager students to engage in this discussion. They either wanted to take the easy way out and say that everything is art (but then why do we value it?) or that it is all relative (but then how do we judge its quality?), or else they would simply shrug their shoulders and refuse to play along at all. As Aristotle might suggest, they did not know enough (or believe they knew enough) about art to enter into a discussion of it. Then, about five years ago, when I was trying to drag a class through this discussion, one of the students noted the similarity between what we were talking about and an episode of *The Simpsons* he had recently seen. Fortunately, I was familiar with the episode, as were several of the students in the class.

The gist of the episode is that Homer purchases and tries to assemble a backyard barbecue pit, which he bungles terribly, resulting in a grotesque clump of bricks and metal. He drags the monstrosity behind his car back to the store to try to return it, but is refused. While he is pulling it home, the towrope breaks and it smashes into an art gallery owner's car. She tracks Homer down and tells him that the disfigured barbecue pit is a work of art and offers him a show in her gallery, much to the dismay of Marge, who has formally studied art and whose paintings, as Homer points out, actually look like the things she is trying to paint. Homer creates more "outsider art" and is briefly praised by the art world as a great artist, but his second show fails, even though he does essentially the same things he did the first time. Finally, after Lisa tells Homer about some of the large, imaginative art projects by Christo, Homer floods the entire town to replicate the canals of Venice. Surprisingly, everyone in Springfield is thrilled with this final art project.[6]

Once the debate was framed in the context of this episode, the classroom exploded with questions and observations. Is Homer's barbecue art? Why or why not? It took no skill to produce, but as the gallery owner points out, it is an expression of his emotion (in his case, rage). What is the role of the viewer/audience? Are Marge's paintings art even though no one sees or appreciates them? Does Homer's acceptance by the art community make him an artist? Does he stop being an artist when they reject him? Is Homer's final project art (or as Bart suggests, vandalism)? What is the value of art? Is it worth destroying property for (as Homer does) or even sacrificing human lives (Lisa tells Homer that a few of Christo's yellow umbrellas blew over and killed some people)? It was suddenly a wonderful class, full of high-level thinking and conversation. Since then, I have always used this *Simpsons* episode ("Mom and Pop Art") as an example when framing this discussion; in fact, I have occasionally even made the teleplay required reading, which has led to consistently more thorough discussions of the question than I had seen previously. It is apparent that the students simply required a familiar pathway into the abstract and esoteric topic.

Religion is another area that I have generally had difficulty generating healthy classroom discussions about, not because the students are unfamiliar with it (indeed, many of the students at University of Wisconsin–Waukesha are openly religious, most of them Christian), but because some students seemed unwilling to have their beliefs questioned or challenged, while others seemed to know that this was a "hot-button" issue which led to arguments that made them uncomfortable. Of course, these were some of the reasons that I wanted them to think and talk about religion, especially in my Composition II course, which focuses largely on creating and supporting arguments with evidence that is meaningful to one's audience (in other words, they need to learn that "because I believe it to be true" is not good enough support for a claim). For several semesters, I devoted one unit of the class to the debate between science and religion, which I, rather naively at first, thought they would embrace because of its obvious social significance as well as their apparent interest in Christianity. These discussions weren't as painstaking as the ones about "what is art?," but the students still weren't digging into the issue to the depth I had hoped. They often appeared to be repeating lines of reasoning that they had been taught, instead of seriously pondering the related questions and engaging in serious critical thinking. Then I introduced "Lisa the Skeptic."

"Lisa the Skeptic" is a surprisingly complex *Simpsons* episode that quite impressively delves into a wide variety of questions and issues related to the science versus religion debate. The episode starts with intellectual and socially conscious Lisa learning that a new shopping mall is being built in a field where fossils had previously been found. She hires a lawyer to force the mall owners to halt the project until an archaeological study of the area can be completed. The owners comply, and the students of Springfield Elementary School, led by Lisa, are sent to the area to dig for fossils. After hours of labor they uncover a skeleton of what appears to be an angel (a human with wings). The townspeople appear, and most assume it is in fact an angel. Lisa remains alone in her skepticism but is hard-pressed to come up with a plausible scientific explanation. Homer quickly steals the skeleton and sets it up in a makeshift shrine in his garage, charging people money to come see it and selling them crude religious artifacts ("no one gets into heaven without a glow stick"). Frustrated with the town's lack of logic (including her own mother, who admits she believes in angels), Lisa takes a bone fragment from the skeleton to Stephen Jay Gould for scientific testing. Her devotion to science upsets the townspeople, causing them to go on a rampage, during which they destroy the Springfield Museum of Natural History. Gould later reports that the tests were inconclusive (though we learn at the end of the episode that he never ran the tests, possibly because Lisa didn't have much money to pay him). Then the skeleton disappears, and the townspeople assume Lisa destroyed it and have her arrested and put on trial, which supposedly is going to settle the age-old question of science versus religion. However, before the trial can get going, the skeleton reappears at the top of a hill with a message that "the end will come at sundown." Everyone—except Lisa—assumes that this is a prediction of the apocalypse, and they begin preparing for Judgment Day. They all gather around the skeleton at sundown to witness the end of the world, only to find that the whole thing is a publicity stunt concocted by the owners of the new shopping center (now called the "Heavenly Hills Mall"). The townspeople are momentarily upset that their faith was manipulated in this manner but are quickly placated when they find out the mall has a Pottery Barn and there is a 20 percent off sale going on.[7]

What is remarkable about "Lisa the Skeptic" is how thoroughly it presents the science versus religion issue. The episode not only points out the obvious ways in which greedy people like Homer and the mall owners can exploit people's religious beliefs (Ned Flanders eagerly purchases four of Homer's glow sticks) and the foolish violence that petty religious differences can lead to (Lenny and Carl come to blows over whether it is the Angel of Peace or the Angel of Mercy), but it subtly points out the flaws with science. The fact that Gould never runs the tests on the bone fragments—whether out of greed, laziness, or simply whim—reminds us that science is only as reliable as the humans who are conducting it, and humans are often unreliable. Similarly, early in the episode, the writers remind us of the evils that science can bring through Marge's comment that the air conditioner in the new mall is "more powerful than a million hydrogen bombs." And, of course, the episode exploits the selfish hypocrisy of religious people like Moe, who is injured while destroying the science museum and then says, "Oh, I'm paralyzed; I just hope medical science can cure me," and the entire mob, who feel so strongly about their beliefs that they destroy a museum and have a little girl arrested but then quickly abandon those beliefs for a discount at the new mall.

What is even more remarkable is that while my students were unwilling to talk about religion in America, they were more than willing to discuss and critically analyze religion in the animated world of Springfield. They quickly identified and began analyzing both Lisa's stance and her detractors' beliefs. With prodding, they began to see the subtleties of the debate described above. They not only saw religion/belief more clearly, but gained a more nuanced understanding of science as a process that is used by humans in a variety of ways. Their fear of the controversial topic dissolved, and they stopped speaking in clichés and oversimplifications. I am convinced that the familiar backdrop of a popular television show helped them feel more comfortable, and I suspect that the fact that the issue was moved out of the real world into an obviously artificial one gave them a sense of distance from the debate that helped them gain a different perspective than the one they entered the classroom with, regardless of whether they were believers or nonbelievers.[8]

These two benefits—providing people with better pathways into discussions of complex abstract topics and helping them feel comfortable discussing controversial issues—are necessary steps along the path toward greater sociopolitical understanding. Although popular culture certainly cannot provide this pathway to every American, given the media-saturated world that most young people have grown up in, it seems reasonable to assume that, when they walk into college classrooms, they are more like Binx Bolling than Aunt Emily. And, in truth, there is no compelling argument against using popular culture as a tool for understanding politics. There is no evidence that popular culture makes us take politics less seriously; indeed, it may well cause people to take it more seriously once they see how deeply politics is entwined into their lives already. Furthermore, the understanding of politics that Americans are getting from popular culture is not as superficial as some might suspect. According to a 2004 National Annenberg Election Survey, viewers of late-night talk shows knew more about the positions of presidential candidates than nonviewers. In fact, regular viewers of Comedy Central's satiric talk show *The Daily Show with Jon Stewart* knew more about election issues than people who regularly read newspapers. The naysayers may have tradition on their side, certainly, but that's the same weak defense Aunt Emily would raise for race/class superiority. Thus it seems to be best not to roll our eyes at Americans' knowledge of *V for Vendetta* and *Chappelle's Show* and *The West Wing,* but to use this knowledge as a pathway to understanding American politics well enough to become the stronger moral beings and more responsible citizens that the American Political Science Association honorably strives to create.[9]

Notes

1. Walker Percy, *The Moviegoer* (New York: Vintage Books, 1962), 226; Michael Berube, "The 'Elvis Costello Problem' in Teaching Popular Culture," *Chronicle of Higher Education,* August 13, 1999, chronicle.com/weekly/v45/i49/49b00401.htm (accessed May 29, 2007).

2. Marshall Gregory, "The Value of a Liberal Arts Education at Butler University," *Liberal Arts Matters,* 2004, http://www.butler.edu/las/ValuestatementGregory.aspx (accessed May 30, 2007); and "A Liberal Arts Education," University of California, Berkeley, April 24, 2007, http://ls.berkeley.edu/?q=about-college/liberal-arts-education (accessed May 30, 2007); William Bradshaw, "Review of *Goals for Political Science,*" *Journal of Politics* 14, no. 3 (1952), http://www.jstor.org/view/00223816/di976483/97p0328s/0 (accessed July 14, 2007).

3. "Mission," *McCormick Tribune Freedom Museum,* http://www.freedommuseum.us/ (accessed July 23, 2007). The five members of the Simpson family are Homer, Marge, Bart, Lisa, and Maggie. The five protections guaranteed by the First Amendment are freedom of religion, freedom of speech, freedom of the press, the right to assemble, and the right to petition the government for a redress of grievances. The three judges on *American Idol* are Simon Cowell, Paula Abdul, and Randy Jackson.

4. Percy, *The Moviegoer,* 224.

5. Jerilyn Marshall, "What Would Buffy Do? The Use of Popular Culture Examples in Undergraduate Library Instruction," *ERIC,* March 13, 2002, eric.ed.gov (accessed June 2, 2007); Archana Ram, "New Courses in Pop Culture Offer Modern Look at Society," *Daily Northwestern,* March 2, 2004, www.dailynorthwestern.com (accessed May 29, 2007); Anna Tomasino, *Discovering Popular Culture* (New York: Longman, 2007), ix.

6. The complete teleplay of this episode is available at "Mom and Pop Art," *The Simpsons,* April 11, 1999, http://www.snpp.com/episodes/AABF15 (accessed June 2, 2007).

7. The complete teleplay of this episode is available at "Lisa the Skeptic," *The Simpsons,* November 23, 1997, http://www.snpp.com/episodes/5F05 (accessed June 2, 2007).

8. The efficacy of this strategy was shown in the students' ability to apply the ideas from *The Simpsons* to their papers responding to a number of articles we had read about science and religion. My own belief that this was successful was supported by a colleague who visited my class on a day I was teaching "Lisa the Skeptic"; she commented specifically how impressive it was that students "made frequent reference to the other readings on this subject."

9. Bryan Long, "*Daily Show* Viewers Ace Political Quiz," *CNN,* September 29, 2004, http://www.cnn.com/2004/SHOWBIZ/TV/09/28/comedy.politics/ (accessed August 6, 2007).

2

R FOR REVOLUTION

Hobbes and Locke on Social Contracts and Scarlet Carsons

Dean A. Kowalski

> People should not fear their governments; governments should fear their people.
>
> —"V," in *V for Vendetta*

The Wachowski brothers are remarkable filmmakers. After their cultish break-through film, *Bound* (1996), they wowed us with the seminal *Matrix* movies. All three films are artful, stylish, and provocative. But the awesome special effects of *The Matrix* (1999) and its sequels make it easy to overlook the Wachowskis' prowess as screenwriters and indeed fledgling philosophers. Each of the *Matrix* films skillfully conveys different philosophical themes: skepticism, free will, and existentialism, respectively. As screenwriters for *V for Vendetta* (2005), the Wachowskis set their sights on political philosophy. The goal of this essay is to explain how the Wachowski adaptation of the Alan Moore and David Lloyd graphic novel deftly expresses important tenets of classic social contract reasoning, especially those pertaining to the debate between Hobbes and Locke regarding the state of nature, the role of the sovereign, and the justifiability of political revolt by the citizens.[1] Having accomplished this, Locke's substantial influence on American political thought becomes obvious.

The "Ulcered Sphincter of Ass-erica" and the State of Nature

The film begins with Lewis Prothero (Roger Allam), the politically charged "Voice of London," providing the viewer with his rousing account of world events. Prothero's tone is caustic as he informs his viewers that the *former* United States recently sent goodwill tokens of wheat and tobacco across the Atlantic—presumably as a desperate plea for British aid. He believes that England should dump it into the sea as fitting recompense for the Boston Tea Party. Prothero shares his scorn for the former United States and the war it started. If it started abroad, it now ravages American soil. (Later in the film, we learn that the United States' foreign policies have triggered a second civil war, and that the ripples of this reached the shores of Great Britain.) He calls the United States the world's largest leper colony, referring to a plague that "the colonists" apparently created. Prothero further reminds his viewers that only twenty years ago America had everything; they were the most powerful country on Earth. Now the nation is a shambles. In fact, it is no longer a nation.

Prothero's commentary provides us an opportunity to consider what it might be like to live in a world without *any* established governments. This hypothetical state of affairs preoccupied political philosophers of the Enlightenment, including Thomas Hobbes and (later) John Locke. They called it the "state of nature." Hobbes's depiction is particularly striking. He believes that, lacking a strong government to deter our inherently egoistic impulses, the state of nature would be a constant struggle. Fueling our adversarial interactions are the facts that resources are limited and that we combatants are more or less equal in ability regarding both the "faculties of body and mind." Regarding the former, Hobbes writes, "For as to the strength of body, the weakest has strength enough to kill the strongest, either by secret machination or by confederacy with others that are in the same danger with himself."[2] Regarding the latter, Hobbes claims, "I find greater equality among men than that of strength. For prudence is but experience, which equal time equally bestows on all men in those things they equally apply themselves unto."[3]

Parity creates the genuine hope of subduing our competitors, which further embroils us in our struggle to gain the upper hand against them. Hobbes vividly continues:

> From this equality of ability arises equality of hope in the attaining of our ends. And therefore if any two men desire the same thing, which nevertheless they cannot both enjoy, they become enemies; and in the way to their end . . . endeavor to destroy or subdue one another. And from hence it comes to pass that where an invader has

no more to fear than another man's single power, if one plant, sow, build, or possess a convenient seat, others may probably be expected to come prepared with forces united to dispossess and deprive him, not only of the fruit of his labor, but also of his life or liberty. And the invader again is in the like danger of another.[4]

Thus any advantage one person may achieve in the state of nature ultimately makes him a target. Others will soon conspire against him. Thus retaliation and re-retaliation is a never-ending cycle that breeds fear, contempt, revenge, mistrust, and more fear.

It is now easier to see why Hobbes believes that existing in the state of nature is tantamount to enduring a state of "war of every man against every man." Life in this condition would be bleak indeed. There would be no property, technology, leisure, or any comforts whatsoever. This leads to the rather famous passage from *Leviathan*: "In such condition there is no place for industry, because the fruit thereof is uncertain: and consequently no culture of the earth; no navigation, nor use of the commodities that may be imported by sea; no commodious [suitable] building; no instruments of moving and removing such things as require much force; no knowledge of the face of the earth; no account of time; no arts; no letters; no society; and which is worst of all, continual fear, and danger of violent death; and the life of man, solitary, poor, nasty, brutish, and short." Clearly, living in the state of nature is to be avoided at all costs. Our livelihoods—and our very lives—depend on it.

Three Waters and Avoiding the State of Nature

Following the lead of Moore and Lloyd, the Wachowskis paint a bleak picture of the fictive near future. War, terrorism, and general chaos surround England, apparently triggered by American foreign policy. Britain was not completely immune to terrorist attacks. A subway station ("tube station") was bombed, killing innocent people. The death toll spiked dramatically when St. Mary's grammar school, the Three Waters water treatment facility, and a tube station were simultaneously targets of biological terrorism. The unleashed virus caused eighty thousand deaths. England took appropriate action. Prothero might say that England "did what it had to do," and thereby in his mind avoided divine judgment and wrath (unlike the United States). Britain closed the subways, and took the further measures of expelling foreigners and subduing political activists. It evacuated its Muslim constituency (and presumably its other marginalized faiths). It began quarantining "social undesirables," including homosexuals and those suffering from various diseases. Britain sealed off its borders and achieved homogeneity in the hopes of protecting itself from the rest of the world. As a result, British society remained stable. As Prothero might say, "Good guys win, bad guys lose, and England prevails."

Hobbes (as we will see) is likely to be sympathetic to these political maneuverings, given Britain's potential return to the state of nature. Nevertheless, his answer to avoiding the state of nature presupposes that no strong governments exist. He in fact believes that forming strong governments is imperative in avoiding it. The first step is to become fully aware of our best interests.

Hobbes believes that those in the state of nature soon come to realize that forming contracts (compacts, covenants) with one another is the key to our well-being. The crucial first step is to seek out others who also desire peace, safety, and prosperity. This is Hobbes's self-proclaimed first law of nature. He writes, "Every man ought to endeavor peace, as far as he has hope of obtaining it; and when he cannot obtain it, that he may seek and use all helps and advantages of war."[5] To secure our best interests, we must seek peace. Rational people should—and inexorably will—come together for everyone's mutual benefit. This first step leads the group of peace-seekers to Hobbes's second law of nature, namely, "That a man be willing, when others are so too, as far forth as for peace and defense of himself he shall think it necessary, to lay down this right to all things; and be contented with so much liberty against other men as he would allow other men against himself."[6] The contracts that we form should be such that individuals agree to refrain from certain (especially hostile or threatening) behaviors so long as others also agree to avoid such behaviors. The contract is in effect a promise not to harm others on the condition that others promise not to harm you. Entering into such agreements is the second necessary step in avoiding the state of nature.[7]

Even granting Hobbes's assumption that rational people will eventually enter into contracts vowing to limit hostile behavior, he nevertheless believes that we will continue to act from self-interested motives. Hobbes thus thinks that we will never pass up a chance to violate our contracts, so long as we benefit (more) from doing so and we are reasonably sure that our violation will go undetected. Hobbes in effect holds that the contract entered into *all by itself* is nothing but empty words. For the contract to be operatively binding, it has to include allegiance to a governing body Hobbes calls a "sovereign." Hobbes believes that allegiance to a politically powerful sovereign is necessary for stability and thus justice. He writes, "Before the names of just and unjust can have place, there must be some coercive power to compel men equally to the performance of their covenants [contracts], by the terror of some punishment greater than the benefit they expect by the breach of their covenant . . . and such power there is none before the erection of the commonwealth [state]."[8] The sovereign, as the political head of state, is to deter any and all contractual violations. His successfully doing so will ensure the state's stability and integrity; the alternative is to return to the state of nature. But because leaving the state of nature was the goal of entering into the contract in the first place, the sovereign must be allowed any means necessary to keep the contract(s) intact.

Hobbes indeed believes that the sovereign's political power is unlimited.[9] He seems to further believe that anything less than this prevents a true commonwealth from forming. Hobbes writes: "The only way to erect such a common power [sovereign], as may be able to defend them [citizens] from the invasion of foreigners, and the injuries of one another, and thereby to secure them . . . and live contentedly, is to confer all their power and strength upon one man, or upon one assembly of men, that may reduce all their wills, by plurality of voices, unto one will . . . and therein to submit their wills, every one to his will, and their judgments to his judgment."[10] Only by empowering a monarch-type leader (or perhaps an oligarchy) with unlimited political power can we avoid a state of nature. This type of government is necessary to literally save us from ourselves. Because we cannot trust ourselves to keep our contracts, we must transfer our will to the sovereign. He now speaks for us. Once delivered from ourselves, we can then and only then enjoy the benefits of security and peace of mind that come with living in a stable society.

High Chancellor Sutler as Hobbesian Sovereign

In *V for Vendetta*, Adam Sutler (John Hurt) rises to political power as England's Undersecretary of Defense. His job was to protect British citizens. A stalwart of the ultraconservative political party "Norsefire," he did so zealously and without remorse. He quickly sponsored the bill that resulted in closing the subway system after the terrorist biological attack. Prior to the bioterrorist attacks, and in an act of uncanny foresight, he had spearheaded a preemptive special project to search for biological weapons in England. Both governmental measures were enacted swiftly, under the auspices of natural security. And although the St. Mary's virus ravaged England before he could locate the culprits, the undersecretary would not be deterred, and he would not falter. He would defend Britain at all costs.

Fearful of the consequences of America's war and the threat of further biological attacks, the British people needed a champion. They longed for security and peace of mind and thus someone who could provide it. That year, Sutler was the Norsefire candidate for prime minister. The staple of his platform was the newly penned "Articles of Allegiance." Electing him and pledging to these articles were the sole tickets to quash further threats to British soil. He won in a landslide victory. Soon after, a cure for the St. Mary's virus was developed in British laboratories. Many British citizens saw this as a sign from God. The Almighty had confirmed their decision to elect Sutler and he was thus duly anointed Britain's savior. A new political office was created for him. As high chancellor, his role transcended that of prime minister. By providing his new office with limitless political power, England will prevail.

Upon being appointed high chancellor, Sutler expeditiously wielded his new powers. He established a citywide curfew in London for minors and adults. Anyone on the streets after 11:00 P.M. is liable to be arrested. He erected security cameras throughout the city. These allow Sutler—via his subordinate Mr. Heyer (Guy Henry)—to have near complete video surveillance of London and presumably all of Britain. This technology was soon upgraded to include retinal scanning for immediate identification of anyone deemed suspicious. Similar audio surveillance was established by tapping phone lines and implementing constant radio sweeps of the city. Such monitoring technology soon included the "Interlink" and personal e-mail exchanges. Sutler, through a different subordinate, Mr. Etheridge (Eddie Marsan), can thus eavesdrop on any audible or electronic conversation in the country. In addition to a traditional police force led by Mr. Finch (Stephen Rea), Sutler created a special, covert police force—the Fingermen—led by Mr. Creedy (Tim Pigott-Smith). They are charged with controlling the more insidious threats to England's future. Sutler also took control of media outlets, most notably the British Television Network (BTN). Along with Mr. Dascomb (Ben Miles), who controls the day-to-day functions, Sutler authorizes what is broadcast to the public. In fact, the BTN seems to be the only remaining broadcasting station in the county. It is clearly the only station that may carry emergency broadcasts. These interrupt whatever program viewers are currently watching. (If citizens are not watching the "tele," the audio of the emergency broadcast is provided via the public loudspeaker system.) Of course, all of these new machinations were deemed necessary for national security. They were the price of security and peace of mind in a chaotic, terrorism-infected world. England prevails.

Hobbes certainly would have agreed with Sutler's political station. With the pending threat of returning to the state of nature, electing Sutler provided consent for his Articles of Allegiance. This, in turn, changed the social contract between the British government and its citizens. Making Sutler high chancellor solidified Britain's new political turn and ensured that everyone would abide by the new articles—all in the hope of reestablishing stability and peace of mind. With constant and extensive surveillance by the government, the likelihood of someone breaking a contract undetected is nil. By reducing the modes of public transportation and the hours at which people may travel freely, governmental surveillance is that much more effective. With a sovereign inclined to zealotry and mercilessness, punishments for noncompliance are swift and harsh. Thus the common good is tightly secured. Whether this approaches tyranny would not bother Hobbes. He believed that nothing else would suffice. Tyranny is better than anarchy, he believed, and without a Hobbesian sovereign securely in place, anarchy is exactly what we face.

"Strength through Unity, Unity through Faith"

The first time the viewer encounters High Chancellor Sutler, it is November 5, 4:00 A.M. Four hours have passed since the terrorist only known as "Codename V" (or simply "V") has bombed the Old Bailey justice building. Sutler has assembled his "undersecretaries," all of whom are handpicked, loyal Norsefire party officials. He appears to them on a huge, two-way projection screen; the room is dark, with the only light coming from Sutler's looming image and from small desk lamps in front of each undersecretary. Sutler glares down on them, demanding, "Gentleman, you have had four hours. You had better have results."

Sutler first quizzes Mr. Creedy about his response to this latest terrorist threat. Creedy responds that the area has been quarantined and any potential witnesses have been detained for questioning. Next, Mr. Etheridge begins by informing the high chancellor that the music playing over the public loudspeakers of the central emergency broadcast system during the explosion was Tchaikovsky's *1812 Overture*. Sutler curtly replies, "Add it to the blacklist. I never want to hear that music again." Nodding, Etheridge reports that random radio sweeps have been doubled and phone surveillance is being carefully scrutinized, sharing that his findings "indicate a high percentage of conversation concerned about the explosion." Sutler immediately asks Mr. Dascomb what is being done about this concern. He informs the high chancellor that the BTN is calling it an "emergency demolition." Dascomb has arranged for spin coverage on the television and the Interlink, including the reports of "several experts who will testify against the Bailey's structural integrity." To this plan, Sutler adds, "I want Prothero to speak tonight on the dangers of these old buildings and how we must avoid clinging to the edifice of a decadent past. He should conclude that the New Bailey will become the symbol of our time and the future that our conviction has rewarded us." Mr. Heyer next reports that the security cameras captured several images of the terrorist, but that his Guy Fawkes mask made retinal identification impossible. Photos also revealed that a young woman accompanied the terrorist. Sutler turns to Mr. Finch, wanting to know what he knows about the girl. Finch replies that he is exploring a few leads on her identity.[11] After reporting that the explosives were homemade with over-the-counter chemicals, Finch concludes, "Whoever he is, chancellor, he is very good." Sutler immediately interjects, "Spare us your professional annotations, Mr. Finch, they are completely irrelevant."

Sutler quickly sums up the situation: "Gentlemen, this is a test. Moments such as these are matters of faith. To fail is to invite doubt into everything we believe, everything that we have fought for. Doubt will plunge this country back into chaos, and I will not let that happen. . . . Gentlemen, I want this terrorist found and I want him to understand what terror really means. England prevails." Again we see the complete reign that Sutler has over the country. He meets with his aides in the middle of the night in secret conference rooms. They speak only when spoken to and report only the facts. All other commentary is irrelevant. Sutler has instituted a blacklist of music, as well as (we find out later) of books and art. Possessing these illegal items carries severe punishment. He provides the final word on how the news is to be reported and gives explicit orders as to what the "Voice of London" will say. When the terrorist is found, he will not merely be faced with criminal charges, but will be the subject of state-sanctioned terror himself. Sutler in effect provides unity for Great Britain, as his will in the only one that is realized. Through this unity, England remains strong, and England prevails.

Interestingly enough, there is another aspect of Sutler's rule that Hobbes countenances. Sutler and his Norsefire ultraconservative party have seemingly instituted a state-sanctioned religion. Prothero, and thus Sutler, believe that the demise of the United States was ultimately due to divine judgment. America is being punished for "Godlessness," as Prothero puts it. Prothero rhetorically asks his viewers, "Do you think he's not up there? You think he's not watching over this country? How else do you explain it? He tested us but we came through. . . . Immigrants, Muslims, homosexuals, terrorists, disease-ridden degenerates. They had to go! I am a God-fearing Englishman, and I'm proud of it!" England will not crumble because it will not be Godless. Hobbes underscores this political strategy by affirming:

> This fear of things invisible is the natural seed of that which every one in himself calls religion; and in them that worship or fear that power otherwise than they do, superstition. . . . And this seed of religion, having been observed by many, some of those that have observed it have been inclined thereby to nourish, dress, and form it into laws; and to add to it, of their own invention, any opinion of the causes of future events by which they thought they should best be able to govern others and make unto themselves the greatest use of their powers.[12]

For Hobbes, the only difference between religion and superstition is what doctrine the state sanctions. But the sovereign has complete control over which doctrines are to be publicly taught and which are to be suppressed.[13] The driving force in this choice is to establish and preserve peace. Thus, for Hobbes, religion becomes one more mode of the sovereign's political control, and typically an effective one at that.

But preserving the authenticity of a state-sanctioned religion requires a proper figurehead. Among the important features, according to Hobbes, is that the faith of the multitude be focused on "one person, whom they believe not only to be wise, and to labor to procure their happiness, but also to be a holy man, to whom God himself entrusts to declare His will supernaturally."[14] Adam Sutler is a deeply religious man who promises to secure the happiness of British citizens. He is revered by the English people, as demonstrated by the fact that his portrait hangs in places of honor in so many households. He all but prophesied the pending bioterrorist attack. More importantly, once Sutler was elected, God provided British citizens with a cure to the horrific St. Mary's virus. This can only be a sign that God has entrusted England to Sutler. The British are consequently unified in their faith in Adam Sutler and his state-sanctioned religion. England achieves strength through its faith, and England prevails.

Valerie's Story

Evey Hammond (Natalie Portman) is interrogated due to her involvement with the terrorist V. The person in an adjoining cell contacts Evey with a letter written on toilet paper. The author's name is Valerie (Natasha Wightman), and the letter is her autobiography. Valerie fears that she may die in this awful place. She shares her story with Evey as an act of love and support, hoping that Evey will live to escape.

We learn that young Valerie was unlike most other young women. Rather than chasing boys, she was more fascinated with girls. Her first girlfriend was Sarah (Laura Greenwood). Valerie remembers her beautiful wrists. The high school counselor assured the two girls that their mutual infatuation was merely a passing phase. Sarah indeed grew out of it, but Valerie did not. Her interest was not merely some forbidden schoolgirl crush; it was expressive of who (and how) she was. Her next serious girlfriend was Christina (Kyra Meyer). Now a young adult and with Chris by her side, she "came out" to her parents. They disowned her. Valerie recounts, "But I only told the truth. Was that so selfish? Our integrity sells for so little, but it is all we really have. It is the very last inch of us. But within that inch, we are free." Once an actress, Valerie starred in *The Salt Flats*. She shares with Evey that "it was the most important role of my life, not because of my career, but because that is how I met Ruth [Mary Stockley]. The first time we kissed, I knew that I never wanted to kiss any other lips but hers again." The two lovers moved to a small flat in London together. Ruth grew Scarlet Carsons for Valerie in their window box, and thus their apartment always smelled of roses. Those were the best years of her life.

But Valerie's makeshift autobiography becomes foreboding as she recounts how America's war came to London. She wistfully reports, "After that, there were no roses anymore, not for anyone." She further tells Evey that this was the time when the meaning of words began to change. Unfamiliar words like "collateral" and "rendition" became frightening, while "Norsefire" and "Articles of Allegiance" became powerful, but being "different" became dangerous. Even now, she still does not quite understand why the government hated people like her so much. Valerie tells Evey that they took Ruth while she was out buying food; Valerie never cried so hard in her life. It wasn't long before the Fingermen came for her. They barged into her flat while she sat quietly on the couch and hauled her away to a detention facility. She admits that it is strange that her life should end in this terrible place, but "for three years, she had roses and apologized to no one." She accepts that she will die here; every inch of her shall perish—every inch but one. This inch is "small and fragile, and it is the only thing in the world worth having. We must never lose it or give it away, and we must never let them take it away from us."

Evey never knew Valerie apart from the words on the tissue paper. They never met. John Locke never knew or met Valerie either (obviously), but the fictional character and the historical philosopher agree on one thing: the value and importance of human life. The fact of human existence is so important that each of us possesses natural or basic human rights merely in virtue of being human. Locke writes:

> The state of Nature has a law of Nature to govern it, which obliges everyone, and reason, which is that law, teaches all mankind who will but consult it, that being all equal and independent, no one ought to harm another in his life, health, liberty or possessions. . . . Everyone as he is bound to preserve himself, and not quit his station willfully, so by the like reason, when his own preservation comes not into competition, ought he as much as he can to preserve the rest of mankind, and not unless it be to do justice on an offender, take away or impair the life, or what tends to be the preservation of life, the liberty, health, limb, or goods of another.[15]

Locke thus also believes in (normative) laws of nature, but, unlike Hobbes, holds that they are binding in the state of nature, that is, prior to any established government. The operative moral law here is something like "Mankind ought to be preserved and co-exist in peaceful interactions with one another."[16] This law is grounded partly in our rationality—our ability to recognize the dictates of the moral law and why it is important to do so. It is also grounded in our equality. About this crucial idea, Locke further explains that nothing is "more evident than that creatures of the same species and rank, promiscuously [indiscriminately] born to all the same advantages of Nature, and the use of the same faculties, should also be equal one amongst another, without subordination or subjection."[17] Because we are naturally rational and equal in status, each of us is bound by the moral obligation not to impinge on the life and liberty of another.

Because of our ability to understand the moral law, we grasp the supreme significance of respecting our equality and independence. We are thus bound not to harm another person's life, liberty, or possessions because by choosing to harm others in this way, we fail to act in accordance with what is supremely valuable in life. This moral obligation grounds our basic human rights. Possessing a (moral) right is a justified claim against others to respect some moral obligation. We can thus justifiably demand, as is our (natural) right, that others respect our equality and independence. In fact, our ability to do this further grounds our unique status as natural rights possessors. For Valerie, what grounds our uniqueness is our integrity as individuals. Our integrity is our very humanness; it underlies who we are and the projects we undergo. It is supremely valuable. This is why she believes that it is the only thing truly worth having and the only thing that we should never give away. To give it away is to give up being the independent human person we are; this would fail to respect our equal status with others. For others to take it from us is for them to fail to respect our equality. Thus, we have a right to have our integrity—our humanness—respected. Locke calls it being created as rational with the capability to grasp the natural (moral) law; Valerie calls it integrity. However, these terms are merely different ways to articulate the same idea.

Insofar as Locke holds that we ought not to harm another in terms of his or her life, health, limb, liberty, or possessions, we could say that Locke holds we ought not to (unjustifiably) impinge on another's happiness. Thus you have a basic right not to have your happiness infringed upon. Valerie clearly had her happiness infringed upon. She was living quietly with Ruth in a loving, consensual, adult relationship. She and her projects posed no real threat to others. But the newly elected Norsefire political regime imposed its agenda on Valerie, Ruth, and others who were deemed "different" and thus dangerous. Under the blanket of national security, people like Valerie were taken to detention facilities and used in research for advancing England's biological weapons program (of course, without consent), which led to many tragic deaths, including Valerie's. Sutler and his new articles indeed unjustifiably infringed on the happiness of many, if not all, of England's citizenry. The extensive and constant surveillance, the strict curfews for mature adults, the restriction of public transportation, the blacklisting of arts and literature (including statues of the Buddha and copies of the Koran) all work to objectionably curtail the happiness of British citizens. But, for Locke, our happiness is merely a matter of not having our basic human rights unnecessarily infringed upon. Thus, Locke (as does Valerie) would conclude that the nature of the social contract after Sutler takes office violates basic human rights. As we will soon see, this is reason to doubt the genuineness of Sutler's political authority in England.

The so-called terrorist V (Hugo Weaving) also finds Sutler's authority dubious. But V's motives are two-pronged. In a style akin to that of Alexandre Dumas's *Count of Monte Cristo,* he exacts his revenge against those who harmed him. This helps to explain the title of the film (and graphic novel). But once vengeance is satisfied, V places a single Scarlet Carson on each of his casualties. Each of his "victims" was directly responsible for the atrocities performed on Valerie and other "social undesirables" (like V himself, as we later learn, which begins to explain his resolve). The Scarlet Carsons thus embody something greater than merely V's vendetta. They symbolize happiness. As it was taken from Britain, V takes the life of those responsible. The rose is thus a symbol of what is lost. This is why Valerie claims that once Sutler came to power, there were no roses for anyone. This is why the last time we see V, he is riding in a subway car surrounded by Scarlet Carsons. And this is why V makes his vendetta public. He works to demonstrate the inherent tyranny of the Sutler regime.

Sutler as Lockean Tyrant

Locke thus differs with Hobbes about the necessity of subjecting ourselves to tyranny in order to preserve our best interests. He believes that Hobbes offers us a false dilemma: Either subject ourselves to complete tyranny or suffer the ordeals of chaos and anarchy in the state of nature.[18] It is not necessary for us to fear our government; there is a third alternative. Locke does not believe that the state of nature would be an unbearable constant struggle of everyone against everyone. He believes that persons are basically decent and that we regularly will consult the moral law and respect each other's basic rights. But Locke is not naive. He realizes that a few people in the state of nature will invariably choose not to uphold the moral law. Because of this, Locke agrees with Hobbes about the need for government. Our interests are better served if we enter into a social contract with others and erect a stable government.

Locke believes that our interests are better served by the state due to three interlocking facts about human persons and our relationship to the moral law. First, understanding the (normative) laws of nature requires time, effort, and skill, but not everyone is able or willing to commit to grasping them. Second, people are often clouded by self-interest in applying the law and meting out appropriate punishments for infractions of it. Third, even if some individuals accomplish fair and impartial application of the law, not everyone will be able (for various reasons) to execute punishment. These three facts make life in the state of nature unstable and uneasy (although not nasty, brutish, and short). Thus we soon form governments in order to better protect our basic rights.[19] Doing so is clearly in our best interest. We benefit by the establishment of common law, the machinery to settle disputes among interested parties, the elevation of impartial judges to rule over such disputes, and the political means by which to enforce the judges' decisions.

By entering into the social contract, individuals agree not to punish infractions of the moral law themselves; we transfer that power to the state. We thereby agree to uphold the laws of the state generally. However, we are bound to this agreement on the condition that the state works to preserve our liberty and property, which is the common good.[20] But recall that Locke interprets "property" in a broad sense. This includes all that we have a right to—our lives, health, limbs, liberty, and estates. Therefore, when the government extends its power beyond the common good, which is the joint preservation of our basic rights, and begins to infringe on our property (and thus happiness), our duty to recognize the government's authority is rendered null and void.

Cases where the government becomes tyrannical provide the best examples of how our obligation to the state is nullified. Tyranny occurs when governments, under the pretense of political authority, purposively act to violate our basic rights to life, health, limb, and liberty. Locke writes: "Tyranny is the exercise of power beyond right, which nobody can have a right to; and this is making use of the power anyone has in his hands, not for the good of those who are under it, but for his own private, separate advantage. When the governor, however entitled, makes not the laws, but his will, the rule, and his commands and actions are not directed at the preservation of the properties of his people, but the satisfaction of his own ambition, revenge,

The "terrorist" V battles two of Chancellor Sutler's officers to save Evey Hammond, and to reclaim the rights of man from the oppressive Norsefire government. (Jerry Ohlinger's Movie Material Store)

covetousness, or any other irregular passion [tyranny obtains]."[21] When tyranny begins, true government ends. The social contract is effectively dissolved, and the magistrate thereby surrenders his (or her) authority. Acting without authority, the magistrate ceases to be such and may be justifiably resisted, like any other transgressor of human rights.

Sutler's rule certainly seems tyrannical. It is infused with ambition for money and especially power. Sutler and the Norsefire party heads were responsible for developing and unleashing the St. Mary's virus. Norsefire party heads became obscenely rich and powerful once the cure was made public. The party was also responsible for the "social cleansing" that resulted in the persecution and death of additional English citizens. Although Sutler was not high chancellor when these events took place, they remain evidence of the lengths to which he and his undersecretaries (Creedy especially) are willing to go to keep power. Thus, Sutler's covetousness to retain power persists. The "social cleansing" mandates remain in effect. People who are deemed "different" and thus dangerous continue to live in fear, if they live at all. He and Dascomb continue to spin the news and limit the flow of information pertinent to the public good.[22] He has made various "decadent" commodities—like butter—illegal, but he continues to enjoy them. The blacklist grows, with the *1812 Overture* becoming the latest artistic taboo. In fact, the list ballooned so quickly that Sutler instituted a Ministry of Objectionable Materials, which V relies on to furnish his lavish "Shadow Gallery" abode. Whenever Sutler's authority is challenged, be it in the form of Finch's professional annotations, or V's more overt tactics, Sutler responds with vitriol, quick to exact revenge (and not merely retribution) for any affront. When V's timetable for a second terrorist outburst draws near, Sutler charges his undersecretaries "to make everyone remember why they need us!" Creedy doubles arrests. Dascomb fabricates inflammatory news stories, including those about the avian flu. It is reported that a new virus has killed twenty-seven British citizens. If this story is true, it is probably Sutler's doing. If it is false, it is another instance of his regime wielding fear, not justice. Because Sutler exerts political power that he is no longer entitled to, V acts properly to spur the citizens of Britain to oppose him.

Voracious Villain . . . Virtuous Vanguard . . . Vox Populi?

One can now see how V is more of a patriot or freedom fighter than a terrorist (even if his overall character remains morally ambiguous). His attempt to spur a revolution begins with his blowing up the Old Bailey justice building. But V marks the event by playing the *1812 Overture* through the public loudspeakers. Just before the fireworks begin, V tells Evey, "It is to Madame Justice that I dedicate this concerto in honor of the holiday she seems to have taken from these parts, and in recognition of the imposter that stands in her stead." The imposter is most certainly Sutler. By making his will the law, he operates above it. Only hours after destroying the Bailey, V hacks his way into the emergency broadcasting channel at the BTN to make his intentions clear. Over every tele and public broadcasting screen in the country, he provides England his diagnosis of the country's basic problem and urges his fellow countrymen to join him a year from now to enact the cure.[23] But, of course, the citizenry must decide for themselves whether they should enact their right to rise up against the Sutler establishment.[24]

Locke would concur with V's call for mobilization. Governmental authority, for Locke, is ultimately grounded in trust. Citizens entrust their government to protect their rights and thus their interests. When political authority violates its trust, it reverts back to the people and they are at liberty to dissolve the government. Locke writes:

> Governments are dissolved . . . when the legislative, or the prince . . . act contrary to their trust. . . . The legislative act against the trust reposed in them when they endeavor to invade the property of the subject, and to make for themselves, or any part of the community, masters, or arbitrary disposers of the lives, liberties, or fortunes of the people. . . . Whensoever, therefore, the legislative shall transgress this fundamental rule of society, and either by ambition, fear, folly, or corruption, endeavor to grasp themselves, or put into the hands of any other, an absolute power over the lives, liberties, and estates of the people, by this breach of trust they forfeit the power the people had put into their hands for quite contrary ends, and it devolves to the people, who have a right to resume their original liberty, and by the establishment of a new legislative (such as they shall think fit), provide for their own safety and security, which is the end for which they are in society.[25]

Sutler's cartel indeed grasped for themselves an absolute power over the lives, liberties, and fortunes of the British people. This was the very reason that Creedy suggested to Sutler that they unleash the Larkhill-developed bioweapon against the British people. This spawned fear, which allowed the Norsefire party to accomplish its greater, ultraconservative agenda at the expense of their fellow countrymen. Locke would thus agree with V that revolution is appropriate; Sutler's administration clearly violated its trust with the citizenry. That revolution is called for is exactly why V believes that governments should fear their people. The people are the true shareholders in the corporation of society. Like any other corporation, the shareholders empower its executives conditionally. If the executives do not run the company with the best interests of the shareholders in mind, the shareholders retain the right to remove them. Therefore, regardless of what we might think about a man who painstakingly and surgically exacts cold-blooded revenge—and by his own admission it consumed him for twenty years—he is on firm Lockean grounds for rousing the British people to revolt against the tyranny of the Sutler regime.

Locke, Jefferson, and the Wachowski Brothers

It is well known that Thomas Jefferson, himself an astute fledgling philosopher, was influenced by Locke. Even a casual reading of the opening lines of the Declaration of Independence reveals this:

> We hold these Truths to be self-evident, that all Men are created equal, that they are endowed by their Creator with certain unalienable Rights, that among these are Life, Liberty, and the Pursuit of Happiness—That to secure these Rights, Governments are instituted among Men, deriving their just Powers from the Consent of the Governed, that whenever any Form of Government becomes destructive of these Ends, it is the Right of the People to alter or to abolish it, and to institute new Government, laying its Foundation on such Principles, and organizing its Powers in such Form, as to them shall seem most likely to effect their Safety and Happiness.

Thus Locke's influence on America's brand of democracy cannot be overstated. It reaches all the way back to the founding fathers.

But Locke's influence over American political thought doesn't end there. Locke also argues for a separation of political powers, thus ensuring the rubric of a checks and balances system of political authority.[26] There are no checks on Sutler's power. At best, he is a Hobbesian sovereign; at worst, he is merely a tyrannical dictator. Locke also believes in the separation of church and state.[27] He believes the domain of each is sufficiently different that combining them can only become problematic. Indeed, intertwining the two can serve as a powerful tool of oppression, as it does in Sutler's hands. It seems likely that the careful reader could find other connections between Locke, Jefferson, and contemporary American political thought if only she were to look.

Having clarified Locke's influence on American political thought through the lens of *V for Vendetta*, the philosophical talents of the Wachowskis are not merely verisimilitudinous, but verily vindicated as veritas. They have done an admirable job teaching us about Locke's (and Hobbes's) political philosophy. And the movie spurs other philosophical questions not discussed here: Was V a virtuous person? Did he impermissibly treat Evey by subjecting her to torture-type scenarios given the fact that she wished she was a stronger person? It is incredibly unlikely that the Wachowskis will ever become influential American philosophers. Nevertheless, it would be a bit of a shame if their renown remains limited to directing a special effects movie about a guy who emerges from a tub of pink goop only to become the "chosen one." Perhaps this essay did its part to prevent that.[28]

Notes

1. Recall that Moore and Lloyd in the graphic novel profess philosophical anarchy as the proper response to fascist regimes and not Lockean social contract theory. Therefore, it cannot be said that the Wachowskis were merely amplifying philosophical themes that were already present in their source material. This is further testament to their skills as armchair philosophers.

2. Thomas Hobbes, *Leviathan* (London, 1651), chapter 13. Hobbes's prose appears with some stylistic emendations.

3. Ibid., chapter 13. Hobbes continues, "For such is the nature of men that howsoever they may acknowledge many others to be more witty, or more eloquent or more learned, yet they will hardly believe there be many so wise as themselves; for they see their own wit at hand, and other men's at a distance." Hobbes's view here has an interesting parallel to the movie. Arguably, the different party heads each possess different talents and strengths (both physical and mental), but each is terribly distrusting of the others. This remains so even if one believes himself to be more intelligent than another, or a second believes himself to be more cunning and resourceful than the first.

4. Ibid.

5. Ibid., chapter 14.

6. Ibid.

7. It is interesting to note that Hobbes's two laws of nature trade on an ambiguity between descriptive and normative states of affairs. Typically, laws of nature are merely descriptive. According to the law of gravity, objects on earth *will* fall at 9.8 meters per second squared, and on the law of inertia, objects *will* stay at rest (or *will* stay in motion) until acted on by another body (or force). These laws of nature are not at all normative. Normativity is the idea that something should happen a certain way, or that a person should perform a certain behavior. There is no intelligible sense of what physical objects should do, even if we can intelligibly predict what they will do. But Hobbes's two laws of nature do include both descriptive and normative elements. The reason for this is that he is describing the behavior of *rational* animals. Realizing his two "laws," thinks Hobbes, is actually in our best interest, and because we are rational creatures, we will eventually abide by them to the best of our abilities. Seemingly, this is why he calls them laws—we will (eventually) act in accordance with them in roughly the same sense that falling objects act in accordance with the law of gravity.

8. *Leviathan*, chapter 17.

9. There is apparently one small caveat to this. Hobbes believes that the sovereign's political power is limitless assuming that the sovereign acts rationally. That is, the sovereign does not have the authority to act in ways that undermine his power. What sorts of acts Hobbes has in mind isn't always clear, but presumably a sovereign cannot rule the commonwealth if he commits suicide. Thus, the sovereign does not have the authority to take his own life (even if he might have the authority to ask for yours).

10. *Leviathan*, chapter 17.

11. In the graphic novel, Moore and Lloyd accordingly call Etheridge's department the "Ear," Dascomb's the "Mouth," Creedy's the "Finger," Heyer's the "Eye," and Finch's the "Nose." The idea is that Sutler (or Adam Susan in the graphic novel) is clearly the "head" of England, doing all of its thinking. (In the graphic novel, this analogy is tempered by the fact that "Fate," a supercomputer, seems to do most of Susan's thinking for him.) The various factions thus play the role of information gatherers (the eyes, ears, and nose) or enact Sutler's commands (the finger and the mouth).

12. *Leviathan*, chapter 11.

13. Ibid., chapter 18. A careful viewer of the film will recall that although Gordon Deitrich (Stephen Fry) was abducted by Fingermen because the most recent episode of his comedy talk show cast the high chancellor in a bad light, he was killed because Creedy's men found a copy of the Koran in a secret room in his house.

14. Ibid., chapter 12.

15. John Locke, *The Second Treatise of Government* (New York: Barnes and Noble, 2004), chapter 2, section 6. page 4. The first and third segments of section 6 are excerpted here. In the middle section, Locke buttresses his account of basic human rights and moral obligations with an argument grounded in God's role in creating us. The extent to which Locke's moral and political views require religious grounding is controversial. Some scholars believe that Locke offers two distinct defenses of human rights and moral obligation, making his arguments "over-determined." Others believe that Locke's theistic and more naturalistic arguments can be integrated to offer one unified theory to ground his ethical and political views. Even if Locke is necessarily committed to his theistic arguments (another controversial position), there are places in his work (for example, *Second Treatise*, chapter 16, section 195) where he clearly believes that even God must affirm the normative laws of nature, making such laws logically prior to God's will. Therefore, God's role in Locke's ethical and political theory is not one where God invents the moral law by mere fiat. Thus, God is not to be interpreted as some sort of king arbitrarily handing down laws to humankind, a political position that Locke goes to great pains in the *Second Treatise* to avoid.

16. See *Second Treatise*, chapter 2, section 7, page 5. However, note that Locke believes that built into this law is the means to punish those who transgress it. That is, if people willfully choose to violate this law, then they choose to forfeit their security under it. In fact, such transgressors become an enemy to humankind; therefore, by the strictures of the law itself, they must be dealt with accordingly for the preservation of

humankind. A careful reading of the *Second Treatise* will uncover Locke arguing for other qualifiers to this general law as well.

17. *Second Treatise,* chapter 2, section 4, page 3. At the end of this section, Locke adds an apparent qualifier to his basic position about equality, writing, ". . . unless the lord and master of them all should, by any manifest declaration of his will, set one above another, and confer on him, by an evident and clear appointment an undoubted right to dominion and sovereignty." Most scholars agree that Locke adds this clause sarcastically because it pretty clearly refers to something like the "divine right of kings" to rule over subjects. Locke's sarcasm is better understood once the reader (a) recalls that in the *First Treatise on Government,* Locke dismantled the most persuasive argument for the divine right of kings (arguments Locke recapitulates for the reader in the opening lines of the *Second Treatise of Government*) and (b) compares the two halves of section 4 to realize how completely implausible it is to qualify the first half at all (especially given the arguments that Locke subsequently offers in the remainder of the *Second Treatise*).

18. To be fair, the kind of anarchy that Hobbes and Locke (more or less) intend is different from the kind of anarchy that Moore and Lloyd intend in the graphic novel. For more on the latter kind of anarchy, see Robert Paul Wolff, *In Defense of Anarchism* (New York: Harper and Row, 1970).

19. *Second Treatise,* chapter 9, sections 123–27.

20. Ibid., chapter 9, section 131.

21. Ibid., chapter 18, section 199, page 112.

22. Interestingly enough, when the original spin on the Bailey "demolition" airs, Dascomb is asked by a network associate whether anyone will believe it. He smugly replies, "Why not? Our job is to report the news, not fabricate it. That's the government's job." The irony is that Dascomb is part of the government and so he knowingly spins the news and assists Sutler in doing it.

23. V's speech, excerpted:

> There is something terribly wrong with this country, isn't there? Cruelty and injustice, intolerance and oppression. And where once you had the freedom to object, to think and speak as you saw fit, you now have censors and surveillance coercing your conformity and soliciting submission. . . . I know why you did it. I know you were afraid. Who wouldn't be? War, terror, disease. There were a myriad of problems which conspired to corrupt your reason and rob you of your common sense. Fear got the best of you. And in your panic, you turned to the now High Chancellor Adam Sutler. He promised you order, he promised you peace . . . and all he demanded in return was your silent, obedient consent. . . . But if you see what I see, if you feel as I feel, and if you would seek as I seek, then I ask you to stand beside me, one year from tonight outside the gates of Parliament. And together, we shall give them a 5th of November . . . that shall never, ever be forgot.

24. When the year was up, V indeed left the final choice of revolution completely

in Evey's hands (even though Finch's concurrence ultimately allowed Evey to carry out her decision). This might represent the choice that the citizens had to make in opting for political upheaval. The congregants outside the Parliament building bolstered Evey's choice that Britain was better off overthrowing Sutler's regime. The people must decide, carefully and in clear conscience, whether revolution is called for and thus whether they are better off without the current political structure.

25. *Second Treatise,* chapter 19, sections 221 and 222, pages 123–24. Furthermore, see *Second Treatise,* chapter 11, section 137, for a similar argument for the permissibility of political revolution against an "absolute arbitrary political power."

26. Ibid., chapter 12, section 143. However, Locke's division of powers is not quite the familiar one of legislative, executive, and judiciary. See chapter 12, sections 146 and 147 of the *Second Treatise.*

27. In his "Letter on Toleration" (1689), Locke writes:

> I esteem it above all things necessary to distinguish exactly the business of civil government from that of religion and to settle the just bounds that lie between the one and the other. If this be not done, there can be no end put to the controversies that will be always arising between those that have, or at least pretend to have, on the one side, a concernment for the interest of men's souls, and, on the other side, a care of the commonwealth. . . . The care of souls cannot belong to the civil magistrate, because his power consists only in outward force; but true and saving religion consists in the inward persuasion of the mind, without which nothing can be acceptable to God. . . . And, upon this ground, I affirm that the magistrate's power extends not to the establishing of any articles of faith, or forms of worship, by the force of his laws. For laws are of no force at all without penalties, and penalties in this case are absolutely impertinent, because they are not proper to convince the mind.

28. William Irwin is another philosopher who extols the philosophical insights of the Wachowski brothers. See the two volumes he's edited, *The Matrix and Philosophy: Welcome to the Desert of the Real* (Chicago: Open Court Press, 2002) and *More Matrix and Philosophy: Revolutions and Reloaded Decoded* (Chicago: Open Court Press, 2005).

3

POLITICAL CULTURE AND PUBLIC OPINION

The American Dream on Springfield's Evergreen Terrace

J. Michael Bitzer

> Please, please, kids, stop fighting. Maybe Lisa's right about America being the land of opportunity, and maybe Adil's got a point about the machinery of capitalism being oiled with the blood of the workers.
>
> —Homer Simpson

When a little girl's father finishes a free sample of *Reading Digest,* she notices an essay contest: "*Children under 12. Three hundred words, fiercely pro-American.* Sounds interesting." When she can't find her muse for the essay, the little girl rides to the local national forest for inspiration. Sitting amid the towering trees that allow rays of sunlight to beam down, the little girl solicits the landscape: "Okay, America, inspire me." As she gazes out to the snow-capped purple mountain majesties, a bald eagle lands on a tree branch in front of her (notably between leaves that look akin to an olive branch in one talon and the shafts of arrows in the other). Spreading its wings and cocking its head to one side, the vision awes the little girl, and she proceeds to write her essay.

Along with her father, the little girl presents her essay at the Veterans of Popular Wars hall, right after another child presents his defense of burning the American flag. In her essay, entitled "The Roots of Democracy," the little girl recounts her vision of America: "When America was born on that hot July day in 1776, the trees in Springfield Forest were tiny saplings, trembling towards the sun. And as they were nourished by Mother Earth, so too did our fledgling nation find strength in the simple ideals of equality and justice. Who would have thought such mighty oaks or such a powerful nation could grow out of something so fragile, so pure?"[1]

Once the judges confirm that she, and not her father, wrote the essay, the little girl and her family win an all-expense-paid trip to Washington, D.C., to compete in the finals. While visiting a memorial to a leading women's rights pioneer, the little girl overhears her hometown congressman taking a bribe to permit logging in the same forest where she found her inspiration. Disillusioned, she tears up her essay and envisions the capital morphed into a trough of pork barrel projects and legislative pigs stuffing their snouts with bribes.

A different muse, one of a muckraker exposing graft, payola, and corruption, drives the little girl to write a new essay on what she has witnessed. She reads, "The city of Washington was built on a stagnant swamp some 200 years ago and very little has changed. It stank then and it stinks now. Only today, it is the fetid stench of corruption that hangs in the air." Amid the audience's gasps, the disillusioned little girl continues her torrid portrayal of the nation's capital: "And who did I see taking a bribe but the 'honorable' Bob Arnold. But don't worry, Congressman, I'm sure you can buy all the votes you need with your dirty money. And this will be one nation under the dollar with liberty and justice for none."

Following a call by one of the competition's judges, the Federal Bureau of Investigation conducts a sting operation of the crooked congressman, who is expelled from the legislature and serves time in prison (where he miraculously becomes a born-again Christian). Upon hearing the news, the little girl gasps, "I can't believe it. The system works."

This episode from the third season of *The Simpsons*, "Mr. Lisa Goes to Washington," advocates more than what Homer observes: "Oh, Marge, cartoons don't have any deep meaning. They're just stupid drawings that give you a cheap laugh," upon which he stands up and exposes his "rear cleavage." This episode, along with many others in the long-running animated series, espouses the virtues, vices, and varieties of American political culture, public opinion, and ultimately the American Dream. Through the skillful use of satire, *The Simpsons* demonstrates insights into the underlying political culture and public opinion of the United States' governing system (and, more broadly, society at large). This chapter presents an overview, as well as the differing ideas, of the concepts of political culture, public opinion,

America's most "nuclear" family, the Simpsons, provides insight into the different attitudes, ideologies, and values prevalent in American democracy in the longest running animated series in history. (Jerry Ohlinger's Movie Material Store)

and the "American Dream," all through the medium of the Fox Network's series *The Simpsons.*[2]

Culture and Politics

Both the umbrella concept of "culture" and the particular concept of "political culture" share common ideas and purposes; nevertheless, scholars have differing ideas and definitions of what constitutes culture and political culture. In general, a broad view of culture can be seen through what Walter Lippmann, a famous American journalist and political commentator, wrote in 1914: "Culture is the name for what people are interested in, their thoughts, their models, the books they read and the speeches they hear, their table-talk, gossip, controversies, historical sense and scientific training, the values they appreciate, the quality of life they admire. *All communities have culture. It is the climate of their civilization*" (emphasis added).[3]

All societies have some kind of culture that represents a people's way of life. Culture is characterized best by a variety of components, such as values, beliefs, symbols, languages, norms, and even physical matter. Values serve as important components of culture by defining desirable and important principles or ideals within a society; values are the thoughts about what ought to be in a society, and as Seymour Martin Lipset describes, are "well-entrenched, culturally determined sentiments."[4] Beliefs are seen as common concepts of a society and its people about what is true. Each society has core values that serve as its foundational basis; often these values center on the role and importance of the individual citizen, their responsibilities and protections within the society, and the role and importance of the collective grouping of citizens. An example is the freedom of speech, which is a value respected and cherished in the United States, as is the value of tolerating all viewpoints. However, these two values can conflict with each other when the freedom to speak unpopular ideas challenges the value of tolerating different viewpoints.

Along with these two important concepts, symbols and language are considered to be reflections of these values and beliefs, by embodying a society's values and beliefs within concrete terms and actions. For example, the preamble to the U.S. Constitution asserts that all political power rests with its citizens: "We the People of the United States, in Order to form a more perfect Union, . . . do ordain and establish this Constitution." This language gives concrete form to the value that political sovereignty, or the principle of legitimate power and authority, rests with "the people." Along with symbols and language, norms are generally considered to be rules, or guidelines, by which a society enforces its values and beliefs upon its citizens.

All of these intangible concepts (values, beliefs, and norms) may be identified, reinforced, and promoted through such tangible physical products as automobiles. When one sees an automobile as a product, or artifact, of a society's culture, one associates certain values and attitudes within that society with the artifact, such as mobility, individualism, and exploration. Even television shows and movies can serve as artifacts that demonstrate the values, beliefs, even attitudes that constitute a society's culture. As Allan McBride and Robert Toburen assert, the "images that are saved and broadcast on magnetic tape provide clues about . . . our society in social, political, and economic terms."[5]

Beyond these basic components, different types of culture may emerge within a society. This book's key argument centers on the differences between popular culture, defined as commercial entertainment produced for mass consumption, and high culture, or entertainment produced for an elite class for very exclusive consumption. What appeals to elites, such as Robert Underdunk Terwilliger (a.k.a. Sideshow Bob), might be the staging of the operetta *H.M.S. Pinafore,* while the lowbrow comedy of Krusty the Klown and the violent escapades of *The Itchy and Scratchy Show* may appeal to the masses (most notably Bart and, ironically, Lisa). Along with popular and high culture, other forms of culture may exist, such as economic culture, religious culture, sub-cultures, and, for the purposes of this chapter, political culture.

Within the political science discipline, the study of political culture mirrors the diversity of what constitutes the political way of life of a society. For example, in 1956, Gabriel Almond contended that "every political system is embedded in a particular pattern of orientations to political action," what he called political culture.[6] Later, in a now classic work, Almond and Sidney Verba defined political culture as "specifically political orientations—attitudes toward the political system and its various parts, and attitudes toward the role of the self in the system."[7] These attitudes have an impact on what citizens know about their political and governing system, what their feelings are toward that political system, and how they judge their political system.

Almond and Verba contend that there are three types of political culture that ultimately make up a broader concept of "civic culture." The first, participant political culture, is when citizens are highly in tune with the political activity and events of their society and they actively participate in political life: "members of the society tend to be explicitly oriented to the system as a whole and to both the political and administrative structures and processes."[8] This type of political culture is evident in the *Simpsons* episode "Much Apu About Nothing," when local citizens, outraged by supposedly constant bear attacks in Springfield, march to City Hall and demand that the mayor do something. Once the citizens get their Bear Patrol, complete with a stealth bomber, they are outraged by the taxes to pay for the patrols. Under siege at City Hall with citizens chanting "Down with Taxes!," Mayor "Diamond Joe" Quimby asks an aide, "Are these morons getting dumber, or just louder?" "Dumber, sir. They won't give up the bear patrol, but they won't pay taxes for it either," remarks the aide.[9]

Unlike active citizen involvement found in participant culture, a second form is that of subject culture, where citizens believe that they have little impact on their society's political life, so they choose not to participate in political activities. An example of this is alluded to in "Lisa's Substitute," in which Bart runs for class president against Martin Prince and is so far ahead in terms of popularity that no one in the class—including Bart—bothers to vote, except for Martin and his friend Wendell. The students all assume a Bart victory is a foregone conclusion, and that their participation is not needed. Therefore, none of them bother to get involved.[10]

Finally, parochial political culture is when a society's citizenry focus their attention on themselves and disregard any involvement in centralized political participation, since citizens have no expectation of the larger political system aiding them in any way. In the episode "The Bart Wants What It Wants," Principal Skinner embodies the parochial culture as he begins to steal lab equipment from the Springfield Preparatory School and justifies it by saying to a shocked Lisa, "Welcome to Dick Cheney's America," before making his getaway.[11]

Analogous to Almond and Verba's definition, Daniel Elazar, in his 1966 study of the United States, describes political culture as "the particular pattern of orientation to political action in which each political system is imbedded" which is "rooted in the cumulative historical experiences of particular groups of people." Contending that a society can have numerous political cultures and that these cultures may overlap with one another, Elazar characterizes three distinct types of American political cultures: moralistic, individualistic, and traditionalistic.[12]

In his conceptualization of moralistic political culture, Elazar presents an approach to politics that exercises power and authority for the betterment of all citizens in order to achieve "some notion of the public good and . . . the advancement of the public interest." Citizens who adhere to this approach believe that it is their duty to actively participate in political life and that government should be more actively involved in both "the economic and social life of the community." This type of culture is exemplified in "Sweets and Sour Marge," where Marge gets a judge to ban the import and distribution of all sugar into Springfield after it weighs in as America's fattest city ("Woohoo! In your face, Milwaukee!") in the *Duff Book of World Records,* and in the "Weekend at Burnsie's" episode, when Ned Flanders leads a campaign for a government ban on medical marijuana.[13]

A second political culture, an individualistic one, values the principal importance of the individual within a society; therefore, government and politics should be "means by which individuals may improve themselves socially and economically." Within this culture, political activity is seen as "a specialized one, essentially the province of professionals, of minimum and passing concern to laymen, and no place for amateurs to play an active role." "Trash of the Titans" demonstrates this culture when amateur politician Homer Simpson defeats long-sitting sanitation commissioner Ray Patterson, and immediately botches the job by spending his yearly budget in less than one month. To resolve the deficit, Homer has other cities pay Springfield to take their trash; only when the trash begins to explode out of golf holes and manholes do the citizens fire Simpson and decide to relocate Springfield.[14]

Finally, Elazar contends that a third political culture, what he terms traditionalistic, exists primarily in the southern United States, where an ordered hierarchy within society determines the role and relationship of citizens. Those who are at the top of the social system, sometimes referred to as elites, are expected to play a significant role in government, while those in the lower end of the society are "not expected to be even minimally active as citizens . . . [in fact], they are not even expected to vote." Government, within this culture, is designed to promote and continue traditional values and beliefs within the society and the interpersonal relationships that have developed over time. This type of hierarchical culture is embodied in "They Saved Lisa's Brain," when Lisa and other local Mensa leaders assume the leadership of Springfield (their reign is ended, however, when an angry mob comes to overthrow them, and Stephen Hawking has to swoop in and save the day), and in the episode "Homer the Great," when a society of influential men in Springfield, known as the Sacred Order of the Stonecutters, controls all aspects of politics and society, including hiding the truth about extraterrestrials, keeping the metric system down, and even making Steve Guttenberg a movie star.[15]

All of these approaches emphasize the fact that different concepts can explain political culture; however, a different approach taken by political scientists comes from studying political culture as an explanatory factor, rather than being defined by outside forces. Following his work in defining political culture by particular actions, Gabriel Almond, in writing a study with Bingham Powell, wrote that political culture impacts "the conduct of individuals in their political roles, the content of their political demands, and their responses to laws." This approach contends that political culture is not just "what a group has" in the forms of beliefs, attitudes, and values, but also "what a group is."[16] John Street notes that while some define political culture as being "the judgments citizens pass on political behaviour," others characterize political culture as "the language through which politics is conducted." Ultimately, Street argues that culture can be seen as "more than attitudes people hold to politicians and political institutions" (or the structures of government), but as "made up of a complex of feelings and images, deriving from the home and work, from manifestos and popular culture."[17]

In an important study of American states and their political culture, Erikson, McIver, and Wright determine that the political identity and ideological characteristics of a state, from Alabama to Wyoming, can be traced back to the state's political culture, and that government actions, or policy adoptions, can be linked to the same.[18] Compare, for example, the differences in sociopolitical priorities due to differences in political culture between Springfield and Shelbyville in "The Seven-Beer Snitch," where Shelbyville enjoys a thriving cultural arts community and Springfield cannot even sustain their short-lived Frank Gehry–designed cultural center.[19]

The conflict over what defines and what constitutes political culture, as well as the impact it has on society, continues to demonstrate the variety and variations surrounding the core issues of what make up a society's political and governing system. This expression of "a people's political way of life" has a significant relationship in the expression of those "people's" beliefs and attitudes about their political system. Conversely, changes in people's beliefs and attitudes can impact and evolve a society's political culture. As any society and its citizens mature, attitudes and beliefs can evolve and change as well. While the underlying beliefs and attitudes within a society about its politics and government serve as its political culture, the day-to-day (and often year-to-year) attitudes and beliefs about politics and government are a society's public opinion. Both political culture and public opinion interact with one another; the attitudes of political culture serve as the foundation to a society's political and governing system, while public opinion serves as important and necessary component to the daily political system, particularly within the United States.

The Power to Shape, and Be Shaped by, Public Opinion

Just like political culture, public opinion is often viewed in different ways. Public opinion can be seen as the collection, distribution, and summation of the public's preferences on issues, events, and personalities, most notably within the political and governing system. Typically, public opinion is measured by polls, which tend to categorize public opinion in different ways:

direction, or the issue's support or opposition among the public; whether the public's opinion on an issue or concern is stable or not; the intensity, or the gradation of support or opposition; and the issue's salience, or importance of the given issue among the public. In addition to these characteristics, once public opinion is measured, it can reflect varying attributes, such as consensus or agreement on an issue; a permissive attitude, where the public is open to persuasion on the issue; or divisiveness, where the issue provokes strong opinions on both sides of the issue, as is the case for abortion and gun control.

Like culture, different types of public opinion exist. In 1950, Gabriel Almond observed three distinct types of "publics": the general public, or those citizens who don't know or care about issues beyond immediate concerns that affect them (Homer, Lenny, Carl, Moe, Barney); the attentive public, or those citizens who are typically better-educated and who follow abstract political issues and concerns (Lisa, Flanders, Sideshow Bob, Mr. Burns, Principal Skinner); and the elite public, or the individuals, such as elected officials, journalists, and policymakers, who can be highly influential on the other types of publics, and thus shape "public opinion" (Mayor Quimby, Governor Mary Bailey, Kent Brockman, Reverend Lovejoy, Birchabald "Birch" T. Barlow).[20] With the increasing range of the media and the emergence of other venues, such as the Internet, another form of public has emerged known as "issue publics." These are individuals who follow narrow and specific issues, as evidenced in Springfield by the proliferation of interest-specific newspapers responding to Burns's monopoly of mainstream media in the award-winning fifteenth season finale, "Fraudcast News."[21]

Not only has the increased power of television, radio, and the Internet spawned new types of publics, but these venues have also prompted an easier way to manipulate and energize public opinion. In the summer of 2007, the U.S. Senate was debating an extensive overhaul of U.S. immigration laws. While most public opinion polls reflected support for major provisions within the proposed legislation, critics of the measure utilized not only talk radio, but also the Internet to energize and coalesce a grassroots backlash against the bill. When the "grass roots roared," the immigration plan stalled and eventually was defeated.[22]

For their eighteenth season finale, *The Simpsons* went after this ability of private individuals to funnel their outrage against the media, and how the media and government may join together to shape public opinion. In this four hundredth episode, entitled "You Kent Always Say What You Want,"

Ned Flanders responds to news anchor Kent Brockman's use of a profane word on air by using the Internet to mobilize "people I never met to pressure a government with better things to do to punish a man who meant no harm for something nobody even saw." Ultimately, Brockman is fired, and employs the same medium that brought him down to fire back at his former profession. In an appearance reminiscent of the 2005 movie *Good Night, and Good Luck*, Brockman declares to a webcam broadcast: "Friends, the press and the government are in bed together in an embrace so intimate and wrong, they could spoon on a twin mattress and still have room for Ted Koppel. Journalists used to question the reasons for war and expose abuse of power. Now, like toothless babies, they suckle on the sugary teat of misinformation and poop it into the diaper we call the 6:00 news. Demand more of your government! Demand more of your press! Vote out your so-called representatives! Reject your corporate masters!"[23]

Although private individuals can affect the media, it is the media that largely shapes and influences public opinion in three distinct ways. First, the media engages in agenda setting, or determining which issues or concerns are "newsworthy" and influencing citizens to consider those issues or concerns above others. This was evident in Kent Brockman's entire broadcast dedicated to the "Lisa Lionheart" doll that created buzz for the Malibu Stacey rival. Second, there is framing, or the ability to influence the way citizens interpret events and issues. The power of framing was shown in the *Simpsons* episode "Mr. Spritz Goes to Washington," when Fox News interviews a Democratic congressional candidate and places devil horns on him, puts a Soviet flag in the background, and tells him that he has made a "very adulterous point" to paint him as an evil, unethical communist to the viewing public. Finally, the media engages in priming, presenting issues in a similar manner over time in a way that prepares citizens to come to specific conclusions about issues, events, and even candidates for public office. This is demonstrated in the four hundredth episode *of The Simpsons*, when a Fox News commentator, in his "Liberal Outrage" segment, announces that it "seems that liberals want to give NASA the right to abort space missions whenever they feel like it." Homer deplores "Liberals! I hate them so much!"[24]

The power to shape public opinion can come not only from the media and private individuals and groups, but also from the government itself. As Sven Steinmo has noted, "Governments do not simply wait for citizens to demand public policies, they also set the agenda."[25] In "Much Apu About Nothing," Mayor "Diamond Joe" Quimby must deal with an angry mob over the "constant bear attacks" in Springfield and subsequent higher taxes to pay for the Bear Patrol. In dealing with the higher taxes issue, Mayor Quimby convinces the angry mob that it is illegal immigrants who are causing their higher taxes and pledges a ballot referendum on deporting illegal immigrants. Caught up in the fervor, the citizens of Springfield actively support the proposition's passage. Moe observes, "You know what really aggravateses me is them immigants. They want all the benefits of living in Springfield, but they ain't even bothered to learn themselves the language." Homer responds, "Hey, those are exactly my sentimonies." What Homer doesn't realize is that voting for Prop 24 would affect his favorite Kwik-E-Mart clerk, Apu Nahasapeemapetilon, who is an illegal immigrant. After discovering this fact, Homer reflects to himself, "I got so swept up in the scapegoating and fun of Proposition 24, I never stopped to think it might affect someone I care about." Turning to his friend Apu, Homer takes him by the shoulder and says, "You know what Apu . . . I am really, really gonna miss you."[26]

Not only do elected officials and policymakers have an impact on public opinion, but so do those running for public office. As Leonard Steinhorn describes it, modern-day candidates are akin to big business when they engage in the "political sell": "political advertising—at least the positive kind—is all about . . . defining and branding candidates, turning their lives and beliefs and backgrounds into a story so engaging and appealing that voters want to associate with it through their vote." Steinhorn goes on to argue that the "most common and emotionally satisfying narrative links the candidate to the American Dream—as an individual who either triumphed over adversity or rose above modest means to become a national leader."[27]

When Montgomery C. Burns, Sideshow Bob, and even Homer Simpson seek public office, they all attempt to shape public opinion through their campaigns. In "Two Cars in Every Garage and Three Eyes on Every Fish," Burns seeks to use his vast fortune to win the governor's mansion and override the penalties imposed on his nuclear plant by state inspectors (after it was discovered that Bart caught a three-eyed fish in the local stream adjacent to the power plant). Through a campaign of smear tactics and deriding "those bureaucrats down there in the state capital," Burns is able to go from a 98 percent "despicable or worse" rating to even with the incumbent governor. His campaign fails only when, on the eve of the election, Burns joins the Simpson family for dinner and Marge serves one of the three-eyed fish that started the investigation of the Springfield Nuclear Plant. Burns, with campaign consultants urging him to eat the fish, spits it out before live cameras, dooming his run for office. As he leaves the Simpsons' house, Burns observes the irony of his doomed campaign: "This anonymous clan of slack-jawed troglodytes has cost me the election. And yet, if I were to have them killed, I would be the one to go to jail. That's democracy for you."[28]

Unlike his fellow Republican, Sideshow Bob wins his election bid, defeating Springfield's six-term mayor, "Diamond Joe" Quimby. Bob's victory comes through a combination of first appealing to Springfield's citizens from jail, and upon release, hitting the campaign trail, where he attacks Quimby as a "flip-flopper," and actually does back-flips to impress his audience of school children. To counter Bob's campaign antics, both Bart and Lisa jump into Quimby's lap before the cameras and reporters in an effort to show the public Quimby's softer side. Campaign ads dot the airwaves, with Quimby's campaign spots ending with "If you were running for Mayor, he'd vote for you," while Bob's negative ads attack Quimby for being soft on crime; the ads even point to the fact that Quimby pardoned Bob, to which the ad rhetorically asks, "Can you trust a man like Quimby?" Only after it is shown that Bob stuffed the ballot box with votes from dead people (and pets) does Quimby return to office.[29]

Most interestingly, a successful campaign ensues after Homer insults the garbage collectors and picks a fight with the sanitation commissioner. After his campaign stumbles at a U2 concert, Homer goes to Moe's Tavern and seeks the bartender's advice for his stagnant campaign. Moe says that Homer needs to "think hard and come up with a slogan that appeals to all the lazy slobs out there." Homer then hits upon his campaign slogan of "Can't Somebody Else Do It?" and promises of round-the-clock trash pickup and doing all the "messy jobs," which lead him to an astonishing victory over the efficient and able incumbent. The citizens of Springfield expect the sanitation department to do all sorts of things that they don't want to do; yet when Homer goes on a $4.6 million spending spree to fulfill his campaign pledge, Mayor Quimby denounces him for blowing his annual budget within a month.[30]

Whether it is through campaigns, or through government policies, or through the power of the media, public opinion ultimately is the key linkage between the governed and the government. In his classic work, *Public Opinion and American Democracy*, V. O. Key portrays public opinion as being "the product of an interaction between political influentials and the mass of the people," in which the elites of society must work to develop within the public guarantees not to follow the base instincts and easy pathways that will lead toward the destruction of a democratic system of governance.[31] In *Coming to Public Judgment: Making Democracy Work in a Complex World,* Daniel Yankelovich relates the importance of public judgment to the soul of the American Dream: throughout the nation's history, "one of the most persistent themes in American political thought has been how to create a community in which all Americans participate fully as citizens. This is the Dream of Self-governance—of free people shaping their destiny as equals." Ultimately, Yankelovich follows Key's argument by advocating not public opinion, but "public judgment" that marries the general public with the nation's elites, so that in order for "democracy to flourish, it is not enough to get out the vote. We need better public judgment, and we need to know how to cultivate it." Once the gap between the experts and the masses can be bridged, then, Yankelovich contends, the American Dream of a successful democratic practice will be solidified. But just ensuring the practice of the American governing system is not the only way to envision the American Dream; in fact, like public opinion and political culture, the American Dream has its own variations.[32]

The American Dream at 742 Evergreen Terrace

Just as there are variations to the understanding of political culture (whether it can truly explain or be explained) and public opinion (does it drive the actions of government, or does government drive the opinions of the public?), so too are there variations on the conception of "The American Dream." Scholars have debated and discussed the core ideas of, and even if there is such a thing as, an "American Dream." The conflict over an American Dream often focuses on the ideal versus the reality of such a notion. An early proponent of such a concept was James Truslow Adams, who wrote in 1932 that "there has . . . been the *American dream,* that dream of a land in which life should become fuller for every man, with opportunity for each according to his ability or achievement." He ended his work focusing on the conflicting reality of classism within America, by pointing out that "those on top, financially, intellectually, or otherwise, have got to devote themselves to the 'Great Society,' and those who are below in the scale have got to strive to rise, not merely economically, but culturally. We cannot become a great democracy by giving ourselves up as individuals to selfishness, physical comfort, and cheap amusements."[33]

Along with this belief in a fuller life, scholars have debated the core characteristics of the American Dream. In what he calls the "American Creed," noted political culture scholar Seymour Martin Lipset describes the characteristics as being "liberty, egalitarianism, individualism, populism, and laissez-faire." As a society that abhors the use of government to instill and mandate, it is primarily left up to the individual to achieve success in the end; the United States is seen as "a country that stresses success above all, [and] where people are led to feel that the most important thing is to win the game, regardless of the methods employed in doing so. American culture applies the norms of a completely competitive society to everyone."[34]

In their study of American political culture, Herbert McClosky and John Zaller argue that all societies suffer from conflicting values, and that within the United States those values are of democracy and capitalism. While the economic system of capitalism "is primarily concerned with maximizing private profit," the political system of democracy "aims at maximizing freedom, equality, and the public good."[35] Daniel Elazar contends that while the United States broadly shares a general political culture, that culture is "rooted in two contrasting conceptions": the first is the "marketplace[,] in which the primary public relationships are products of bargaining among individuals and groups acting out of self-interest," while the second is that of a "commonwealth," where "citizens cooperate in an effort to create and maintain the best government in order to implement certain shared moral principles." This battle over individualism versus the collective is often seen as the center of political battles in American politics, and can certainly been seen within the lives of the family on Springfield's Evergreen Terrace.[36]

In the episode "Scenes from the Class Struggle in Springfield," the tension of trying to demonstrate a family's achievement of the American Dream is satirically and expertly played out through Marge Simpson. Upon discovering a $2,800 Chanel suit marked down to $90 at an outlet mall, Marge buys the dress and wears it to the Kwik-E-Mart, where a snobbish high school acquaintance sees her and invites her to the Springfield Country Club. Mingling with the upper crust of society and ignoring her family, Marge must constantly redesign her Chanel suit until the evening when she and her family are invited to a gala ball, where they will be invited to become members of the club. Having gone through several renditions, the dress is destroyed, and Marge goes out to purchase an expensive replacement, to ensure that she will fit in with the elites. Warning her family that there will be "no vulgarity, no mischief, no politics" on the eve of their being accepted by high society, Marge reflects on the fact that she's more comfortable in a place like Krusty Burger than a country club. Besides, she notes that "I wouldn't want to join any club that would have *this* me as a member."[37]

Other approaches to understanding the American Dream have sought to explain not just the ideals, but the realities of what former President Bill Clinton observed: "If you work hard and play by the rules you should be given a chance to go as far as your God-given ability will take you." In her work, Jennifer Hochschild contends that the American Dream rests on four tenants: that everyone, no matter their background, can achieve the dream; that everyone can have a reasonable anticipation of achieving the dream; that everyone can achieve the dream "through actions and traits under one's own control"; and finally, that "true success is associated with virtue." But in looking at the realities, the dream is more of a fantasy and "less than perfect." Hochschild argues that the notion of an American Dream is too focused on "radical individualism," while defining success in achieving the dream often boils down to money and power. Looking at the pursuit of the American Dream through the perspective of minorities, for example, Hochschild argues that whites trust the American Dream, even though that same dream "encourages people not even to see those aspects of society that make the dream impossible to fulfill for all Americans."[38]

Another scholar contends that multiple forms of the American Dream have been evident through history. According to Jim Cullen, the American Dream is "a complex idea with manifold implications that can cut different ways," and the different visions of the American Dream give it strength to carry on through time: "Ambiguity is the very source of its mythic power, nowhere more so than among those striving for, but unsure whether they will reach, their goals." Cullen points to certain aspects of U.S. history—the Puritans, the Declaration of Independence, the dreams of upward mobility, equality, and home ownership—as constantly redefining and elaborating upon the basic characterization of the American Dream.[39] Richard Ellis also notes that American history exemplifies different political cultures, and that among the characteristics that define these cultures are egalitarianism, or social equality, individualism, hierarchy, fatalism, and hermitude, or the attempt to withdraw from society to "live a life of austere self-sufficiency."[40] Some, such as James A. Morone, contend that, beyond identifying specific characteristics, American political culture is, like public opinion and culture itself, "almost constantly contested and continuously evolving."[41]

Within the town of Springfield, one family seems to be in a constant battle to achieve some semblance of the American Dream's attributes. Yet ironically, in the episode "Homer's Enemy," the writers of the show demonstrate that Homer, Marge, Bart, Lisa, and Maggie have achieved some levels of success that many average Americans have not. In an episode that many observers have noted as one of the series' darkest and funniest social commentaries, viewers are introduced to Frank Grimes, a Springfieldite who survived a silo explosion at the age of eighteen, who learned how to hear again during the painful recuperation, and who studied science by mail, eventually earning his correspondence school diploma in nuclear physics. After Mr. Burns witnesses Grimes's moving story, Frank begins a career at the Springfield Nuclear Power Plant. In trying to make friends with his new coworker, Homer invites Grimes (whom Homer has nicknamed "Grimey") over for dinner. Upon seeing the Simpsons' house, Grimes exclaims that "it's a palace," and is astonished that Homer has photographs of himself with former President Gerald Ford, on tour with the Smashing Pumpkins, and even from when he went into outer space. Comparing the Simpsons' residence to his apartment (which has bowling alleys above and below it), Grimes goes ballistic, declaring that "I've had to work hard every day of my life, and what do I have to show for it? This briefcase and this haircut. And what do you have to show for your lifetime of sloth and ignorance? . . . A dream house, two cars, a beautiful wife, a son who owns a factory [that Bart bought with one dollar], fancy clothes, and lobsters for dinner!" Grimes goes on to contend that Homer epitomizes what is wrong with America: "You coast through life, you do as little as possible, and you leach off decent, hard-working people—like me. If you lived in any other country, you'd have starved to death long ago." "He's got you there, Dad," remarks Bart.[42]

The Simpsons: Pop Culture Evidence of Variations on the American Dream

In our modern society, many different artifacts can be utilized to demonstrate the idea of American political culture, public opinion, and the ultimate goals that most Americans strive for. Yet going back to the perceptions of a French philosopher on the young American republic, Alexis de Tocqueville sought to understand why citizens of the United States were so restive in the midst of apparent success:

> One can conceive of men having arrived at a certain degree of freedom that satisfies them entirely. They then enjoy their independence

without restiveness and without ardor. But men will never found an equality that is enough for them.

Whatever a people's efforts, it will not succeed in making conditions perfectly equal within itself. . . .

However democratic the social state and political constitution of a people may be, one can . . . count on the fact that each of its citizens will always perceive near to him several positions in which he is dominated, and one can foresee that he will obstinately keep looking at this side alone. When inequality is the common law of a society, the strongest inequalities do not strike the eye; when everything is nearly on a level, the least of them would be hurt by it. That is why the desire for equality always becomes more insatiable as equality is greater.

In democratic peoples, men easily obtain a certain equality; they cannot attain the equality they desire. It retreats before them daily but without ever evading their regard, and when it withdraws, it attracts them in pursuit. They constantly believe they are going to seize it, and it constantly escapes their grasp. They see it from near enough to know its charms, they do not approach it close enough to enjoy it, and they die before having fully savored its sweetness.[43]

Through the use of popular culture artifacts such as *The Simpsons,* one can envision the differing perceptions of political culture, public opinion, and notions of what constitutes the American Dream. The rebellious individualism of Bart, the intellectualism and social consciousness of Lisa, Homer's constant craving for success (albeit usually in the form of a donut or Duff beer), the caring concern of Marge, even the quiet certitude of Maggie—all contribute in some fashion to serving as a reflection of the ways Americans live their lives. But even though, as de Tocqueville observed, Americans are achieving success, they ultimately yearn for something beyond that achievement—and perhaps that is the best conceptualization of political culture and public opinion that leads to the American Dream, as reflected in the not-so-quiet little town of Springfield, U.S.A.

Notes

Epigraph: "The Crepes of Wrath," Production Code: 7G13, Original Airdate: April 15, 1990.

1. The "defense of flag burning" essay is offered by resident bully Nelson Muntz, who ends his essay with the definitive argument of "but if you do [burn the flag], you better burn a few other things. You better burn your shirt and your pants. Be sure to burn your TV and car. Oh yes, and don't forget to burn your house, because none of those things could exist without six white stripes, seven red stripes, and a *hell of a lot of stars.*"

2. "Mr. Lisa Goes to Washington," Production Code: 8F01, Original Airdate: September 26, 1991.

3. Walter Lippmann, *A Preface to Politics* (New York: Mitchell Kennerley, 1913), reproduced in full by Matt Whittaker, Juliet Sutherland, and the Project Gutenberg Online Distributed Proofreading Team, http://www.gutenberg.org/files/20125/20125-h/20125-h.htm (accessed July 1, 2007).

4. Seymour Martin Lipset, *American Exceptionalism: A Double-Edged Sword* (New York: Norton, 1996), 25.

5. Allan McBride and Robert K. Toburen, "Deep Structures: Polpop Culture on Primetime Television," *Journal of Popular Culture* 29, no. 4 (1996): 181–200.

6. Gabriel A. Almond, "Comparative Political Systems," *Journal of Politics* 18, no. 3 (1956): 391–409.

7. Gabriel A. Almond and Sidney Verba, *The Civic Culture: Political Attitudes and Democracy in Five Nations* (Princeton: Princeton Univ. Press, 1963), 11.

8. Ibid., 15–18.

9. "Much Apu About Nothing," Production Code: 3F20, Original Airdate: May 5, 1996.

10. "Lisa's Substitute," Production Code: 7F19, Original Airdate: April 25, 1991.

11. "The Bart Wants What It Wants," Production Code: DABF06, Original Airdate: February 17, 2002.

12. Daniel Elazar, *American Federalism: A View from the States* (New York: Thomas Y. Crowell Company, 1966), 84–93.

13. "Sweets and Sour Marge," Production Code: DABF03, Original Airdate: January 20, 2002; "Weekend at Burnsie's," Production Code: DABF11, Original Airdate: April 7, 2002.

14. "Trash of the Titans," Production Code: 5F09, Original Airdate: April 26, 1998.

15. "They Saved Lisa's Brain," Production Code: AABF18, Original Airdate: May 9, 1999; "Homer the Great," Production Code: SF09, Original Airdate: January 8, 1995.

16. Gabriel A. Almond and G. Bingham Powell, *Comparative Politics: Systems, Process, and Policy* (Boston: Little, Brown, 1978), 25; Lisa Wedeen, "Conceptualizing Culture: Possibilities for Political Science," *American Political Science Review* 96, no. 4 (2002): 713–28.

17. John Street, "Political Culture—From Civic Culture to Mass Culture," *British Journal of Political Science* 24, no. 1 (1994): 95–113.

18. Robert S. Erikson, John P. McIver, and Gerald C. Wright Jr., "State Politi-

cal Culture and Public Opinion," *American Political Science Review* 81, no. 3 (1987): 797–814; see also their book: Robert S. Erikson, John P. McIver, and Gerald C. Wright Jr., *Statehouse Democracy: Public Opinion and Policy in the American States* (New York: Cambridge Univ. Press, 1993).

19. "The Seven-Beer Snitch," Production Code: GABF08, Original Airdate: April 3, 2005.

20. Gabriel A. Almond, *The American People and Foreign Policy* (New York: Harcourt, Brace, 1950).

21. "Fraudcast News," Production Code: FABF18, Original Airdate: May 23, 2004. The Writer's Guild of America recognized this episode with the Paul Selvin Award, which honors works with a focus on First Amendment issues.

22. Julia Preston. "Grass Roots Roared and Immigration Plan Collapsed," *New York Times,* June 10, 2007.

23. "You Kent Always Say What You Want," Production Code: JABF15, Original Airdate: May 20, 2007.

24. "Lisa vs. Malibu Stacey," Production Code: 1F12, Original Airdate: February 17, 1994; "Mr. Spritz Goes to Washington," Production Code: EABF09, Original Airdate: March 9, 2003; "You Kent Always Say What You Want," Production Code: JABF15, Original Airdate: May 20, 2007.

25. Sven H. Steinmo, "American Exceptionalism Reconsidered: Culture or Institutions?" in *The Dynamics of American Politics: Approaches and Interpretations,* ed. Lawrence C. Dodd and Calvin Jillson (Boulder, Colo.: Westview, 1994), 128.

26. "Much Apu About Nothing," Production Code: 3F20, Original Airdate: May 5, 1996.

27. Leonard Steinhorn, "Ads Are Us: Political Advertising in a Mass Media Culture," in *Campaigns and Elections: American Style,* 2nd ed., ed. James A. Thurber and Candice J. Nelson (Boulder, Colo.: Westview, 2004), 117.

28. "Two Cars in Every Garage and Three Eyes on Every Fish," Production Code: 7F01, Original Airdate: November 1, 1990.

29. "Sideshow Bob Roberts," Production Code: 2F02, Original Airdate: October 9, 1994.

30. "Trash of the Titans," Production Code: 5F09, Original Airdate: April 26, 1998.

31. V. O. Key, *Public Opinion and American Democracy* (New York: Knopf, 1961), 557.

32. Daniel Yankelovich, *Coming to Public Judgment: Making Democracy Work in a Complex World* (Syracuse: Syracuse Univ. Press, 1991), 1.

33. James Truslow Adams, *The Epic of America* (Boston: Little, Brown, 1932), 404 (emphasis in original).

34. Lipset, *American Exceptionalism,* 19, 47.

35. Herbert McClosky and John R. Zaller, *American Ethos: Public Attitudes toward Capitalism and Democracy* (Cambridge, Mass.: Harvard Univ. Press, 1984), 7.

36. Elazar, *American Federalism*, 85–86.

37. "Scenes from the Class Struggle in Springfield," Production Code: 3F11, Original Airdate: February 4, 1996.

38. Jennifer L. Hochschild, *Facing Up to the American Dream: Race, Class, and the Soul of the Nation* (Princeton: Princeton Univ. Press, 1995), 18, 251.

39. Jim Cullen, *The American Dream: A Short History of an Idea That Shaped a Nation* (New York: Oxford Univ. Press, 2003), 6–7.

40. Richard Ellis, *American Political Cultures* (New York: Oxford Univ. Press, 1996), 142.

41. James A. Morone, "The Struggle for American Culture," *PS: Political Science and Politics* 29, no. 3 (1996): 424–30.

42. "Homer's Enemy," Production Code: 4F19, Original Airdate: May 4, 1997.

43. Alexis de Tocqueville, *Democracy in America*, ed. Harvey C. Mansfield and Delba Winthrop (Chicago: Univ. of Chicago Press, 2000), 513–14.

Part 2

CAST AND CREW

ACTORS AND INSTITUTIONS IN AMERICAN GOVERNMENT AND POLITICS

4

CONGRESS, CORRUPTION, AND POLITICAL CULTURE

Mr. Bulworth Goes to Washington

John Grummel

Although frequently portraying the executive branch of the government, Hollywood has paid scant attention to the legislative. However, one of the most famous films regarding American politics, *Mr. Smith Goes to Washington,* concerns the U.S. Congress. Jefferson Smith, the main character in *Mr. Smith Goes to Washington,* is the embodiment of American values and ideals. He comes to the U.S. Senate as a replacement appointment for a senator that died in office. He is expected to do nothing while he is there, he "can't ask any questions or talk out of turn," but Smith becomes somewhat disillusioned by the influence of the party machines and ends up crusading for the ideals and values on which the United States was founded.[1]

A more contemporary film about Congress, *Bulworth,* focuses on incumbent senator Jay Bulworth's final days campaigning for California's Democratic nomination for the U.S. Senate. Senator Bulworth, after making a deal with an insurance lobbyist, sets up a hit on himself and then flies out to California to finish his primary campaign. Once in California, he begins to question the way things are done in Washington, D.C. Bulworth, through his various campaign and television appearances, addresses problems with American politics and policymaking, and provides a critique of the political environment in Washington and problems with campaign finance and the power of large political interests. In the beginning, he does this because he is going to be killed, so he has nothing to lose, but even after he decides he wants to live, Bulworth continues with the same message.[2]

Frank Capra's 1939 film, *Mr. Smith Goes to Washington,* brings attention to several themes concerning Congress. The film provides a basis for examining certain aspects of the legislative process, highlighting problems of corruption. This is relevant considering the recent number of corruption-related charges and convictions brought against members of Congress and congressional lobbyists, most notably Tom DeLay and Jack Abramoff. Tom DeLay (R), who represented the 22nd district in Texas and served in the U.S. House of Representatives from 1984 to 2006, was indicted in Austin, Texas, on September 28, 2005, on criminal charges of conspiracy to violate election laws in 2002 by a Travis County, Texas, grand jury. The following week, on October 3, he was indicted yet again on a money laundering charge. The allegations stemmed from the involvement of DeLay's PAC, TRMPAC, in funneling corporate contributions to state campaigns during the 2002 election cycle. Jack Abramoff, a high-powered Republican lobbyist, in January 2006, reached a plea agreement with federal prosecutors in which he pleaded guilty to numerous felonies, including defrauding Indian tribal clients, conspiring to bribe members of Congress, evading taxes, conspiracy, and wire fraud, and agreed to cooperate with the authorities.[3]

This theme of corruption is also evident in the 1998 film *Bulworth.* Although *Bulworth* centers on Bulworth's California Democratic primary election campaign, the film provides little insight concerning congressional campaigning. Instead, *Bulworth* is a vehicle to illustrate how political culture and the political environment in Washington, D.C., limit and constrain the alternatives that Congress may consider in solving the nation's problems and in making public policy. In fact, *Bulworth* allows for a closer look at the political environment in Washington, D.C., including the influence of powerful interests and lobbyists on legislating in the U.S. Congress.

Legislating in the U.S. Congress

Senator Smith has just returned to his office after a meeting with the senior senator from his state, Senator Paine. Senator Paine recommended to Smith that he propose a bill concerning a boy's camp. Smith mentions this to his secretary, Miss Saunders, and wants to get started right away, but Saunders feels it necessary to explain to Smith the legislative process.

Saunders: My dear Senator, do you have the faintest idea what it takes to get a bill passed?

Smith: No, no, you're going to help me. . . .

Sanders: Senator, do you mind if I give you a rough idea of what you're up against?

Smith: No, no, no, go ahead.

Saunders: Well, a senator has a bill in mind, like your camp, right? . . . He has to sit down first and write it up. The why, when, where, how, and everything else. Now, that takes time. . . . So we knock it off in record-breaking time of let's say 3–4 days.

Smith: Oh, a day!

Saunders: A day?

Smith: Yes, just tonight.

Saunders: . . . It's dawn, your bill is ready. You take it over there and introduce it.

Smith: How?

Saunders: You get to your feet in the Senate and take a long breath and start spouting, but not too loud, because a couple of the senators might want to sleep. Then a curly-headed page boy takes it up to the desk where a long-faced clerk reads it, refers it to the right committee.[4]

The lawmaking function of Congress is not entirely as described in this scene, but it is not far from what actually happens, either. There are some parts that are left out, but it still provides an excellent starting point. Anyone, senators, congressmen, lobbyists, cabinet secretaries, White House staff, or private citizens, can write a piece of legislation, but only a member of Congress can introduce a bill. So, although most legislation originates outside of Congress, mostly in the executive branch, from the White House and the various cabinet departments, the legislation must be introduced by either a member of the House of Representatives or the Senate. This is done in a manner similar to what was described above by Senator Smith's secretary. Her description starts in the Senate, but bills could be introduced into the House of Representatives first, or even introduced into the House and Senate nearly simultaneously.[5]

Once introduced, the bill is referred to the relevant committee or committees. As noted by Saunders to Senator Smith, committees are "small groups of senators [that] have to sift a bill down, look into it, study it, and

Senator Jefferson Smith (Jimmy Stewart) embodies the idyllic myth of the maverick congressman standing up for the American people to battle graft and corruption within the political system in the Frank Capra classic *Mr. Smith Goes to Washington*. (Jerry Ohlinger's Movie Material Store)

report to the whole Senate. You can't take a bill nobody ever heard about and discuss it among ninety-six men." These are known as standing committees. There are currently nineteen standing committees in the House of Representatives and sixteen in the Senate. Standing committees are permanent committees that have been created either by public law or by the House and Senate rules and that generally have legislative jurisdiction, but they are not the only types of committees found in Congress.[6]

Other committees include joint, conference, and select or special committees. Select committees are usually temporary panels that go out of business after the two-year life of the Congress in which they were created. Some select committees, such as the House Permanent Select Intelligence Committee, take on the attributes of permanent committees. Select committees usually do not have legislative authority; they can only study, investigate, and make recommendations. Joint committees include members from both chambers and have been used for such purposes as studying, investigating, and oversight, as well as routine activities. Conference committees are used to reconcile different versions of the same bill passed by the House and Senate.

The full standing committee refers the bill to one of its more specialized subcommittees, which is a subunit of a committee established for the purpose of dividing and managing a committee's work, and it is in the subcommittee that most of the work on a bill is done. It is important to note that several thousand bills and resolutions are referred to committees during each Congressional session. Committees only select a small percentage for consideration, and those that are not addressed often receive no further action; in other words, these latter bills die in committee. The chair of the subcommittee sets the subcommittee's agenda and chooses the bills that will be considered, and the bills that are reported out of committee help set Congress's agenda. A subcommittee can do a number of things when considering a bill. First, it asks relevant executive agencies for written comments on the measure. Second, it holds hearings to gather information and views from noncommittee experts. Whether or not hearings will be held and who will appear before the subcommittee is determined by the subcommittee chair. Most hearings are open to the public and, ideally, the purpose would be to acquire more information concerning the bill under consideration, but this is not always the case. Given the power of the subcommittee chair, the minority usually has to work informally with the chair to invite witnesses representing their point of view. At subcommittee hearings, these witnesses summarize submitted statements and then respond to questions from the senators.

After the hearings, the subcommittee meets to perfect the measure by making amendments to the bill, while noncommittee members sometimes attempt to influence the language. This is known as markup, and it is defined as a meeting of the subcommittee or committee to debate and consider amendments to a measure under consideration. The markup determines whether the measure pending before a committee will be recommended to the full House or Senate, and whether it should be amended in any substantive way. Sometimes a committee may make only minor changes, while at other times a committee may completely rewrite a bill. Once the markup is finished, it is voted on by the committee. If the language is agreed upon, the committee sends the measure back to the full Senate, usually along with a written report describing its purposes and provisions. This is the sifting down and studying of a bill referred to above by Saunders.

This is where the procedures between the House of Representatives and Senate differ. At this point in the House of Representatives, the bill is sent to the Rules Committee, while in the Senate there is the possibility of a hold. Addressing the Senate procedure first, a hold is when a senator wishes to be informed about a bill. This is euphemistic language, for often the senator placing the hold has a problem with the bill. A hold is an informal practice by which a senator informs his or her floor leader that he or she does not wish a particular bill or other measure to reach the floor for consideration. Now, the Majority Leader need not follow the senator's wishes, but is certainly on notice that the opposing senator, the senator placing the hold, may filibuster any motion to proceed with consideration of the measure. In such cases, a compromise would have to be worked out so that the bill can proceed to the floor.

In the House of Representatives, a bill goes to the Rules Committee after being reported out of its appropriate standing committee. The Rules Committee is the "right hand" of the Speaker, and it places the bill on the calendar and gives the bill a rule. The time of debate and whether or not amendments can be offered, and the number of amendments that can be offered, are set by the rule. Amendments that can be offered must be germane—that is, relevant to the bill being considered. Since it would be nearly impossible for 435 representatives to discuss each and every bill, the Rules Committee also sets the time of debate for each bill to be considered. When the bill's time on the calendar arrives, it is considered by the full House.[7]

Unlike in the House of Representatives, the number of amendments and time of debate in the Senate is not limited. There is the possibility of filibuster, a means by which action on the floor of the Senate may be delayed by basically talking a bill to death. Jefferson Smith, in what is probably one of the most memorable scenes of *Mr. Smith Goes to Washington,* made use of the filibuster in his battle against the influence of Mr. Jim Taylor and the party machine. As stated by a reporter on the scene, "Half of official Washington is here to see democracy's finest show, the filibuster. The right to talk your head off, the American privilege of free speech in its most dramatic form. The least man in that chamber once he gets and holds that floor by the rules can hold it and talk as long as he can stand on his feet, providing always, first he not sit down, second that he does not leave the chamber or stop talking."[8]

During Mr. Smith's filibuster, he reads from the Constitution, the Declaration of Independence, and works of literature. This is not uncommon during a filibuster. During one of the most famous filibusters, Strom Thurmond, who held the floor for over twenty-four hours, read from (among other things) the Washington, D.C., phonebook. It is important to note that a filibuster is often used more as a threat to bring about compromise or get concessions. There is only one way to end a filibuster, and that is by a cloture motion. In order to invoke cloture, it is first necessary for those who wish to bring about the cloture motion to collect sixteen signatures from their fellow senators. Once the signatures have been collected, the motion is voted on. It requires sixty votes to limit debate. If the cloture motion passes, members of the Senate may spend no more than thirty additional hours debating the legislation under consideration.

Saunders' description of lawmaking continues: "[in the House, there are] more amendments, more changes, and the bill goes back to the Senate. The Senate doesn't like what the House did to the bill, they make more changes. The House doesn't like those changes. Stymie. . . . So, they appoint men from each house to go into to a huddle called a conference and they battle it out." The members of subcommittees in the House and Senate that considered the bill are appointed to any conference committee created to reconcile differences between the House and Senate versions of the bill. After the differences have been ironed out, the bill, then known as a conference report, is sent back to the floors of the House and Senate for a vote. After the same identical bill has been passed by the House and Senate, it is sent to the president for his signature or veto.[9]

Miss Saunders's description of how a bill becomes a law ends with the following statement, "Finally, if your bill is still alive after all this vivisection, it comes for a vote. Yes, the big day finally arrives and Congress adjourns. Catching on, Senator?" This is an important point since very few bills ever become law, only about 5 to 10 percent. Most bills, as implied above, die before even reaching the floor of either chamber, in committee. This is not unusual since the path a bill must take is a series of multiple veto points. It is much easier for opponents of a bill to kill it than for proponents to get a bill passed.[10]

This is not the case with all bills, of course. Many bills pass with little difficulty whatsoever. However, the more controversial or widespread a bill is in its policy implications, the more difficult it is to get such a bill passed. In both cases, it is often necessary for deliberation and compromise to be involved. This is particularly true of bills with widespread policy implications, such as an energy policy bill. It might be difficult to get a majority of representatives and senators to agree on all parts of such a comprehensive bill. Thus, what often appears to the general public as a tedious process of debate, deliberation, and possibly even compromise occurs over the contested parts of the bill. Since it is these types of bills that receive the most media attention, this is why it appears that Congress has great difficulty getting anything done.

Congress and American Political Culture

Both films, but *Bulworth* in particular, suggest that American political culture and the political environment in Washington, D.C., affect the type of policy alternatives that can be proposed. Political culture is defined as "commonly shared attitudes, beliefs, and core values about how government should operate," and it defines the boundaries of political action and shapes what most people expect from politics and how politics is conducted. Political culture originates in a country's political and social practices as well as its political myths, ideals, and symbolic positions. American political culture is composed of values, such as freedom, democracy, individualism, and majority rule, that most Americans hold dear.[11]

The character of Mr. Smith exemplifies several of these values in their most idealistic form. He comes to Washington, D.C., naive and idealistic. He is mesmerized by the monuments and memorials and what they stand for in American political history. He recites Jefferson and Lincoln. Before visiting the Senate he visits Mount Vernon to get in the mood. His seat in the Senate was once Daniel Webster's, and Smith is in awe. After proposing a bill that is in conflict with another bill that was set up by powerful interests, Smith begins to investigate suspicions of graft. Saunders, afraid for what will happen to Smith, asks him, "Why don't you go home? Tell about your little streams, about the camp and the home of the free. This is no place for you. You are half-way decent. You don't belong here. Now, go home!" Smith's investigation leads to attacks on Smith by these powerful interests and agents in Senate, in particular the senior senator from Smith's state, Joseph Harrison Paine. But Smith is never entirely disillusioned, as is evident from his speech toward the end of his filibuster. He states:

> There is no compromise with truth. That's all I got up on this floor
> to say. . . . Just get up off the ground. That's all I ask. Get up there

with that lady that's up on top of the capital dome, the lady that stands for liberty. Take a look at this country through her eyes if you really want to see something. And you won't just see scenery. You'll see the whole parade of what man has carved out for himself after centuries of fighting, and fighting for something more than just jungle law. Fighting so he can stand on his own two feet: free and decent. The way he was created, no matter what race, color, or creed. That's what'll you see: No place out there for graft, or greed, or lies, or compromise with human liberties.[12]

Political culture can limit the types of proposals that are made by Congress to solve the nation's problems. Political culture contains not only those values that are considered good, but also judgments concerning those that are not accessible or bad. For example, Bulworth states, "Now everybody's gonna get sick someday but nobody know how they gonna pay. Health care, managed care, HMOs, ain't gonna work, no sir, not those. Cause the thing that's the same, every one cause of this, those mother fuckers there, the insurance companies.... You can call it single payer, or Canadian way, only socialized medicine will ever save the day. Come on now, let me hear that dirty word, 'socialism'!" Since capitalism and free enterprise are seen as the best economic system for the United States and in direct opposition to socialism, which is often associated with communism and former Cold War adversary the Soviet Union, proposals of socialized medicine have been met with harsh resistance, as was the case in 1993 with the attacks against the Clinton administration's attempts to bring about comprehensive, national health care reform.[13]

The prevalence of this belief about business is evident from another statement made by Bulworth. He states, "You want to know why the health care industry is the most profitable business in the United States, because the insurance companies take 24 cents out of every dollar that's spent. You know what it takes the government to do the same thing for Medicare, 3 cents out of every dollar. Now, what is all this crap that they hand you about business being more efficient than government?" Because of the power and emphasis on business in the United States and its perceived ability to do things more efficiently, such statements as made by Jay Bulworth, although they may contain some truth, are not necessarily believed by most Americans because of their distrust of government.[14]

American political culture and the political environment in Washington,

In the 1998 movie *Bulworth,* Senator Jay Billington Bulworth (Warren Beatty) trades in suit, tie, and political pretense to become a voice and spirit of representation for poor and oppressed communities often underrepresented in the American Congress. (Jerry Ohlinger's Movie Material Store)

D.C., have also limited what Congress has been able to do in other policy areas as well, such as welfare and employment, particularly concerning minimum wage and outsourcing. This real-life problem is highlighted in the film when Bulworth, appearing in a television interview more like he is a member of a gang rather than a politician, states:

> We got babies in South Central [Los Angeles] dying as young as they do in Peru. We got public schools that are nightmares. We got a Congress that ain't got a clue. We got kids with submachine guns. We got militias throwing bombs. . . . We got factories closing down. Where the hell did all the good jobs go? Well, I'll tell ya where they went. My contributors make more profit . . . hiring kids in Mexico. Ole brother can work in fast food if he can't invent computer games, but what we used to call America, that's going down the drain. How's a young man going to meet his financial responsibility working at mother fucking Burger King? He ain't! And please don't even start with that school shit, there ain't no education going on in that mother fucker. Obscenity? We got a million brothers in prison, I mean the walls are really rocking, but you can bet your ass that they would all be out if they could pay for Johnnie Cochran. The Constitution is supposed to give them an equal chance. Well, that ain't gonna happen for sure. . . . The movies, the tabloids, TV, and magazines they tell us what to think and do and all our hopes and dreams. All this information makes America fat, but if the company is out of the country, how American is that? But we got Americans with families can't even buy a meal. Ask a brother that's been downsized if he's getting any deal. Or a white boy busting ass till they put him in his grave. You ain't gotta be a black boy to be living like a slave. Rich people have always stayed on top by dividing white people from colored people.[15]

Bulworth makes a number of points here that are relevant to political culture and to Congress, particularly the problems that Congress has been addressing for decades, but also the demographics of Congress. He primarily addresses the problems of African Americans in the inner city, including crime, poor education, and poverty, but these problems, as Bulworth remarks, are not just problems for African Americans, but for lower- and middle-class whites, Hispanics, Asians, American Indians, and all others as well. Also, contained in this quote, particularly the last sentence, is part of the reason why solving these problems is so difficult.

Bulworth claims that rich people have stayed in power by dividing whites and African Americans, as well as other minorities. This hypothesis has been implied by several notable political scientists, such as Thomas Dye and William Domhoff. This quote, as well as earlier remarks quoted by Senator Bulworth, suggests that America has problems, but what problems are dealt with and how is controlled by those in power, particularly the rich. There is evidence to suggest that there is some truth in this, since almost 70 percent of all interest groups on Capital Hill are economic or business groups. It has also been suggested that solving such problems as those mentioned above is extremely costly, and as such might not be in the interest of the rich, since it may cut into their own income and profits. Why this close connection between the rich and Congress? Part of the answer is found by looking at the composition of Congress.[16]

What is the composition of Congress? Demographically, it is as Bulworth *might* say a bunch of rich white guys along with a few rich white women and minorities. Congress is disproportionately populated by white males. Members of Congress tend to be better educated and to have higher incomes than the average person in the United States. Nearly two hundred members are millionaires. Of the 535 members of the 110th Congress, 458 are white and 465 are men. In the 110th Congress, there are 41 African Americans, 26 Hispanics, and 70 women. Furthermore, with regard to candidate recruitment, parties want to recruit people who not only appeal to voters but are able to raise funds. Given the costs of campaigning, potential candidates as well as current public officials tend to be well connected with wealthy interests, thus increasing the potential for corruption.[17]

Congress and Corruption

In the months prior to the 2006 midterm elections, Jeffrey H. Birnbaum commented that this "might be the biggest wave of congressional scandals in a generation." Several members of the House of Representatives and the Senate, as well as several high-powered congressional lobbyists, were being investigated at this time, but accusations of corruption in Congress are not a recent phenomenon. *Mr. Smith Goes to Washington* focuses on the corruption of the 1930s, and *Bulworth* highlights the corruption of 1990s, but, in essence, they are films that speak directly to the type of corruption that still exists today. In the case of *Mr. Smith Goes to Washington,* it is the corruption of the party machines that Jefferson Smith rallies against. The power of party machines has long since diminished, but the power of the large economic interests and lobbies that have been present since the country's founding is a major topic of both films.[18]

This connection is due, in part, to the amount of money required to be reelected. Because of the fear of losing future funding, public officials might be more likely to vote more along the lines of their rich contributors. In a few instances, officials may become corrupted by this environment. According to opinion polls, most Americans believe that Congress is corrupt, but not necessarily *their* member of Congress. In an April 2006 *USA Today*/Gallup poll, voters were asked whether they believed their member of Congress was corrupt and then whether members of Congress generally were corrupt. On the first question, 22 percent said they believed their member of Congress was corrupt, while 67 percent of respondents disagreed. On the second question, 47 percent of the sample said most members of Congress were corrupt, while 46 percent said they were not corrupt. An August 2006 Harris poll showed that 77 percent of Americans had a negative view of Congress, while a May 2006 Gallup poll indicated that 83 percent of Americans considered corruption a serious issue, and 64 percent believed that dealing with corruption should be a high priority for Congress.[19]

Bulworth makes reference to the connection and influence of business and economic interests on Congress throughout the film:

> . . . Now it ain't that funny, you contribute all my money.
> You make your contribution and you get your solution.
> As long as you can pay I'm gonna do it all your way.
> Yes, the money talks and the people walk.
> . . . Big Money . . . One man, one vote, now is that really real?
> The name of our game is let's make a deal.
> Now the people got the problems, the haves and the have nots.
> But the ones who make me listen, pay for thirty-second spots
> . . . Yo! Bank of America, this table over here.
> Wells Fargo and CitiBank, you're really very dear
> Loan billions to Mexico and never have to fear
> because taxpayers, taxpayers take it in the rear
> . . . Yo, over here we have our friends from oil
> They don't give a shit how much the wilderness is spoiled

They tell us they are careful, we know it's all a lie
As long as we keep driving cars and let the planet die
. . . Exxon, Mobil, the Saudis in Kuwait,
if we still got the Middle East, the atmosphere can wait.
The Arabs got the oil, we buy everything they sell,
but if the brothers raise the price, we'll blow them all to hell.[20]

In this campaign "rap" given to an audience of rich contributors, Bulworth describes the relationship between economic interests, in this case banking and oil interests, and Congress. He suggests that Congress is likely only to help those that help finance their campaigns. This is evident in another part in the film, when Bulworth is questioned at an African American church about a particular health insurance bill, favored by many of those attending, and why he did not support it. Bulworth's response is: "Because, you really haven't contributed any money to my campaign, have you? Do you have any idea how much these insurance companies come up with? They pretty much depend on me to get a bill like that and bottle it up in my committee during an election, and that way we can kill it when you are not looking."[21]

Bulworth suggests that the cost of campaigning for reelection is part of the reason why large economic interests have greater influence than most other interests in the United States. He states, "I am a senator, I've got to raise $10,000 a day everyday I'm in Washington. I ain't getting it in South Central. I'm getting it in Beverly Hills. So I am voting in the Senate the way they want me to and I'm sending them my bills." The average campaign costs during the 2001–2002 electoral cycle for the House and Senate were $667,000 and $3.6 million, respectively. Bulworth further suggests that it is due to this relationship between rich economic interests and members of Congress that things will not change unless Congress changes the laws concerning campaign fund-raising. He says:

I got a simple question that I would like to ask of this network that pays you to carry out your task. How come they got the airwaves? They're the people's aren't they? They'd be worth 70 million to the people today if some money-grubbing Congress didn't give them away for big campaign money. It's hopeless, you see, if you're running for office without no TV. If you don't get big money you get a defeat. Corporations and broadcasters make you dead meat. You've been taught in this country there's speech that is free, but free do not get you no spots on TV. If you want to have senators not on the take, then give them free airtime, they won't have to fake.[22]

As declared by California's legendary boss Jess Unruh, "money is the mother's milk of politics." *Bulworth* suggests the same. This continual quest to remain in power takes money—as noted above, large amounts of money. The need to raise increasingly large amounts, particularly for campaign advertising, in order to retain power creates an environment that is fed by money. But it takes more than money to win elections; it takes votes. To get votes, candidates must also cater to the masses, but (as suggested by the above quote) only to get your vote. Although it is a minority of congresspersons who become corrupt, due to gray areas in campaign legislation, the laws do not seriously deter candidates from using questionable means to raise funds.[23]

Conclusion

These two films provide an excellent starting point for addressing various aspects of Congress. In particular, corruption in Congress has been around for many years and has taken different forms, from the party machines of *Mr. Smith Goes to Washington* to corrupt lobbyists and politicians in *Bulworth*. These films provide only limited insight into the difficulty of passing legislation, but do illustrate the effects of the institutional constraints in Congress and the environmental constraints of the American political system on the legislative process. In particular, these films illustrate how political culture and the political environment in Washington, D.C., might influence the types of problems that Congress deals with and how they deal with them. As suggested by both films, powerful political and economic interests appear to control the agenda and thus what issues will be dealt with seriously. Lastly, the character of Mr. Smith does provide hope for all Americans. Most congresspersons are not corrupt but are honest and honorable people working for their constituents, as was Senator Smith. Unfortunately, the focus of the media on the corrupt aspects of Washington often overshadows the hard work of these public officials.

Notes

1. *Mr. Smith Goes to Washington*, Dir. Frank Capra (Culver City, Calif.: Columbia Pictures Corporation, 1939), VHS. Quote spoken by Senator Paine in conversation with

Taylor, leader of the state party machine, concerning the man who should replace the senator who died, Senator Foley.

2. *Bulworth,* Dir. Warren Beatty (Los Angeles, Calif.: Twentieth Century-Fox Film Corporation, 1998), DVD.

3. DeLay's highest office in the House of Representatives was Majority Leader. After his indictment, in accordance with Republican Caucus rules, DeLay temporarily resigned from his position as House Majority Leader, and later, after pressure from fellow Republicans, announced that he would not seek to return to the position. On April 4, 2006, DeLay announced that he would be stepping down from his seat in Congress by early June. He appeared a final time on the House floor on June 8 before leaving his office the following day.

4. *Mr. Smith Goes to Washington,* Dir. Frank Capra.

5. As per the Constitution, revenue bills must first be introduced in the House of Representatives. Otherwise, bills may be introduced into either chamber.

6. *Mr. Smith Goes to Washington,* Dir. Frank Capra.

7. When considering legislation on the floor of the House of Representatives, House members may form the committee of the whole. This is designed to expedite legislation, given the size of the House of Representatives, allowing for the House to pass legislation with only one hundred members present.

8. *Mr. Smith Goes to Washington,* Dir. Frank Capra.

9. Ibid.

10. Ibid.

11. Karen O'Connor and Larry Sabato, *Essentials of American Government: Continuity and Change, 2006 Edition* (New York: Pearson Education, 2006), 9.

12. Both quotes from *Mr. Smith Goes to Washington.*

13. *Bulworth,* Dir. Warren Beatty. Information on the Clinton Health Care Plan can be found at www.ibiblio.org/nhs/NHS-T-o-C.html (accessed March 2, 2008). Information concerning the debate surrounding the Clinton health care plan can be found at www.upenn.edu/pnc/ptbok.html (accessed March 2, 2008). A critique of Clinton's Health-Care Plan, "Cradle-to-Grave Slavery," by Jarret B. Wollstein, can be found at www.fff.org/freedom/0194c.asp (accessed March 2, 2008).

14. *Bulworth,* Dir. Warren Beatty. The Green Party USA contends that Medicare offers 98¢ of coverage for every dollar brought in, while private insurers at best provide 70¢ of coverage for every dollar. Scott McLarty and Starlene Rankin, "Democrats and Republicans Downplay Health Care Crisis," Green Party USA, Washington, D.C., August 24, 2006, http://www.gp.org/press/pr_2006_08_24.shtml (accessed March 3, 2008). Likewise, a 2005 study by *Health Affairs* indicates that while Medicare provides 97¢ worth of care coverage per dollar, the private health care insurance industry in California provides only 66¢ of coverage per dollar, with 21¢ covering the cost of paperwork. Victoria Colliver, "Paperwork Is 21% of Health Care Costs," San Francisco Chronicle, November 11, 2005, http://www.sfgate.com/cgi-bin/article.cgi?f=/c/a/2005/11/11/BUGM8FM8I11 .DTL (accessed March 3, 2008).

15. Ibid.

16. This connection between the richest Americans and their leaders has been a theme of such works as Thomas Dye, *Who's Running America?* (New York: Prentice Hall, 2007); William Domhoff, *Who Rules America Now?* (Long Grove, Ill.: Waveland Press, 1997); and C. Wright Mills, *The Power Elite*, new ed. (New York: Oxford Univ. Press, 1999). See also Peter Bachrach and Morton Baratz, *Power and Poverty: Theory and Practice* (New York: Oxford Univ. Press, 1970), concerning how the political agenda is controlled by the wealthy. It is suggested in James Anderson's work *Public Policy Making* (Boston, Mass.: Houghton Mifflin, 2005) that actual as well as perceived cost can have an inhibiting effect on policymaking.

17. O'Connor and Sabato, *Essentials of American Government*, 179.

18. Jeffrey H. Birnbaum, "In the Loop: On K Street: Wave of Corruption Fails to Move Congress to Act on Ethics Legislation," *Washington Post* online edition, Monday, May 29, 2006, http://www.washingtonpost.com/wp-dyn/content/article/2006/05/28/AR2006052800795.html (accessed March 2, 2008).

19. Polling reported in Chris Cillizza's "The Fix: Parsing the Polls on Congress and Corruption," *Washington Post* online edition, May 10, 2006, available at http://blog.washingtonpost.com/thefix/2006/05/parsing_the_polls_on_congress.html (accessed March 3, 2008), and Citizens for Responsibility and Ethics in Washington (CREW), "Beyond Delay: The 20 Most Corrupt Members of Congress," Washington D.C., 2007, available at http://www.beyonddelay.org/report (accessed March 2, 2008).

20. *Bulworth*, Dir. Warren Beatty.

21. Ibid.

22. Both quotes from *Bulworth*. Data concerning costs of the 2001–2002 election cycle are from Roger H. Davidson and Walter J. Oleszek, *Congress and Its Members*, 9th ed. (Washington, D.C.: CQ Press, 2004).

23. Jess Unruh, quoted in Davidson and Oleszek, *Congress and Its Members*, 9th ed., 68.

5

THE PRESIDENT AS HERO

Don't Blame Me, I Voted for Bartlet

Jennifer J. Hora

At the heart of the NBC series *The West Wing* (1999–2006) was Josiah "Jed" Bartlet (Martin Sheen), a president portrayed as all things to all people. The series romanticizes the politics of the presidency and the executive branch and in particular creates a "president-as-hero" image for its viewers. Government actors and political scientists applaud the attention this award-winning series drew to national politics, but is President Bartlet's leadership and the executive branch politics portrayed in the series a realistic depiction of the presidency?

This essay examines the portrayal of executive politics, leadership, and the president-as-hero image in *The West Wing*. While the media often focuses on the worst leadership attributes of real-life presidents (Bush's need for secrecy, Clinton's reliance on polling to make decisions, Reagan's hands-off attitude), *The West Wing* presents a very different side of presidential leadership. Jed Bartlet is a character much like the biblical King Solomon, with the perfect solution that no other political actor could produce. This political hero is above the fray, above politics.

A common theme of the show involved the president's hardly being seen for most of the episode and then Bartlet breezes in at the end, quickly making a tough decision. Voila! The problem is solved, with little reliance on staff for the decision-making process. Bartlet's ability to speak his mind with a level of honesty and carelessness not seen in today's successful politicians also creates this image of a hero president, a president who does not pay the political price for being frank or short with those around him.

The West Wing's creator, Aaron Sorkin, admits his characters have a heroic dynamic. This essay examines Bartlet's president-as-hero model and compares it to the real dynamics of presidential leadership and politics. How does the idealized President Bartlet stand up against today's politicians?

The Final Call—The Right Call

Nothing promotes the president-as-hero image more than the many episodes where President Bartlet was rather removed from a situation and then swept in to solve the crisis. For example, in the episode "H. Con-172," the staff scamper around to find a way to avoid a censure of the president for concealing his multiple sclerosis in the presidential campaign. The president then sweeps in at the end and takes the deal offered by Congress. The president takes responsibility, accepts the censure, and admits he was wrong so the country can move on to other issues, even though the staff was pushing the president to fight the censure. The president allows his staff to pursue a variety of options on this issue while he works on other governing business. However, Bartlet steps in at the end and pursues a radically different option.[1]

As a problem solver, President Bartlet also specializes in multitasking. In "Celestial Navigation," the entire episode focuses on three senior staff members and each of them trying to solve their individual problem. Despite endless brainstorming, Chief of Staff Leo McGarry (John Spencer), Press Secretary C. J. Cregg (Allison Janney), and Deputy Chief of Staff Josh Lyman (Bradley Whitford) fail to find solutions to their respective problem. While he works on his own issues in the Oval Office, all three senior staff members come to see him at the same time. The president, however, hastily solves all three major problems in thirty seconds to end the show. What three senior staffers fail to settle in an hour, he resolves as rapidly as each can present the problem.[2]

Continuing with the president-as-hero image presented by making the right decision at the right time, viewers watch as President Bartlet solves problems almost effortlessly; he even solves problems in his pajamas. Much like in "Celestial Navigation," in "Mandatory Minimums" the president solves problems for the press secretary, the chief of staff, and the deputy communications director, Sam Seaborn (Rob Lowe), but this time the president's one-minute appearance is while he is in bed, and he still manages to fix what the staff saw as irresolvable problems.[3]

In "Shibboleth," the president single-handedly solves a problem involving one hundred Chinese Christians seeking asylum. While staff work on the problem throughout the episode, the president solves it by himself, thinking of a unique solution. President Bartlet calls the governor of California and devises a plan to allow the asylum seekers to escape, thereby avoiding an international crisis. Bartlet solves the problem without input from any advisers.[4]

President Bartlet impresses his staff with his ability to multitask; in fact, he leaves them in awe of his abilities to deal with so many complex issues all at the same time. There are numerous examples of this. One of the more entertaining episodes, "Hartsfield's Landing," involves the president playing two chess games at the same time while also dealing with a crisis between Taiwan and China.[5]

Not only does the president act heroic in terms of solving the problems of the country, but he also resolves various personal crises and settles dis-

The television series *The West Wing* helped to highlight the increased power and expectation heaped upon the modern executive branch by portraying President Josiah "Jed" Bartlet (Martin Sheen) as being part Solomon, part savior, and part superhero. (Jerry Ohlinger's Movie Material Store)

putes for staff members. Bartlet fixes a problem between his chief of staff and his daughter as well as problems between C. J. and the press core, in his own family, and of course between various staff members. From small to large, President Bartlet solves it all. Maybe more importantly, Bartlet takes responsibility for solving the problem: no small issue is beneath him.

Concerning this hero aspect, that of making the final call, the television show *The West Wing* reflects the real West Wing in representing the way the final decision does rest with the president. Staff members provide advice; presidents make the final call. However, *The West Wing* slightly stretches this hero-like quality. The George W. Bush administration is perhaps least like the fictional Bartlet White House of the recent administrations. First, most accounts of the Bush administration show one in which the president relies heavily on staff advice for making decisions. Bush's style is often compared to that of former President Ronald Reagan, who relied heavily on staff but also was accused of being out of touch. Some authors even go as far as to claim Bush is susceptible to criticism for being "underbriefed and understudied" because of his known dislike of long briefing papers. Second, President Bush purposely appointed trusted and known advisors. He typically relies on them heavily, as most presidents in the past have done as well. It is a rare occasion when a president does not seek and heed advisers' suggestions.[6]

President Clinton was the person to make final calls and decisions during his administration; however, even he typically relied on advice rather than acting independently on each major decision. Clinton often relied on his unappointed, unelected wife as his closest adviser, but rarely made decisions without thorough consultation of staff members familiar with the situation. Despite these consultations, however, Clinton developed a reputation among his staff for having a wealth of knowledge on issues that added a unique personal stamp on policy. The Clinton administration George Stephanopoulos describes in his book gives several examples of President Clinton's making the right call. Stephanopoulos describes how the Clinton staff was often in admiration and awe of the president's policy and political savvy. Many memoirs of President Richard M. Nixon's staff members describe how, as president, he took endless briefing papers with him to the residence each evening and thoroughly read all of them by early the next morning. President Nixon was known for his ability to process great amounts of information and asked difficult questions to experts in their area of expertise. All presidents are responsible for making the final decision and being the one to make tough judgments—it is part of executive leadership. In this manner, *The West Wing* was remarkably accurate in reflecting the reality of the job for most presidents.[7]

Also, on a more intimate level, *The West Wing* tends to overemphasize the personal attention the president devotes to the private lives of the White House staff. There is no evidence President George W. Bush dedicates a significant amount of time and attention to handing out relationship advice to Chief of Staff Joshua B. Bolten or Press Secretary Dana Perino. As far as the public knows, President Clinton never played matchmaker for his staff members either.

Going It Alone

A second hero-like image projected by *The West Wing*'s President Bartlet is the impression that the president can go it alone, and often chooses to do so. The president has hand-picked staff at his disposal and is the head of the entire bureaucracy. However, repeatedly in *The West Wing,* this president chooses actions not only without relying on available assistance, but going against measured advice. President Bartlet makes choices following his own (sometimes unexplained) logic rather than the reasoned recommendations of his advisers. This is true on numerous issues, including choosing Supreme Court nominees, hiring decisions, and especially foreign policy.

President Bartlet shows his go-it-alone attitude early in the series and continues to show this mind set through each season. Starting in season one, the president bucks the conventional wisdom and advice from all advisers when choosing his first Supreme Court nominee. President Bartlet could pick an easy Supreme Court nominee for Senate confirmation; the candidate who all staff and Congress agree will receive a quick and easy confirmation hearing. However, he has second thoughts about this easy choice, provoked by a current Supreme Court justice's accusing the president of not picking the best candidate. In the end, the president changes his mind and makes a tough and unusual selection. He picks a candidate he knows will not receive an easy confirmation.[8]

Another example of President Bartlet going it alone is his decision to hire an uncompromising Republican lawyer to work in the White House Council Office. After seeing the lawyer humiliate his own White House staff member on a *Meet the Press*-type show, President Bartlet decides it would be a wise move to hire this smart Republican to perform research from an opposition perspective for the administration. Each and every member of the White House staff, along with a furious attorney general, raises concerns and strongly advises against this choice, but the president plows ahead and does it anyway. There is no stopping him. Of course, this decision proves to be a wise one when the lawyer, young Ainsley Hayes (Emily Procter), makes significant contributions to the administration.

Foreign policy gives many examples of Bartlet's go-it-alone approach to governing. A U.S. spy satellite watching a nuclear storage site in Russia crashes. Foreign policy advisers believe the storage site is being used to store nuclear materials and are afraid the materials will end up on the black market. When Bartlet talks to the Russian president, everyone—Leo, the national security adviser, the chairman of the Joint Chiefs of Staff, etc.—wants him to pretend it was a weather satellite. President Bartlet does this at first, but then shrugs the advice and tells the Russian president the truth, against the wishes of all other decision-makers, even though most of them are in the Oval Office at the time of the phone call and quite demonstrative in how strongly they feel the president should avoid this revelation. Following his own intuition, Bartlet manages to gain agreement from the Russians, allowing the Americans to recover the satellite.[9]

Perhaps the best example of President Bartlet's "going it alone" heroesque performance comes when the president is dealing with an Israeli–Palestinian–United States crisis. At the end of season five and the beginning of season six, the president faces a tough decision about how to react to Palestinian terrorists' attacking envoys from the United States, causing the deaths of two U.S. senators and a former chairman of the Joint Chiefs of Staff. All the president's advisers, including Leo, Josh, Toby Ziegler (Richard Schiff), the current chairman of the Joint Chiefs of Staff, the Speaker of the House, a majority of Congress, and the American people (polling indicated nearly 80 percent) demand swift military action as a response. President Bartlet, however, resists all pressures and pushes forward with diplomacy. The story continues over four episodes, and the president maintains his position of solo tenaciousness while being continually beleaguered by those around him to pursue military action. The president persists, and manages to broker a peace accord between Israel and the Palestinians at Camp David while minimizing the military conflict. Bartlet is the only politician who thinks his plan has a chance; by going it alone he is able to claim a personal victory when the plan succeeds.[10]

The "going it alone" aspect of President Bartlet is perhaps the hero characteristic that least reflects real politics. Clinton Rossiter describes the president as "a magnificent lion who can roam widely and do great deeds," and there are many famous pictures of presidents standing in the Oval Office pondering the difficult decisions they were facing—alone (remember JFK? and of course LBJ during Vietnam? and Clinton at the end of his term?). The reality, though, is that most of the time presidents rely heavily on research, opinions, and advice from every resource available. Presidents routinely seek out White House staff members, cabinet members, national security advisers, and endless bureaucrats for any and all information available. All presidents heavily rely on staff for information to guide decisions. And while each president is the one to make the final decision (as explored above), he does not make that decision alone or without using the input of valuable political assets. There might be disagreements among staff and differing opinions of action, but it is rare for a president to go against the wishes of all other policy makers involved in the decision. Even when there is disagreement between advisers and/or institutions on a course of action, and the media might be highlighting these contradictory plans of action, presidents usually have numerous staff backing their decisions. President Bush, who pushed forward with his decision on the involvement in Iraq, found many political advisers willing to support his plans of action, even though he was going against public opinion and a Democratically held Congress after the November 2006 elections.[11]

Martin Sheen, who plays the role of president in *The West Wing*, says he sees his character as the combination of the best qualities of Presidents Kennedy, Carter, and Clinton. But even President Carter, known for avoiding delegation and maintaining control over policy, used his staff's opinions and advice when making decisions. President Kennedy was so concerned with receiving high-quality and trustworthy advice that he appointed his brother as attorney general. President Clinton sought help from a variety of sources when forming policy, even including his wife on health care reform. On most policies most of the time, each and every president seeks out and follows advice from numerous sources.[12]

Jokes, Jokesters, and Excessively Detailed Random Stories

One of the more unusual ways of presenting President Bartlet as a hero is by focusing on his sense of humor. No matter how stressful the situation nor how many people are waiting for him in the White House Situation Room, the president always has time to tell a joke or a long, detailed story.

In "Game On," where President Bartlet is engaged in heavy preparation for the only presidential debate before the general election, Bartlet takes the time to play a practical joke on his communications director, Toby. Bartlet stages an elaborate joke involving several other staff members, where the president blunders a well-rehearsed question and response just to watch Toby explode. In "Impact Winter," the president continues to joke with family and staff while suffering a major multiple sclerosis attack and is virtually unable to move. Even when the president is busy and dealing with serious issues, he finds time to put those around him at ease, as a hero would.[13]

In addition to President Bartlet's love of a joke or funny story is his obsession with imparting random and useless information to staff members or anyone else who happens to be in the room. The president, often at an inappropriate time, brings up stories that entertain him and bore his audience. President Bartlet seems to enjoy torturing staff members with long stories packed with detailed esoteric historical information. In "Enemies," the target of his lecture is Josh, who receives an earful on the historical development of the U.S. National Park Service. All through his lecture, Josh pleads that the president stop sharing information, but Bartlet plows forward with even more National Park details. In the various State of the Union episodes, Barlet rambles on about the history of the address. While able to complete the task at hand, this president manages to be funny and prove his incredibly vast knowledge of the relevant and irrelevant.[14]

One of Bartlet's favorite subjects to drone on about in the trivial category is food and its ingredients. "Dead Irish Writers" begins with party preparations for the First Lady's birthday and the president remembering all details of the food being served, including sauce, appetizer, and dessert—where Bartlet lists the full menu of each course. Bartlet also knows all the details of the food being served at "The State Dinner," even though he is simultaneously dealing with an impending hurricane and FEMA preparedness, a truckers' strike, and an FBI hostage situation. He also takes responsibility for finding the perfect spice combination for the Thanksgiving turkey and calls the Butterball Turkey Hotline for cooking advice. While any president would have numerous staff members available to pay attention to these details and is engaged in governing decisions virtually every waking hour of the day, this president manages to joyfully lecture on esoteric topics and plan menus.[15]

The time and energy spent on making jokes and relaying irrelevant stories is the manner in which the television show least reflects reality. Real-life presidents simply do not have time to constantly entertain their staff and remember every fact learned in a fifth-grade U.S. history class. Most presidential profiles show a person short on time and often short on patience. Pictures show beleaguered presidents struggling to keep up with the tasks of running the country. Toward the end of every president's term, especially two-term presidents, media outlets always show pictures exhibiting the physical changes the president underwent—the graying and thinning hair in particular.

The paradox of this idea of "president as hero," being both one of the people yet above the people, was explored by Thomas Cronin and Michael Genovese. The public wants presidents who are the best and the brightest, yet easily able to identify with the people. Given these opposing expectations, a president such as Nixon was harshly judged as not living up to expectations. President Nixon was known for high intelligence and especially his ability to process information, devour reading materials, and ask the tough questions. However, lacking the "common touch" led to strong criticism from the media and the public alike. President George H. W. Bush received endless coverage for seemingly being amazed by a grocery store scanner long after they were in virtually every small town store. The "common touch" test reverberates in presidential elections as well; it is discussed by analysts and sometimes candidates are asked outright if they know the price of a gallon of milk. Rudy Giuliani was the target of criticism when he was off three-fold on the price of a gallon of milk, and almost as much on the price of a loaf of white bread. The public expects their presidents to be able to handle international crises while still knowing what it is like to walk to the 7-Eleven to get their own Slurpee.[16]

The West Wing does an excellent job of showing the day-to-day stress and the hectic schedule of the commander in chief, but President Bartlet's hero-type qualities seem to make him psychologically immune to the pressures of the job. In contrast, President Clinton occasionally jogged to McDonald's and vacationed on Martha's Vineyard, President Bush (the first) played with his grandchildren, and President Bush (the second) chopped wood. However, most media reports and firsthand accounts of real presidents indicate very limited time for relaxation and not many examples of having time to play practical jokes on staff members. Even presidential vacations to Kennebunkport are often interrupted with much official business. However, for the heroesque President Bartlet, he routinely has time for joining his staff in relaxation activities—even cooking all of them a chili dinner when the First Lady is out of town.[17]

On the other hand, demonstrating a joking president was one strength of the television series because it presented a human side to the man. Viewers saw him laughing with his wife and daughters, complaining about boring meetings, and making fun of other politicians. *The West Wing* often showed President Bartlet struggling with decisions and full of self-doubt, which is an accurate portrayal of a president's decision-making. For example, history shows the struggles of both Presidents Johnson and Nixon to resolve the Vietnam War honorably and swiftly.

And the Administration, Too

In addition to presenting the president as a hero-type character, the creators of *The West Wing* also present other members of the administration in a hero-like light. In virtually every episode viewers see at least one meeting of President Bartlet and the senior staff: Leo (chief of staff), C. J. (press secretary), Josh (deputy chief of staff), Toby (communications director), and Sam (deputy communications director). And in these senior staff meetings, the staff members are always shown fully debating all issues and going to heroic lengths to accomplish what is morally right, even if it is impossible for the administration to achieve at the time. In "Five Votes Down," for instance, the president is almost incoherent because of a combination of back pain medications. The staff, however, laudably manages to deal with an important policy issue facing a Congressional vote. Five Democratic members who are voting for the administration's bill change their mind, and Josh and Leo (with the help of the others) manage to discover whose votes they lost, and win them back. Sometimes the senior staff meetings involve the administration going to heroic lengths to directly help the president, as is shown in "Manchester, Part II," where the staff strategize about the best reelection plan.[18]

Outside of meetings, *The West Wing* routinely shows staff working endless hours, sacrificing personal relationships, neglecting family duties, and suffering effects of having a stressful career. One example of these hero-like efforts is shown in how they respond to a senator's filibustering a bill. In "The Stackhouse Filibuster," every member of the staff has plans to be out of town for the weekend—a very unusual situation where the staff actually plans to not work on Saturday and Sunday. Instead, Josh, Leo, C. J., and Donna Moss (Janel Moloney) work nonstop until they discover the cause of the filibuster and come up with a creative solution to help Senator Stackhouse accomplish his goal, even if it means delaying the bill, and delaying their weekend plans.[19]

In addition to being heroesque in their support of the best solution for the country, in their efforts to help the president win, and in their willingness to sacrifice personal free time, the White House staff are shown as heroes defending the president against detractors. For example, in "And It's Surely to Their Credit," C. J. Cregg goes to extremes to try to keep a high-ranking Army general from trashing the president as the general retires from the military. Other episodes regularly show staff members trying to protect the president's image or time. Concerning policy and political issues, the staff determinedly seek to help President Bartlet.[20]

One of the most powerful aspects of *The West Wing* is its accurate representation of the role and dedication of the White House staff. *The West Wing* illustrates the complexity of the schedule of the president and all those who surround him. The television show very accurately portrays the personal sacrifices and struggles of the staff members and their commitment to the job and country. In particular, Leo, in the role of chief of staff, demonstrates the constraints and pressures on White House staff. Leo's wife divorces him in the first season because of the difficulties of being a spouse of a White House staff member. In the sixth season Leo suffers a stress-induced heart attack. In seasons four and five, C. J.'s father is coping with Alzheimer's, yet she has almost no time to travel home to Ohio to visit him. Virtually every staff member cancels dates and misses family events. A running joke on the show is Donna's having to cancel and reschedule dates, sometimes at odd hours (such as dinner at 11:30 P.M.), because of the demands of her job. In many different ways, members of the administration make heroic sacrifices of themselves for the president and the country.

In real life, many political memoirs mirror the staff dedication presented by *The West Wing*. Many staff members move to D.C. and live apart from their spouses and children. White House staff members often arrive at work before the president and leave hours after he retires to the residence. Tony Snow continued his dedicated service to President Bush after a second diagnosis of colon cancer. Stephanopoulos wrote of many examples of his long hours dedicated to making the Clinton administration as successful as possible. Dick Cheney had his first heart attack shortly after serving as chief of staff under President Ford. Countless political autobiographies repeat stories of working virtually 24-7 as part of the White House staff. The series

The West Wing very accurately portrays the heroic dedication of members of the administration.

Culture Influencing *The West Wing*, *The West Wing* Influencing Culture

Unlike a book, a movie, or a song, there is an interaction between a television series and the real world in which day-to-day realities can influence the show just as the show can influence the day-to-day realities. In the case of *The West Wing*, this interaction with culture was over a seven-year period, from 1999 to 2006, and in some ways continues today through reruns and DVD rentals. The incorporation of current domestic and foreign events was part of the public appeal of *The West Wing* while it was on primetime network television. Cultural events impacted *The West Wing* and often were written into episodes. The series followed many typical political cycles as well as unusual one-time events.

An example of these recurring political events was shown by each season's having an episode about the president's annual State of the Union address: some seasons covering the writing process, others policy formation, and others the post-speech celebrations and ramifications. Other standard events the series covered included the primary election season for both the presidential races as well as congressional races. Viewers of *The West Wing* also saw fund-raising for the campaigns. An especially routine aspect of the political cycle that viewers saw regularly on *The West Wing* was legislative negotiations with Congress. Many routine current events were worked into each episode.

On the other end of the spectrum, *The West Wing*'s writers also incorporated real-life one-time events into the show; sometimes these events were extremely current, other times the show drew on political incidents from the previous decade. Two different *West Wing* events reflected the Monica Lewinsky scandal. First, at the end of season two, President Bartlet revealed his multiple sclerosis, which he had hidden from the public during the election. The secrecy of the Clinton-Lewinsky incident was demonstrated with a fictional medical concealment. Ultimately, President Bartlet accepted a censure for his actions. A second Monica-gate-like event written into the series was a sex scandal involving the vice president, forcing the VP to resign. After September 11, 2001, *The West Wing* ran a special episode dealing with radical Islamic militants. (Perhaps a more impressive illustration of *The*

West Wing's culture connection was the reference to Osama bin Laden a year before September 11.) And after the 2000 Florida voting debacle, Donna, assistant to the deputy chief of staff, had problems with her ballot when voting absentee in "Election Night." *The West Wing* even included a Senator Jim Jeffords–like defect from the party in control of the Senate. In "Constituency of One," a conservative Democrat from Idaho hands Josh a letter to be given to the president announcing his intent to resign from the Democratic Party so that he might run as a Republican in his next election. Just as Jeffords did, the fictitious senator swings control of the Senate from one party to the other.[21]

Along with culture influencing the television show, *The West Wing* also influenced culture. Viewers felt familiar with positions in the administration previously unheard of by most citizens. In conversation, people identify the real-life press secretary as "the C. J. Cregg of the real White House" and the current chief of staff as "the Leo role." As part of discussion, people refer to "West Winging it" when talking about engaging in behind-the-scenes negotiations and bargaining. *The West Wing* made it acceptable, even trendy, to understand and reference terms such as filibuster, estate tax, and the electoral college, as well as acronyms including the GAO, the OMB, and FEC. People previously not engaged in following politics started to pay attention to the front page of the newspaper. Viewers of *The West Wing* also gained respect for the pace and schedule of the White House and even an understanding of unknown staff positions, such as the White House communications director.

Looking at how the show affected culture, one of the strongest impacts was creating and reinforcing an understanding of the complexities presidents face as national policy leaders. As acknowledged in "Talking Points," there is a difference in being a candidate and an elected official; public officials "campaign in poetry, govern in prose." Both the reelection of President Bartlet in season three and the open seat campaign for a new president in seasons six and seven showed the juxtaposition of campaigning and governing. Throughout both of these campaigns the series did an excellent job of showing the complex relationship between campaigning and governing. Astute viewers of the show gained new appreciation for a president's difficulty in following through on campaign promises.[22]

The "President-as-Hero" Image: Why It Matters

Academic literature and the media create an image of "president-as-hero." As Thomas Cronin writes in "Superman: Our Textbook President," political scientists help create an image of an omniscient, omnipotent president capable of handling any task. Cronin continues dissecting the created president-as-hero image in his later work. The "superman" image created by political scientists and relayed through the media leads the public to harshly judge presidential performance. Public expectations are simply too high for one single person to ever meet.[23]

The media also contribute to this heroic portrayal of presidents. They perpetrate the image of president-as-hero by focusing on the individual president dealing with crises, rather than an entire administration and Congress. The president becomes the face of all national crises, from hurricanes to bridge collapses, from high energy prices to education scores. The president is the lead story on the nightly network news and on the front page of newspapers more often than not. In many ways, the media contributes to the creation of this fictional "character" of a president, then turns around and degrades him because he is unable to live up to the mythical creation.

Given the unrealistic portrayal of the president by political scientists and the media alike, it is not surprising that the public has high expectations. Thus, the president-as-hero image was not created by *The West Wing*; the series simply reinforced the image of the president already formed by experts. The public already viewed real-life presidents through this lens. With the creation of *The West Wing,* the public has an additional standard by which to judge the performance of the president sitting in the White House. The television series encourages the paradox by fostering an image that is unattainable by any public servant, making it seem like failure when the president does not live up to these standards. Presidents are unable to live up to this president-as-hero image, and that in turn strikes a blow to their confidence.

Academics, the media, and *The West Wing* all help create a president-as-hero image, and this image becomes the measuring stick by which presidents are judged by the public. Indeed, the public views the president, as portrayed, as a hero. Citizens place a tremendous amount of trust and confidence in the president's ability to make tough choices and carry out difficult policies. It is almost inevitable that presidents will fail to live up to this overblown level of trust. When assessing presidents' actions and abilities, it is important to acknowledge the impossibly high standards by which they are judged.

Notes

A special thanks to Joseph Foy for his comments and editorial suggestions.

1. "H. Con-172," Production Code: 227211, Original Airdate: January 9, 2001.

2. "Celestial Navigation," Production Code: 225914, Original Airdate: February 16, 2000.

3. "Celestial Navigation," Production Code: 225914, Original Airdate: February 16, 2000; "Mandatory Minimums," Production Code: 225919, Original Airdate: May 3, 2000.

4. "Shibboleth," Production Code: 226208, Original Airdate: November 22, 2000.

5. "Hartsfield's Landing," Production Code: 227215, Original Airdate: February 27, 2002.

6. Douglas S. Wood, "The Bush Style," *CNN Specials—Democracy in America* (2000), http://www.cnn.com/SPECIALS/2000/democracy/bush/stories/bush.style/ (accessed July 3, 2007); Peri E. Arnold, *Making the Managerial Presidency: Comprehensive Reorganization Planning, 1905–1996* (Lawrence: Univ. Press of Kansas, 1998).

7. George Stephanopoulos, *All Too Human* (New York: Little, Brown, 1999).

8. "The Short List," Production Code: 225908, Original Airdate: November 24, 1999.

9. "Evidence of Things Not Seen," Production Code: 175319, Original Airdate: April 23, 2003.

10. "Gaza," Production Code: 176070, Original Airdate: May 12, 2004; "Memorial Day," Production Code: 176071, Original Airdate: May 19, 2004; "NSF Thurmont," Production Code: 2T5001, Original Airdate: October 20, 2004; "The Birnam Wood," Production Code: 2T5002, Original Airdate: October 24, 2004.

11. Clinton L. Rossiter, *The American Presidency* (New York: Harcourt, Brace, 1956).

12. "In POTUS We Trust," in *The West Wing: The Complete Sixth Season*, Tommy Schlamme, Dir. Warner Home Video, 2006.

13. "Game On," Production Code: 175306, Original Airdate: October 30, 2002.

14. "Enemies," Production Code: 225907, Original Airdate: November 17, 1999.

15. "Dead Irish Writers," Production Code: 227216, Original Airdate: March 6, 2002; "The State Dinner," Production Code: 225906, Original Airdate: November 10, 1999; "The Indians in the Lobby," Production Code: 227208, Original Airdate: November 21, 2001.

16. Thomas E. Cronin and Michael A. Genovese, *The Paradoxes of the American Presidency* (Oxford: Oxford Univ. Press, 2003); Craig Gordon, "Giuliani's Price-Test: Milk, Bread?" *Chicago Tribune*, April 11, 2007.

17. "The Crackpots and These Women," Production Code: 225903, Original Airdate: October 20, 1999; "Mr. Willis of Ohio," Production Code: 225905, Original Airdate: November 3, 1999.

18. "Five Votes Down," Production Code: 225903, Original Airdate: October 13, 1999; "Manchester, Part II," Production Code: 227202, Original Airdate: October 17, 2001.

19. "The Stackhouse Filibuster," Production Code: 226217, Original Airdate: March 14, 2001.

20. "And It's Surely to Their Credit," Production Code: 226205, Original Airdate: November 1, 2000.

21. "Election Night," Production Code: 175308, Original Airdate: November 6, 2002; "Constituency of One," Production Code: 176055, Original Airdate: October 29, 2003.

22. "Talking Points," Production Code: 176069, Original Airdate: April 21, 2004.

23. Thomas E. Cronin, "Superman: Our Textbook President," *Washington Monthly,* October 1970, 47–54; Thomas E. Cronin, "The Presidency and Its Paradoxes," in *Classics of the American Presidency,* ed. Harry A. Bailey (Oak Park, Ill.: Moore Publishing, 1980).

6

SEEKING JUSTICE IN AMERICA'S TWO-TIERED LEGAL SYSTEM

"I Plead the Fif"

Kristi Nelson Foy and Joseph J. Foy

Based on the principle of the rule of law, the judiciary was designed arguably to be the most dispassionate, equalizing branch of American government. Indeed, the judicial branch of American government is premised on the ideas that "all men are created equal," that there is "justice for all," and that "justice is blind." Undoubtedly, these are essential principles, and they provide support for the foundation of the American legal system. Yet today, over two hundred years from America's founding, these principles are aspirations, not actualized goals. While all people may be created equally, they are not currently treated as such in the legal system. Striking examples of disparity and inequality abound, particularly in the criminal justice system. Certain segments of America's population, such as racial minorities and those in lower socioeconomic tiers, are disproportionately represented in prison populations, are much more likely to have criminal records, and are less likely to serve on juries to judge the guilt or innocence of their peers. In 2001, for example, 64 percent of America's state prisoners were members of racial or ethnic minorities; in 1996, almost half of jail inmates surveyed reported incomes of less than $600 per month, or $7,200 annually, prior to incarceration.[1]

Dave Chappelle, in his *Chappelle's Show*, called attention to these disparities in the criminal justice system in the guise of a comic spoof of the popular *Law and Order* series. Calling into question the validity of the theoretical virtues of the American legal system, Chappelle used this sketch as a forum for airing profoundly astute grievances against the biases of the legal system that work against racial minorities. Concomitantly, this sketch illuminated the crosscutting problem of poverty that afflicts many minorities that are in the criminal justice system. Unfortunately, many of these highly attuned insights and reflections went largely overlooked by fans and critics alike in favor of his more popular sketches (a mock *Frontline* episode about a blind African American who grows up to be a white supremacist, a "racial draft," Samuel L. Jackson advertising his own brand of Sam Jackson beer, and the perhaps best known of all, "Charlie Murphy's True Hollywood Stories," which inspired a generation of young men to proclaim, "I'm Rick James").[2] This chapter, however, seeks to revisit Chappelle's *Law and Order* spoof and use it as the basis for exploring the role of the courts in American politics within the context of race and class issues. Using this sketch as the basis of inquiry, it is clear that when it comes to color and money, lady justice isn't blind.

The American Courts and Systems of Law

Before delving into the problems and inequalities within the judicial branch of government exposed by *Chappelle's Show*, it is important to understand the courts and their various functions. This is imperative because the different roles the courts play in dealing with criminal and civil matters have an impact on racial politics in the United States. And, although Chappelle focuses solely on discrepancies within the criminal system, many of his observations provide a deeper understanding of the judicial system as a whole.

To begin, just as the other branches of the federal government have a state counterpart, so too does the judicial branch. There are both federal and state courts, and all of these courts hear both criminal and civil cases. The federal judicial system is composed of ninety-four judicial districts, including at least one district in each state, the District of Columbia, and Puerto Rico. These district courts funnel into twelve regional circuits, each of which has a court of appeals. For example, there are two district courts in Wisconsin, three district courts in Illinois, and two district courts in Indiana. All of these district courts are encompassed by the U.S. Court of Appeals for the Seventh Circuit. From the appellate courts, a losing party may attempt to appeal to the U.S. Supreme Court. The U.S. Supreme Court is the highest court in the federal system, and it hears a very limited number of cases each year. Similarly, every state in the nation has its own court system. State systems typically mimic the federal system, with each state having numerous trial courts, a few courts of appeal, and one Supreme Court. California, for instance, has fifty-eight trial courts, six appellate districts, each having a court of appeal, and one Supreme Court.

Both federal and state courts hear two kinds of cases, civil and criminal. Civil cases involve lawsuits between two private parties, and the award for the victorious party in the lawsuit is typically monetary damages. Criminal cases are brought by the government against an individual, and if the government is successful in its prosecution of the case, the defendant receives a fine, is incarcerated, or both. The other significant difference between civil and criminal cases is the standard of proof a party must meet to win its case. In criminal cases, because the losing party faces a deprivation of personal liberty (i.e., imprisonment), the standard of proof is high. The prosecution must prove its case beyond a reasonable doubt. In civil cases, since only monetary damages are at stake, the standard is somewhat lower. The prevailing party must prove its case by a preponderance of the evidence (it is more likely than not that a particular act or omission occurred). Due to these different standards in criminal and civil cases, it is possible for a defendant to be acquitted of criminal charges, but then lose a civil case arising from the same incident. Perhaps the most famous example of this juxtaposition is the O. J. Simpson case. In his criminal trial, the bloodied glove provided by the prosecution did not fit Simpson, so he was acquitted of murder charges in the death of his ex-wife, Nicole Brown Simpson, and her friend Ron Goldman. However, O. J. then lost the civil wrongful death and battery suits brought by the Brown and Goldman families and was ordered to pay the two families a total of $33.5 million in damages.

Although Chappelle focuses on the inequalities of the criminal court system, his observations about the unequal application of justice in the United States can be applied to all levels of the court system (federal and state) and all types of cases (civil and criminal). It is important to note, however, that many social critics argue that although there are disparities within the criminal court system, the civil courts have been used to expand minority rights. For instance, Paula McClain and Joseph Stewart Jr. posit that "racial and ethnic minority groups have frequently turned to the courts in an attempt to improve their positions because victories in the courts are more likely to be determined by what is right than merely what is politically popular."[3] An example of their rationale is the landmark case *Brown v. Board of Education of Topeka* (1954), in which the NAACP Legal Defense and Education Fund used the courts to desegregate public schools—a critical victory for the civil rights movement.[4] This case was so influential that other minority groups, including the Mexican American Legal Defense Fund, the Asian Pacific American Legal Consortium, and the Native American Rights Fund, have followed the NAACP's model of using the courts to actively pursue the recognition and expansion of group rights. Thus, there are certainly examples, primarily during the twenty-year period of 1954 to 1974, where the courts were used to further the rights of minorities.

However, as Lucius Barker, Mack Jones, and Katherine Tate explain, the composition of the actual justices populating the courts has more to do with the relatively brief period in American history in which the courts were used for positive change than do the promises of equal treatment under the law. In fact, they argue, "the situation began to change during the Burger Court. The Supreme Court's leadership and strong support of civil rights and civil liberties became much more uncertain. . . . [S]uch change in judicial policy depends in large measure on *who* is appointed to the Court."[5] If one looks to court rulings prior to the decision in *Brown,* the courts were not nearly as ready to advance the rights of minorities. It was the courts, after all, that ruled in 1856 that blacks, be they free or slave, could never be considered to be full citizens of the United States, and therefore were not afforded the same legal protections as whites.[6] *Brown* itself was a case that dealt with the legacy of the 1896 case *Plessy v. Ferguson,* in which the Supreme Court established the original doctrine upholding "separate but equal" accommodations for whites and blacks, and in *Korematsu v. United States* (1944) the Court upheld the right of the U.S. government to create internment camps for the detention of Japanese Americans.[7] Thus, although the Warren Court was largely responsible for a number of significant advances within minority rights, subsequent Courts have been far less permissive. Despite the brief period when the civil courts may have helped advance minority rights, that period proves to be the exception rather than the rule, and these courts remain just as open to criticism as their criminal counterparts.

Race and Class in the Criminal Court System

Turning more directly to the inequalities within the criminal courts, the Chappelle sketch clearly illustrates the common themes associated with discrepancies between racial groups in the legal system. Known most commonly for its edgy, politically incorrect humor, *Chappelle's Show* prompted criticism that it produced too much superficial laughter at the sensitive cultural issues to which it was calling attention.[8] However, despite these critiques, the show actually provides compelling insights into many aspects of American society and politics. In looking at the legal system specifically, the fact that *Chappelle's Show* confronts these issues so directly and unapologetically enables a clear forum from which to examine the too often hushed conversations about race and class that are ongoing in the United States. The real power of Chappelle's comedy is that it taps into the latent distrust of the legal system in America by racial and ethnic minorities, as well as by citizens living in lower socioeconomic conditions across the United States. Thus, it provides a forum for bringing issues of inequality and legal disparities to light.

In the fifth episode of *Chappelle's Show* season two, Dave Chappelle

Although it only ran for three seasons, including the "Lost Episodes," Dave Chappelle's wildly popular *Chappelle's Show* helped to spotlight ongoing problems of racial disparity within the United States, including in the judicial system, by spoofing the legal drama *Law and Order.* (Moviegoods)

starts the show by discussing the rampant corporate corruption that was making headlines across the United States in the wake of the Enron, Tyco, and WorldCom scandals. In discussing the corporate scandals, Chappelle seems bewildered at how the executives of these major companies were able to "rip everybody off" but "get no time in jail." Initially, Chappelle alludes to underlying racism within the American legal system to explain the differential treatment of corporate officials, saying, "I've got to get in on this being white thing." However, as he transitions from his opening monolog into the first sketch, a spoof on the popular television drama *Law and Order,* Chappelle also begins to tap into problems of wealth and the disparity across classifications of crime in the United States to highlight what he perceives as problems in the legal system. He sets up his spoof by saying, "Its like there's two legal systems. . . . It would be better if for like three days they actually put those guys through the same legal system that we all have to go through, and then they put like crack dealers . . . through the legal system that they go through. Wouldn't that be something?"

Chappelle then launches into his special edition of *Law and Order* by bringing back the character "Tron Carter," a flamboyant, black cocaine dealer from the season one sketch "The Mad Real World," and "Charles Jeffries," the priggish, but underhanded, white CEO of the fictional corporation Fonecom who is illegally manipulating company pensions. Chappelle uses a story paralleling the experiences of these two characters to expose what he perceives to be a two-tiered legal system in the United States. During Chappelle's version of *Law and Order,* Carter is treated like the white-collar criminal, while Jeffries is manhandled like a street thug. The result is a profound look into the disparities within the American criminal justice system.

The sketch begins with Jeffries in his bedroom with his wife. He begins telling her about the accountants "getting on them" about misleading the stockholders and blowing employee pensions. He dismisses the accountants, saying, "Come on, people, this is business, right?" Just then, a smoke bomb rolls under the bedroom door, and a cadre of police officers burst in like a SWAT team. The officers shoot Jeffries's dog, even though the dog is lying calmly on the floor in the corner of the bedroom, spraying blood all over Jeffries's wife. The officers then shove Jeffries onto the bed, subdue him, and handcuff him.

On the other side of town, a Dade County police department detective calls Tron Carter to tell him that there is an outstanding warrant for his arrest for cocaine trafficking. Carter responds that they have to be careful how they handle this situation, since they cannot embarrass someone like him in front of his family and community. Carter asks when he can turn himself in, offering to come into the station on Thursday between 2 P.M. and 6 P.M. The detective thanks Carter for his help and apologizes for the inconvenience.

Jeffries is now at the police station, being interrogated by two cops. He asks what he is being charged with, and one of the cops retorts, "Like you don't know, you little bitch." The officers continue questioning Jeffries, and when he complains about one of the cops smoking, they put out a cigarette on Jeffries's forehead. Jeffries promptly pees his pants. He then asks for his lawyer, so they allow a legal aid attorney to come into the interrogation room. The attorney enters, dumps a stack of files onto the table, and says that Jeffries is his fourteenth case this week.

Carter, on the other hand, does not report to the police station until nearly midnight, leaving a roomful of detectives to wait for him all afternoon and evening. Once he does arrive, however, he politely compliments the detectives on the "fine spread" of cheeses they have provided for him, some of which he has never even seen before. The detectives tell Carter that they do not want to make a big deal out of his arrest for trafficking since he has done a lot of good for the community. Consequently, they offer Carter a plea deal of two months in "Club Fed," and they ask him to testify before a Senate investigatory committee. When Carter asks if he can still "traffic rocks to the community" when he gets out of jail, the lead detective says, "Absolutely not," and points to the tape recorder on the table. Carter says, "You're right, selling rocks would be wrong." He then starts laughing and proclaims, "Jail's the shit!" Everyone in the room knows that Carter has no remorse for what he has done, and, given the opportunity, he will sell crack again once he is out of jail.

Flashing forward to the Jeffries trial, one of the police officers testifies for the prosecution and claims that Jeffries ordered his dog to "sic" the cops, which is why they had to shoot it, and that after they subdued Jeffries they found pure Colombian heroin in his house. Jeffries, astonished, blurts out that the heroin is not his. His disheveled and overworked attorney does nothing. The outcome of the trial is a foregone conclusion—Jeffries is guilty. This result is confirmed when the camera pans over to the jury of Jeffries's peers, and every single juror is African American. The judge asks Jeffries if he wants to say anything before sentencing, but just as Jeffries begins to speak, the judge cuts him off and refuses to allow him to get one word out. Clearly disgusted, the judge calls Jeffries the "worst kind of scum on the face of the earth," "an animal," and "a filthy, big-lipped beast" in the open courtroom. He orders a mandatory minimum life sentence, ruthlessly commenting that Jeffries will have "plenty of time to lift weights and convert to Islam." The judge then commands Jeffries to "get out of his sight."

The sketch concludes with Carter's testimony before the Senate investigatory committee. In response to every single one of the senators' questions, Carter pleads the "fif" (Fifth Amendment) and winks at his attorneys as he does it. The senators, recognizing the futility of this endeavor, eventually quit asking Carter questions. At the end of Carter's "testimony," one of his attorneys gets his sentence reduced from two months in jail to one month. Carter raises his attorneys' hands into the air in triumph, just as a photographer takes his picture.

And Justice for Some . . .

As noted above, American jurisprudence is founded on the core principle of equality under the law, and justice is supposed to be blind to factors like race, ethnicity, religion, and class. This is why the disparities that arise out of the legal process become such a powerful tool for illustrating the more pervasive problems of inequality in America. Well before *Chappelle's Show*, artists and authors used the criminal justice system countless times when attempting to capture and dramatize race-based inequities in America.

Perhaps one of the most well-known of these depictions is that of the 1961 Pulitzer Prize–winning novel *To Kill a Mockingbird*. In confronting racism in the Deep South, Harper Lee uses a courtroom drama to reveal the legal and social inequalities faced by minorities in a two-tiered system of justice. Atticus Finch (notably played in the film version of the book by Gregory Peck) offers a strong defense for Tom Robinson, a black man in Alabama who is accused of raping Mayella Ewell, a white woman. Finch offers evidence that shows Robinson could not have inflicted the wounds Mayella suffered because of his handicapped left arm and that it was actually Mayella's father, Bob Ewell, who beat her when he found her making amorous advances toward Robinson. However, despite all the evidence to the contrary, the all-white jury finds Robinson guilty and sentences him to death. Atticus later explains how Robinson was shot to death by prison guards in a reported attempt to flee during his exercise period. "Seventeen bullet holes in him," recalls Finch. "They didn't have to shoot him that much."[9]

But perhaps the most powerful examples of racial inequalities within the legal system are the ones that happen outside the pages of novels or the imaginations of film and television producers. They are cases like that of Emmett Till, a black teenager who was savagely beaten, shot, and dumped into a river with a cotton gin fan attached to his neck with barbed wire for whistling at a white woman. The all-white jury acquitted both white defendants, who later bragged openly about committing the crime. The legacy of Till's case and the acquittal of those two men has long been a stain on the American legal system, and the United States is still struggling with the case, as evidenced by the 110th House of Representatives' recently passing "H.R. 923: Emmett Till Unsolved Civil Rights Crime Act." Yet Till's case is but one of many that highlight racial disparities within the legal system. More recently, there are cases like that of Frank Jude Jr., who was beaten severely by off-duty white police officers who were later acquitted on all major charges by an all-white jury in state court. Or the case of Rubin "The Hurricane" Carter, a middleweight boxer who was arrested for a multiple homicide and convicted by an all-white jury based on suspect evidence, but then released twenty years later on appeal.[10] Each of these cases is an example of those overtly dramatic moments when we are directly confronted with the horrific realities of racism, and they serve as illustrative examples of America's two-tiered system of justice.[11]

It is important to note that disparities within the legal system are not just a black-white issue, either. One of the most striking cases of racial inequality is the case of Vincent Chin, a twenty-seven-year old Chinese-American from Detroit, Michigan, who was celebrating during his bachelor party on June 19, 1982, in Highland Park when two men, Ronald Ebens and Michael Nitz, confronted him. Ebens and Nitz, both autoworkers who were angry over the loss of American auto jobs to Japan, instigated an altercation with Chin at a strip club because they presumed he was Japanese. Ebens was heard to have shouted at Chin, "It's because of you . . . that we're out of work." They began yelling, and Chin hit Ebens, which began the scuffle. All parties were thrown out of the club to go their separate ways. Ebens and Nitz, however, hunted Chin down and beat him to death with a baseball bat. The two men pleaded guilty in state court to manslaughter and received three years of probation and a $3,780 bill for a fine and court costs. Neither Ebens nor Nitz spent even a single day in prison for the beating death of Vincent Chin.[12]

In 1984, the Chin case subsequently went before the federal courts. At the trial, Ebens was found guilty on one of two civil rights charges while

Nitz was found not guilty on both counts. Three years later, the decision against Ebens was overturned on appeal. Lily Chin, Vincent's mother, who had become an activist following her son's death, left the United States to return home to China. People who knew and worked with Lily recall how after the acquittal she announced her plans to return to China to "find peace" because "there is no justice in America."[13]

These anecdotal examples illustrate larger national trends. For example, in 2007, although African Americans made up approximately 12 percent of the U.S. population, they accounted for almost 44 percent of all incarcerations. Likewise, a study by the U.S. Department of Justice revealed that in 2001, black males had a nearly 1-in-3 chance (32 percent) of ending up in prison, as did over 17 percent of Hispanic males. However, white males had slightly less than a 6 percent chance of imprisonment. And although there is significantly less chance for women of all three races to end up in prison, the disparities across the races remain similar (6 percent for black women, 2 percent for Hispanic women, and less than 1 percent for white women).[14]

But how is it that the American legal system can go so far astray from the noble principles of equality and rule of law upon which it is based? Although in each of these cases there are a multitude of explanations, three themes consistently emerge in cases of racial and economic disparity in the prisons and courts: improper legal services for the poor, lack of diversity within juries, and misguided sentencing requirements. These themes are clearly highlighted in Chappelle's version of *Law and Order,* as he directly and openly confronts all three to expose the two-tiered system of law that results in such numerous and compelling examples, exposing racial and economic disparities in the American system.

Legal Services for the Poor

The Sixth Amendment to the U.S. Constitution states, "In all criminal prosecutions, the accused shall enjoy the right . . . to have the Assistance of Counsel for his defence." Early on, questions arose as to whether this amendment meant that an accused only had the right to counsel during a criminal trial, whether the accused only had the right to counsel if he or she was charged with a felony offense, and whether the amendment required the appointment of counsel for an indigent defendant. Many states also questioned whether individuals had the right to counsel in state criminal proceedings. It took decades for the courts to resolve all of these questions.

However, an accused now clearly has the right to counsel at all phases of a criminal proceeding in which he or she could be sentenced to time in jail, and the federal Sixth Amendment right to counsel applies to state proceedings as well. Thus, a criminal defendant should have his or her rights protected by counsel during most criminal proceedings, unless he or she waives the right to counsel.

Even though the right to counsel should, in theory, reduce disparities in the legal system by ensuring that the legal process does not overwhelm criminal defendants, the right to counsel actually illustrates such inequalities. Defendants who can afford to retain their own attorney (or team of attorneys) are typically much more successful than indigent defendants who have counsel appointed for them. Funding for public defenders, who represent defendants who cannot afford an attorney, has been stretched increasingly thin over the past few decades. As a result, Chappelle's portrayal of the public defender in his *Law and Order* episode is more truth than spoof. Public defenders have exceptionally high workloads and few resources to assist with a defense, so the quality of representation they can offer suffers. As the Justice Department noted in 2000, the lack of funding for public defenders has resulted in legal representation of such low quality as to amount to no representation at all, as well as delays, overturned convictions, and convictions of the innocent.[15]

Indigent individuals fare no better in civil matters. A 2005 study by the Legal Services Corporation found that 80 percent of low-income Americans who need legal assistance on civil matters do not receive any.[16] The same study found that approximately 1 million cases a year are turned away because legal aid programs lack capacity to handle them. This causes a significant imbalance in the protection of legal rights for the poor in cases ranging from divorce and custody battles to those of housing and employment and benefits claims. The result is that the poor have access to the legal system, but not in any significant way. As the Washington State Bar Association noted on this issue, "Meaningful access to the court without legal representation is as illusory as if the building itself were physically inaccessible to them."[17]

The discrepancies that result from the influence of money (or lack thereof) in the legal system are manifest in unequal justice for the rich and the poor. In both the criminal and civil courts, the lack of financial means often results in the inability for some citizens to properly maneuver through a complex legal system, which denies them access to justice itself. The images of Tron Carter sitting next to his high-profile legal team juxtaposed with Charles

Jeffries's overworked and underpaid legal aid attorney serve to illustrate this point clearly. This is not to say that legal aid does not serve a very important role in providing access to the courts. To the contrary, the services they do provide are important to the system, but the lack of manpower and resources in the face of ever-increasing demands leave them at a severe disadvantage. Thus, the Chappelle message that justice has a price tag, and only those who can afford to pay can receive any meaningful representation, provides an incisive understanding of inequities in the legal system.

Jury of Your Peers

The Sixth Amendment to the U.S. Constitution also guarantees those facing criminal prosecution "a speedy and public trial, by an impartial jury of the State and district wherein the crime shall have been committed." In the common vernacular, this portion of the Sixth Amendment has been recast to mean that we have a right to be judged by a jury of our peers. Unfortunately, in America today, courts have a tremendous problem getting citizens to show up for jury duty. This may not come as a surprise, as the closest most Americans seemingly want to be to a jury box is in reading a John Grisham novel. And, although getting jurors to serve is a problem in general, turnout rates for minorities are even lower than those of white jurors. In Chicago, for example, 60 percent of residents of a black neighborhood did not respond to calls for jury duty, as compared to 8 percent of residents in white neighborhoods.[18] While there are likely many reasons to account for this disparity (income level issues, renters moving more frequently, apathy, inability to miss work, distrust in the system, etc.), the effects of this reality are significant.

As the aforementioned examples of injustice in the case of Emmett Till, Rubin Carter, Frank Jude Jr., Vincent Chin, and countless others demonstrate, race is in and of itself a significant factor in determining guilt or innocence. The problem of an all-white jury with a minority defendant has been criticized for decades. For example, in his controversial retelling of Rubin Carter's story in "The Hurricane," Bob Dylan reflects on the problem of the lack of diversity within jury trials with the lyrics, "The D.A. said he was the one who did the deed / And the all-white jury agreed."[19] Chappelle plays on this theme in his *Law and Order* sketch when he has Jeffries found guilty by an all-black jury.

But perhaps the most famous example in modern history of claims of jury bias was in the 1992 Rodney King trial, in which a jury of ten whites, one Asian, and one Latino acquitted four white officers of the Los Angeles Police Department after they pulled King over after a high-speed chase and beat him for resisting arrest. With several others looking on, the officers shot King twice with a TASER gun and mercilessly struck him with batons and kicked him to allegedly subdue him (although the beatings continued well after he was limp and unmoving on the ground). The defendants' request for a change of venue was granted, and the trial was moved to Ventura County, which was predominantly white and Hispanic. The acquittal of the officers led to a massive racial riot that resulted in enormous amounts of property damage and the deaths of fifty-three people.

The link between the lack of diversity among jury members and a disproportionate conviction rate for minorities is nothing new to scholars of the legal system.[20] However, it is important to note that such results have more complex origins than one might suspect. According to a study released by Samuel R. Sommers of Tufts University, racial diversity is important for improving the deliberation of juries.[21] In a study of twenty-nine mock juries involving over two hundred "jurors," the Sommers study found that "diverse juries deliberated longer, raised more facts about the case, and conducted broader and more wide-ranging deliberations. They also made fewer factual errors in discussing evidence and when errors did occur, those errors were more likely to be corrected during the discussion."[22]

Ironically, when minorities do show up for jury duty, their perceptions of racial inequality in the criminal justice system directly impact criminal convictions. For some minorities, their distrust of the legal system makes them refuse to credit the testimony of police officers or believe the arguments a prosecutor makes during a trial. This, in turn, leads to "not guilty" verdicts. At the same time, jurors who believe that criminal laws are being enforced unfairly, whether the jurors themselves are minorities or not, have engaged in jury nullification so that a criminal defendant is not convicted. Jury nullification is the process by which a jury returns a "not guilty" verdict even though the jury believes that the defendant is actually guilty of the crime with which he or she has been charged. In either of these instances, it only takes one juror who refuses to find a defendant guilty to hang the jury and acquit a defendant.

Misguided Sentencing

After a criminal defendant is found guilty of a crime, the defendant typically appears at a separate hearing in front of a judge for the sentencing phase of the criminal process. Historically, both state and federal criminal laws have had a penalty provision that provides for a range of possible sentences (for example, a minimum of five years of imprisonment but not to exceed twenty years). After hearing the evidence presented at trial regarding the crime committed, a judge would then decide on an appropriate sentence within the prescribed range based on the severity of the crime and the defendant's character (for example, whether the defendant was sorry for his actions, etc.). If there were mitigating circumstances surrounding the criminal act, the judge would also typically factor that into the sentence. This left considerable discretion for judges during the sentencing phase. Not surprisingly, some judges developed reputations as tough judges who would always give a defendant the maximum sentence possible, regardless of any mitigating circumstances in a case, while other judges developed reputations as "softies" who were more lenient during sentencing. Racial disparities in sentencing were also manifest. The end result was that two defendants who committed similar crimes under similar circumstances in the same city could get wildly different sentences, based on the judges assigned to their cases.

In order to diminish some of this judicial discretion in sentencing, Congress created the U.S. Sentencing Commission in the early 1980s and charged it with the task of developing federal sentencing guidelines. This Sentencing Commission eventually created a very complex system of regulations meant to close the gap in sentencing disparities and take away judicial discretion. Generally speaking, during sentencing a judge would look at a sentencing table, where the horizontal axis of the table was a continuum for criminal history and the vertical axis was a continuum for the level of offense. The box at which the two axes intersected (i.e., one past conviction meets a current battery conviction) gave a relatively narrow range of possible sentences, and the judge then sentenced the defendant within that range. Although there were select circumstances where a judge might depart from the sentencing guidelines, few judges did so for fear of being reversed on appeal.

As noted above, the intent behind the creation of the sentencing guidelines was to reduce inequalities and disparities in the sentencing process. Yet, ironically, the sentencing guidelines only served to entrench some of these disparities. The most glaring example of inequality in the sentencing process was the difference between convictions for possession of crack and possession of cocaine. Under the sentencing guidelines, there is a 100:1 quantity ratio between the amount of crack and the amount of cocaine needed to trigger mandatory minimum sentences for trafficking and possession.

For crack cocaine, a conviction of possession with intent to distribute has a five-year sentence if the defendant is caught with five grams of crack. For powder cocaine, a defendant must be caught with five *hundred* grams or more to trigger the five-year sentence.[23] Thus, if sentenced under the federal sentencing guidelines, Tron Carter would have received significantly more time in prison for "trafficking rocks to his community" than Charles Jeffries would have if he would have been trafficking powder cocaine.

The crack/cocaine disparity correlates to racial disparity in several ways. First and foremost, crack is cheaper than powder cocaine, making it accessible to lower socio-economic classes. As crack addiction spread through America's lower classes, crack became associated with minorities living in the slums, while cocaine remained a drug for whites in the suburbs. Crack's negative connotation soon followed: crack is used by "crack whores," while cocaine is used by "cocaine kittens." Second, although drug use rates are fairly similar across racial and ethnic groups, and two-thirds of crack users in the United States are white or Hispanic, 82 percent of crack defendants in 2005 were African American.[24] Not only is there a significant racial disparity in prosecutions of crack possession and trafficking, but more African American drug offenders are sentenced to prison than white drug offenders.[25] The average time served by African Americans for drug crimes also increased by 77 percent from 1994 to 2003, while the average time served by whites for drug crimes during this period increased by only 28 percent.[26]

The crack/cocaine disparity illustrates the fact that the sentencing guidelines have not succeeded in their goal of reducing disparities in the criminal justice system. But, unfortunately, the sentencing guidelines have failed in other respects as well. For example, due to recently created "three-strikes, you're out" guidelines, "a disproportionate number of young black and Hispanic men are likely to be imprisoned for life under scenarios in which they are guilty of little more than a history of untreated addiction and several prior drug-related offenses. . . . States will absorb the staggering cost of not only constructing additional prisons to accommodate increasing numbers of prisoners who will never be released but also warehousing them into old age."[27]

Faced with evidence regarding the shortcomings of the sentencing guidelines, the U.S. Supreme Court in 2005 decided the case of *United States v. Booker.* In *Booker,* the Court found the sentencing guidelines to be unconstitutional because they violated the Sixth Amendment. Specifically, the guidelines took away the right to a trial by jury because a federal judge could consider factors not presented to the jury or proven at trial when determining the appropriate sentence. As a result, the federal sentencing guidelines are now advisory, but not mandatory.

Has the Jury Reached a Verdict? Concluding on the Courts

In 1987, Warren McCleskey petitioned to have his death sentence overturned because of the racially discriminatory way the death penalty was applied in the state of Georgia. Upon examining evidence from the well-known Baldus Study cited by McCleskey's attorneys, the Supreme Court of the United States decided that although evidence does indicate that blacks are disproportionately more likely to receive the death penalty than whites, the study was insufficient to prove that Georgia violated the equal protection of the Fourteenth Amendment in McCleskey's case specifically.[28] In doing so, the Court acknowledged the data showing the ubiquitous racial discrimination that pervades the American legal establishment as being empirically valid. However, the ruling in *McCleskey* indicated that the Court was unwilling to do anything to correct those systemic realities. The inequalities at the state level were, in essence, going to be overlooked at the federal level, and although statistics demonstrate a clear violation of equal protection in general, those figures mean nothing in individual cases. In effect, the U.S. Supreme Court was going to allow such discrimination to continue by doing nothing to stop it.

Not only do disparities within the legal system exist, but they have a spillover effect into other aspects of American politics and government. According to Jamie Fellner and Marc Mauer of the Human Rights Watch, during the 1996 elections, approximately 13 percent of all eligible black male voters (1.4 million) were disenfranchised due to felony convictions, which is a surprising statistic on its own. Compared to the 4.6 million black men who turned out that year, however, the figure is staggering.[29] Thus, disparities within the court system can have the effect of perpetuating disparities within elections, and therefore in representation. Likewise, although Chappelle approaches the issues of discrimination within the legal system in a comedic fashion, the systemic disparities based on race and class breed contempt for police officers attempting to enforce the laws, the judicial system that applies and interprets the laws, and the political superstructure as a whole. Nothing about that scenario is funny. Additionally, rather than turning to politics to help eliminate these ongoing problems of race and class, groups continue to turn away from a system that does not represent their interests.

The *McCleskey* case serves to highlight the discrepancy between the promises of the American legal system and its realities. There is a pledge of equal protection and rule of law, but the empirical realities diverge greatly from such noble promises. This tension between promise and reality is clearly demonstrated in Dave Chappelle's comic send-up of the hit series *Law and Order*. By inverting the experiences of what a black drug dealer and white corporate executive would experience in his understanding of the American legal system, Chappelle reveals the absurdity of racially and class-based discrimination in the courts, and in doing so provides a broader understanding of real issues threatening the promises of American jurisprudence and democracy as a whole. Chappelle's message is clear—it is time the courts hold themselves accountable for such discrimination and stop metaphorically pleading the "fif."

Notes

1. U.S. Department of Justice, Office of Justice Programs, "Criminal Offender Statistics: Summary of Findings" (Washington, D.C.: Bureau of Justice Statistics, 2007), http://www.ojp.usdoj.gov/bjs/crimoff.htm#inmates (accessed June 5, 2007); Caroline Wolf Harlow, "Profile of Jail Inmates, 1996" (Washington, D.C.: U.S. Department of Justice, Bureau of Justice Statistics, 1998), http://www.ojp.usdoj.gov/bjs/pub/ascii/pji96.txt (accessed July 14, 2007).

2. Although the show only ran for two seasons (not including a trio of "Lost Episodes"), *Chappelle's Show* was wildly popular and had a significant impact on American pop culture, receiving numerous Emmy nominations during its run on cable television and becoming one of the all-time best-selling DVD sets. In rerun form, it remains one of the hallmarks of the cable station Comedy Central's programming, which announced in 2007 that it would be teaming up with MGM to put the show into syndication.

3. Paula D. McClain and Joseph Stewart Jr., *Can We All Get Along? Racial and Ethnic Minorities in American Politics*, 4th ed. (Boulder, Colo.: Westview Press, 2005), 118–19.

4. *Brown v. Board of Education of Topeka*, 347 U.S. 483 (1954).

5. Lucius J. Barker, Mack H. Jones, and Katherine Tate, *African Americans and the American Political System*, 4th ed. (Upper Saddle River, N.J.: Prentice Hall, 1999), 172.

6. *Dred Scott v. Sandford*, 60 U.S. 393 (1856).

7. *Plessy v. Ferguson*, 163 U.S. 537 (1896); *Korematsu v. United States*, 323 U.S. 214 (1944).

8. Critic Kam Williams, writing for the online edition of *News Blaze,* noted this concern by writing that the "sketches are so funny you'll forget that they might actually be reinforcing the same deep-seated intolerance in American culture they seek to satirize." With popular sketches ranging from a mock *Frontline* episode about a blind African American who grows up to be a white supremacist, a "racial draft," and a look into the life of a white suburban family with the "N-word" for a last name, Chappelle's irreverent humor attempts to strike a blow at the covert racism in America. However, these sketches raise questions, according to Williams, as to whether people are laughing with Chappelle or at him. Sharing these same concerns, Chappelle walked away from a $50 million contract with Comedy Central and the show. Citing "artistic differences" as the initial reason for stopping production, Chappelle later indicated that he was unsure about whether the show was furthering racist opinions and perspectives, rather than breaking them down (CBS News, "Chappelle: 'An Act of Freedom,'" CBS News, *60 Minutes II* [December 29, 2004], http://www.cbsnews.com/stories/2004/10/19/60II/main650149.shtml [accessed June 25, 2007]; Kam Williams, "Best of Chappelle's Show [Uncensored] DVD Review," *News Blaze* [June 20, 2007], http://newsblaze.com/story/20070620115358tsop .nb/newsblaze/ENTERTAI/story.html [accessed June 25, 2007]).

9. Harper Lee, *To Kill a Mockingbird* (New York: HarperCollins, 2006), 235.

10. In Carter's second trial in 1967, the jury did contain two African Americans, and the result of the trial was again a "guilty" verdict.

11. H.R. 923—110th Congress (2007): Emmett Till Unsolved Civil Rights Crime Act, GovTrack.us (database of federal legislation), http://www.govtrack.us/congress/bill .xpd?bill=h110-923 (accessed March 4, 2008). The death of Emmett Till and arrest and conviction of Rubin Carter are reflected upon often in popular culture. Bob Dylan's songs "The Death of Emmett Till" (1963) and "The Hurricane" (1975) offer reflections on the racial issues involved in both cases. Likewise, in 1999, Denzel Washington gave a powerful performance as Rubin Carter in the film version of *The Hurricane* based on Carter's 1974 autobiography, *The Sixteenth Round: From Number 1 Contender to #45472.* Till's death has been referenced in theatrical productions, literature, and even rap songs, such as Kanye West's "Through the Wire" (2003).

12. Aletha Yip, "Remembering Vincent Chin," *Asian Week* (June 5–13, 1997), http://www.asianweek.com/061397/feature.html (accessed June 2, 2007).

13. Giles Li, "OCA Mourns Death of Lily Chin," Asian American Council, Dayton, Ohio (June 10, 2002), http://iis.stat.wright.edu/AAC-Dayton/news_reported/memorial_ LilyChin.htm (accessed March 4, 2008). During the federal civil rights trial, the fact that Ebens had been drinking to the point of intoxication raised doubts about whether he had the formal intent of harming Chin on the basis of his national origin. That Ebens was drunk helped the defense in its claim that racial antagonism was not the primary factor motivating Ebens. Ebens later settled the civil suit against him out of court for $1.5 million, but upon ridding himself of his assets and fleeing, he has been able to evade officials (Yip, "Remembering Vincent Chin," 1997).

14. Thomas P. Bonczar, "Prevalence of Imprisonment in the US Population, 1974–2001," U.S. Department of Justice, Bureau of Justice Statistics (Washington, D.C.: U.S. Department of Justice, August 2003).

15. U.S. Department of Justice, *Improving Criminal Justice Systems Through Expanded Strategies and Innovative Collaborations* (Washington, D.C.: U.S. Department of Justice, 2000).

16. Evelyn Nieves, "80% of Poor Lack Civil Legal Aid, Study Says," *Washington Post* (October 15, 2005), A09.

17. David Bowermaster, "Should Poor Be Appointed Attorneys in Civil Cases?" *Seattle Times* (May 31, 2007), http://seattletimes.nwsource.com/html/localnews/2003728887_civilattorneys31m.html (accessed June 5, 2007).

18. David Cole, *No Equal Justice: Race and Class in the American Criminal Justice System* (New York: New Press, 1999), 170.

19. Bob Dylan and Jacques Levy, "The Hurricane," *Desire* (New York: Columbia Records, January 5, 1976).

20. See William J. Bowers, Benjamin D. Steiner, and Marla Sandys, "Death Sentencing in Black and White: An Empirical Analysis of Jurors' Race and Jury Racial Composition," *University of Pennsylvania Journal of Constitutional Law* 3 (2001): 171–275; Derek Chadee, "Race, Trial Evidence, and Jury Decision Making," *Caribbean Journal of Criminology and Social Psychology* 1 (1996): 59–86.

21. Samuel R. Sommers, "On Racial Diversity and Group Decision Making: Identifying Multiple Effects of Racial Composition on Jury Deliberations," *Journal of Personality and Social Psychology* (April 2006), http://www.apa.org/releases/0406_JPSP_Sommer.pdf (accessed June 5, 2007).

22. *Science Daily,* "Racial Diversity Improves Group Decision Making in Unexpected Ways, According to Tufts University Research," based on press release issued by Tufts University (April 10, 2006), http://www.sciencedaily.com/releases/2006/04/060410162259.htm (accessed June 5, 2007).

23. The Sentencing Project, *Crack Cocaine Sentencing Policy: Unjustified and Unreasonable,* http://www.sentencingproject.org/Admin/Documents/publications/dp_cc_sentencingpolicy.pdf (accessed March 4, 2008).

24. Ibid.

25. Ibid., citing U.S. Sentencing Commission, *Fifteen Years of Guidelines Sentencing* (Washington, D.C.: U.S. Sentencing Commission, November 2004), 122.

26. Ibid. See also B. S. Meierhoefer, *The General Effect of Mandatory Minimum Prison Terms: A Longitudinal Study of Federal Sentences Imposed* (Washington, D.C.: Federal Judicial Center, 1992), 20. (In 1986, before mandatory minimums for crack offenses became effective, the average federal drug offense sentence for blacks was 11 percent higher than for whites. Four years later, following the implementation of harsher drug sentencing laws, the average federal drug offense sentence was 49 percent higher for blacks.)

27. Craig Haney, Ph.D., and Philip Zimbardo, Ph.D., "The Past and Future of U.S. Prison Policy: Twenty-Five Years after the Stanford Prison Experiment," *American Psychologist* 53, no. 7 (July 1998): 718.

28. *McCleskey v. Kemp,* 481 U.S. 279 (1987).

29. Jamie Fellner and Marc Mauer, "Losing the Vote: The Impact of Felony Disenfranchisement Laws in the United States" (Washington, D.C.: Human Rights Watch and The Sentencing Project, 1998). Although it is unlikely that all 1.4 million African Americans who were disenfranchised would have actually turned out if eligible, many most likely would have. If turnout among these disenfranchised voters was consistent with 1996 rates among black males, it would have added an additional 588,000 votes.

7

MADISONIAN PLURALISM AND INTEREST GROUP POLITICS

Inhaling Democracy, Choking on Elitism

Joseph J. Foy

In 1994, Christopher Buckley wrote the national best seller *Thank You for Smoking* in an attempt to satirize what he described as an overly zealous attack on the tobacco industry (and those who support it) in the "neo-puritanical 1990s." Central in this inquest were not only nonprofit health agencies, but also government officials who were using the tobacco issue to further their own quest for political support and power. In 2006, the novel was adapted into a film directed by Jason Reitman, which, although differing significantly from the book, kept intact the central libertarian themes of Buckley's novel.[1]

Thank You for Smoking is the story of Nick Naylor, the "face of cigarettes." As the senior vice president for communications at the Academy for Tobacco Studies, a front organization to promote the efforts of conglomerated tobacco, Naylor's job is not only to defend big tobacco against attacks from government and nongovernmental actors, but also to engage in efforts to create a positive image for cigarette companies. He takes pride in the fact that he doesn't "have an MD or a law degree," but, rather, "a bachelor's in kicking ass and taking names." Meeting weekly with fellow spokespersons from the alcohol and firearms lobbies, he rounds out a group known as the "MOD Squad" (Merchants of Death) that brainstorms tactics for making inroads into government and the public, all the while comparing death tolls from their products. To achieve his goals of peddling a positive image of big tobacco, Naylor often employs a dual strategy of obfuscation and distraction, misleading his audiences and muddying the scientific waters that report on the dangers of smoking, while professing the libertarian principles of personal responsibility and freedom of choice. Rhetoric is his weapon, and he wields it well. As Naylor himself said of his abilities, "Michael Jordan plays ball. Charles Manson kills people. I talk. Everyone has a talent."

Using strong satire and often irreverent humor as a means of examining the classical market ethics of libertarianism, *Thank You for Smoking* provides a unique look into the world of pluralist politics and poses a valuable illustration of American democracy at its core. Such insights enable an evaluation, not just of how democratic America is, but also of how democratic it is meant to be. Using James Madison's *Federalist* No. 10 as the basis for inquiry, *Thank You for Smoking* helps illustrate foundational principles of American politics as they relate to the important notion of pluralism: the free and open competition among groups for political power and influence. Contrary to the laissez-faire message offered by Buckley and Reitman, *Thank You for Smoking* actually supplies insight into the elitist effects of pluralist competition that distort democratic outcomes. Ultimately, and perhaps contrary to its intent, *Thank You for Smoking* illustrates that while powerfully funded corporate interests have the ability to play the pluralist game, the average citizen is left out because he or she cannot afford the ticket.

Filtering Out the Harmful Effects of Factions

The importance of special interests in American government and democracy is nothing new to even the most casual observer of politics. Thousands of such groups are registered at the national level, and thousands more at the state and local levels. Yet the disproportionate effect interest groups have in the democratic process in the United States has been examined and debated since the political founding. In *Federalist* No. 10, James Madison dealt with the question of special interests in the form of factions: "a number of citizens, whether amounting to a minority or majority of the whole, who are united and actuated by some common impulse of passion, or of interest, adverse to the rights of other citizens, or to the permanent and aggregate interests of the community." Fearing that organized interests may begin to accumulate power enough to usurp the aggregate interests of a democratic society; Madison asked how democracy might guard against the harm caused by factions. On the one hand, the factions themselves are born out of liberty, and are "sown in the nature of man." The activities of groups and individuals in a vibrant civil society will give rise to conflicting passions of differential and competing interests, whether religious, economic, social, political, or otherwise. To ban such activities would mean the oppressive stifling of the very liberty government is meant to protect, which, according to Madison, is a "remedy . . . worse than the disease." Likewise, trying to give everyone the same opinions, interests, and passions is impractical and unworkable. The factional rise of special interests is, therefore, inherent in a democratic regime.[2]

If one cannot control for the causes of faction, what is to be done to prevent these groups from tyrannically working against the interests of democracy? Madison answered this question by noting that if we cannot remove the causes of faction, we might at least control for their effects. He argued that a republic (representative democracy) that is large enough to encompass a great number and diversity of interests could solve for the potentially dangerous effects of factions. In such a system, if a faction were composed of a minority of the whole, then the republican principle of majority rule could prevent the tyranny of the minority by ensuring that such interests are unable to seize control and work against the interests of the majority. Likewise, the way to guard against the potential tyranny by the majority is to have delegates elected who represent a large number of constituents. With a large number of people being represented by a single elected official, there will be a diverse set of interests to which the representative is accountable. This means it is less likely that a single, unifying interest composed of a majority of the whole will form. The way to guard against the harmful effects of faction, therefore, is to divide interests as much as possible through a large republic, and then allow those groups to openly compete for power and influence within the system as a whole.

The free competition of groups articulated in *Federalist* No. 10 is often referred to as the theory of pluralism. Adherents of the pluralist doctrine argue that the open competition of interests results in moderate government actions and policies that reflect the interests of the democratic community as a whole. This moderation is a result of perpetual contest and compromise among a variety of interests who must accommodate enough views and preferences in order to achieve electoral and policy success. Therefore, outcomes in the long run reflect the aggregate desire of the citizenry at-large.[3]

Are "Tobacco Tactics" Bad for Democracy's Health?

The most fundamental criticism of pluralism is the notion that groups have both equal access and ability when it comes to influencing the political system. Of significant concern is the influence of special interest money in the political system. The most important of interest group activities, which is curiously left out of *Thank You for Smoking*, is the direct pressure of interests on government officials through the activity of lobbying. In the six-month period from July to December of 2006, $1,352,639,056 was spent on federal lobbying efforts—an average spending rate of approximately $226 million per month. Among the leading spenders were the Health Care ($218,087,796) and Communication Technology ($177,797,388) sectors, the Finance and Insurance ($160,664,306) and Energy and Natural Resources ($111,460,545) industries, and representatives from Transportation ($104,031,194) and Defense ($68,629,730). Such numbers call to mind the words of E. E. Schattschneider, who once noted, "The flaw in the pluralist heaven is that the heavenly chorus sings with a strong upper-class accent."[4]

The influence of lobbying money is substantial, as it allows interest groups to cultivate access to public officials in ways not held by those unable to donate such significant sums of money, and access produces rewards. According to political analyst Jeffrey Birnbaum, interest groups spend so much money on lobbying efforts because it often yields up to a 1,000 percent return on their investment in the form of legislative benefits. Whether it is through partisan donations, money to campaigns, or just treating the overworked, underpaid staffers of key legislative officials out to a night of free beer and hot wings, lobbying efforts open doors of government officials to interest groups. By establishing these open lines of communication, interest groups, lobbyists, and activists develop a working relationship with key officials who share common concerns about specific issues. These relationships develop into so-called issue networks, which give pressure groups the ability to influence key decisions on policy and governmental action.

At the end of the film, Naylor is able to testify before a Senate subcommittee and profess principles of liberty and personal responsibility because he was identified as a key stakeholder in the decision under consideration by the committee to place a skull and crossbones poison label on cigarettes. Likewise, groups who have cultivated a relationship with key officials are often called upon to give expert and stakeholder testimony before such committees to influence their decisions. This is an important part of how interest groups are able to shape and direct public policy.[5]

But the influence of money on the political process is not entirely left out of *Thank You for Smoking*. For instance, Naylor makes an appearance on the *Joan Lunden Show* (in the novel, *Oprah*) along with representatives from Mothers Against Smoking, the Office of Substance Prevention, Ron Goode (Todd Louiso), an aide to a senator who is making a career out of capitalizing on the anti-smoking fervor brewing in the United States, and Robin Williger (Eric Haberman), a reformed teenage smoker from Racine, Wisconsin, who has cancer and is bald from undergoing chemotherapy. Faced with such opposition on stage with him, and an overwhelmingly hostile crowd, Naylor makes outlandish claims about how the Ron Goodes of the world want young Robin to die so that their budgets increase, while big tobacco wants to keep him alive so they don't lose a customer. He then promises a $5 million anti-teen smoking campaign so as to protect America's greatest resource, its children. At this, the crowd begins to come around,

In the above scene from the 2006 film *Thank You for Smoking*, tobacco lobbyist Nick Naylor (Aaron Eckhart) uses the news media to make a public appeal to the American people on behalf of his product, which helps him cultivate access to Congress by mobilizing constituent pressures on elected officials. (Photofest)

and Nick is able to become the center of conversation (young Robin even enthusiastically shakes his hand).

How does this scene help to underscore the undue influence money plays in the political process? Naylor's claim that big tobacco is so interested in preserving the health and well-being of America's youth that it is willing to spend $50 million dollars on an anti-smoking campaign is a disingenuous claim, since big tobacco's goal is not to get teens to quit smoking. Rather, the purpose of the campaign is to promote a more favorable climate for the tobacco industry in the minds of the electorate, thereby relieving any political pressure that might come from a citizenry mobilized against the industry. This is a classic public strategy of interest groups in American democracy, known as a campaign of institutional advertising. The purpose of these types of efforts is to foster a public climate favorable for creating political advantage for clients in a particular industry. For Naylor, there is no desire to actually have the campaign influence teens to not smoke. When Nick asks The Captain (Robert Duvall) about his reaction to the campaign, The Captain's only response is to jokingly reply, "I hope it's not too effective." (In Buckley's novel, Nick defends his actions by telling his boss, BR, that they could probably expect good press from the ad campaign.)

The role of money in the democratic process is also highlighted in other ways throughout the film. When Nick goes to Hollywood to discuss the idea of having stars smoke in movies, he and film mogul Jeff Megall (Rob Lowe) devise a plan to have the tobacco industry pay $25 million to have Brad Pitt and Catherine Zeta Jones light up after a sex scene in a forthcoming science fiction film called *Message from Sector Six*. They even plan to market a special brand of "Sector Sixes" cigarette to coincide with the release of the film. Likewise, Naylor drives a suitcase full of money up to the house of Lorne Lutch (Sam Elliot), the original Marlboro Man, who is dying of lung cancer from his years of smoking Kools, to keep him from speaking out against the industry. Lorne takes the money, thereby silencing the potentially balancing effect that an opposition voice could play in a pluralist system.

America Is Living in Spin

Thank You for Smoking helps demonstrate how interest groups use money not only to influence government officials through direct lobbying efforts but also to create a favorable public climate through positive advertising and the silencing of critics. What is left unspoken in the film is the obvious counter to the claim made by Megall, who says, "What information there is, is out there. People will decide for themselves." What about the information that is unable to reach the people due to the fact that some groups cannot afford to disseminate it? How are people to make rationally informed decisions when well-funded interests who come up with the sexiest ad campaign or catchiest slogans are sponsoring the truth?

The problem here is that while Buckley and Reitman's libertarian philosophy is rooted in the notion that a person ought to be free to do what he wants to his body, even if it is in some way causing harm, this philosophy is dependent on the principle of informed consent. Competent individuals who are fully educated may make decisions that carry with them potential risks because they are voluntarily engaging in an act with a sufficient base of knowledge about the effects of their actions. However, as Paul Blumberg reveals about campaigns of deception and obfuscation waged by hundreds of businesses and corporations, it is all but impossible for the average American to monitor and check the sources of all the information with which they are confronted on a daily basis when making decisions. Efforts to deceive and manipulate by groups operating in the public sphere are often successful because of the high cost associated with monitoring those groups, not to mention the need for a high degree of specialization necessary to sort through misleading claims and data. Moreover, Blumberg highlights the corrupting effect such efforts can have on democracy, since the constant inundation of misinformation and manipulation in the marketplace leads to a decline in public trust and crumbles the very foundations of interaction in the democratic community. In such cases, regulation and oversight may be a necessary check on irresponsible and unethical attempts by groups to mislead and distort the democratic dialogue. Without such efforts, people may enter into an agreement or activity willingly, but do so only because they lack complete, accurate information.[6]

The ability of special interests to mislead the public, and pollute democratic dialogue and decision-making, is of central consideration in *Thank You for Smoking*. Nick Naylor is clearly not interested in seeking or promoting truth. To the contrary, he takes pride in describing the work of the Academy for Tobacco Studies' chief scientist, Erhardt von Gruppen Mundt, whom Nick considers a "genius" because he could "disprove gravity." His sophist-like mantra to his son, Joey (Cameron Bright), is that "if you argue correctly, you're never wrong." In Buckley's novel, Naylor appears on *Larry*

King Live, where he claims "ninety-six percent of heavy smokers never get seriously ill." When King skeptically asks him where he got his data, Naylor replies, "From the National Institutes of Health, right here in Bethesda, Maryland." What he does not reveal to the public at-large is his follow-up internal monologue, in which he thinks, "Let the NIH deny it tomorrow; tomorrow people would move on to the next thing—Bosnia, tax increases, Sharon Stone's new movie, Patti Davis's latest novel about what a bitch her mother was." To seal the deal, Naylor goes on to lie that the Centers for Disease Control in Atlanta confirmed the data. Truth in advertising is hardly in Naylor's wheelhouse.[7]

Interestingly enough, in defending the market ethics promulgated in the film, director Jason Reitman told ABC, "There are unfortunate cases of people who started smoking far before the data was out there, but at this point we understand it." But is it the case that people fully understood the health risks of smoking after all the data became available? What about the thousands of smokers who got hooked in part because cigarette companies were misleading consumers by attempting to junk the science of medical research that uncovered the negative health risks associated with smoking? After all, like the real-life advertising and lobbying efforts of American tobacco companies, the entire purpose of the Academy for Tobacco Studies in the film was to obfuscate the facts and delay the establishment of a mainstream consensus about the effects of tobacco. And, at the end of the film Nick is seen sharing these tactics with cellular phone company spokesmen, who hope to use his methods to dissuade fears that there is a relationship between cell phone usage and cancer. On this point the film may be closer to reality than satire.[8]

In examining the actual efforts of the American tobacco industry, Christopher Mooney documents a number of ways in which big tobacco attempted to use the tactics of obfuscation and suppression to cast doubt on the overwhelming scientific evidence showing the direct relationship between smoking cigarettes and health problems. For instance, the tobacco lobby employed a systematic strategy of "junking" established scientific evidence related to the harmful effects of smoking. This strategy earned the label "manufacturing uncertainty" to describe its goal of confusing the public and raising doubts about scientific findings about tobacco use. This strategy has been mimicked by other political interest groups who attempt to cast public doubt on evidence that works against their group goals. For example, the tobacco tactic was adopted, according to the Union of Concerned Scientists

(UCS), by ExxonMobil, which distributed approximately $16 million to forty-three different organizations from 1998 to 2005 in an effort to attack and discredit the science of global warming. Alden Meyer, policy director at the UCS, explained how this money, distributed to ideological pressure groups and think tanks, was used for the "spreading of uncertainty by misrepresenting peer-reviewed scientific studies or emphasizing selected facts." His claim was supported by James McCarthy of Harvard University, who indicated that ExxonMobil was trying to make it seem as though there was a "vigorous debate" in the scientific community, where there was not, on the issue of global warming.[9]

Similarly, Mooney provides evidence to show how groups will often fund efforts to suppress information that may be damaging to their cause. Like Naylor handing a dying Lorne Lutch a suitcase full of money to silence his voice of opposition, Mooney details how the Competitive Enterprise Institute, which received nearly half a million dollars from ExxonMobil in 2003, lobbied to suppress the publication of information about the potential implications of climate change. This suggests that money not only helps to provide some interest groups with a louder voice than others, but it can also be used to shut other voices out of the democratic dialogue. It reveals yet another way in which special interests can derail (or at the very least postpone) meaningful deliberation and action.[10]

In addition to employing tactics and deception designed to mislead adult consumers, special interests have tried to sell their messages directly to children as a method of recruitment. *Thank You for Smoking* makes a number of references to "Joe Camel," a cartoon camel used by R. J. Reynolds in an advertising campaign for its product. Not that they had to work too hard at such efforts. As BR (J. K. Simmons) noted to his spin doctors at the Academy for Tobacco Studies, "We don't sell Tic Tacs . . . We sell Cigarettes. And they're cool and available and addictive. The job is almost done for us." Throw "Old Joe" the cartoon camel in this mix, and you have an ad campaign that is quite effective. In 1991, a study appeared in the *Journal of the American Medical Association* that indicated that Joe Camel was more recognizable among five- and six-year-old children than Mickey Mouse. Although R. J. Reynolds denied that the ad campaign was targeting the youth, internal company documents revealed that the advertising campaign was directed at children and teens. The obvious problem here, however, is that the principle of informed consent does not apply to children (especially five- and six-year-olds) who are being targeted through attractive cartoon characters to buy into a product, thereby creating a compelling governmental need to step in and regulate the tobacco industry's attempts at advertising to children.[11]

Cigarette companies are not the only ones attempting to end-run the principles of rational deliberation and informed consent by persuading children with cartoon ads. Interest groups have often adopted the strategy of attempting to recruit and mobilize young people with cartoons. One of the most direct and extreme examples is the ongoing recruitment and mobilization tactics of the special interest group PETA, People for the Ethical Treatment of Animals. Their tactics have ranged from distributing cartoon trading cards with characters like "Tubby Tammy," an obese young girl who gorges herself on buckets of chicken, to distributing "Unhappy Meals" showing children the inhumane processing of chicken and beef into their fast food favorites. The most shocking of PETA's tactics, however, was the distribution of what they refer to as "Comics for Kids" entitled *Your Mommy Kills Animals* and *Your Daddy Kills Animals*. These leaflets portray a blood-stained mother taking sadistic pleasure in stabbing to death a frightened cartoon rabbit, and an angry father gutting a fish while two others watch in pain and terror with hooks in their mouths. The "comics" go on to reveal actual photographs of skinned and maimed animals, and warn children, "Until your daddy learns that it's not 'fun' to kill, keep your doggies and kitties away from him. He's so hooked on killing defenseless animals that they could be next!"[12]

To sustain the health and vitality of a democracy, there is a need for informed deliberation. Democratic discourse and an open exchange of ideas help people to clearly identify and pursue their interests when heading to the polls or mobilizing to express support or opposition to legislation or governmental action. However, interests seeking to promote their cause at any cost, and using any method to achieve victory, often intentionally pollute rational deliberation. Whether it is relying on the tactics of Nick "The Sultan of Spin" Naylor, who complicates, confuses, and conceals information in order to mislead the public into making irrational choices against their interests, or employing the likes of "Old Joe" the camel to target, recruit, and mobilize the most impressionable of youth, these groups undermine the deliberative process so essential in a democratic society. This, once again, highlights the need for regulation and oversight to guard against the harmful effects of unchecked interests competing for power and political influence in the pluralist system.

Cutting through the Smoke

Despite the problems with pluralism described above, there are also benefits to the pluralist models of understanding politics. Taken as an empirical examination of policy-making and political outcomes, rather than a normative recommendation of what a democracy ought to be, pluralism provides a nice explanatory model for decision-making. Dahl's analysis in *Who Governs?* illustrates that interest associations and pressure groups play significant roles in the policy process, and we should not turn a blind eye to this reality. Finally, as Madison reminds us in *Federalist* No. 10, interest groups are a part of democratic life, born out of the liberty that is essential for democracy. To eliminate the liberty that allows interest groups to form and compete for influence is a tyranny that cannot be allowed in a democratic regime. Therefore, pluralist theories of interest group activity do help us better understand how American politics and government operate.

Likewise, the role of interest groups is not always negative, nor should their involvement in politics always be seen as a "necessary evil." It was, after all, the Topeka chapter of the NAACP that recruited plaintiffs and funded their efforts to end segregation in public schools in several cases that led to the landmark Supreme Court decision of *Brown v. Board of Education of Topeka* in 1954, and the Southern Christian Leadership Conference that helped advance housing, voting, public accommodation, and other civil rights throughout the United States in the 1960s. It was the efforts of labor interests in the nineteenth century that helped to create the forty-hour work week, and the combined efforts of groups representing physicians, pharmacists, women's clubs, and unions that led to the development of federal food and drug safety codes and the passage of the Wiley Act, which created the Food and Drug Administration. Today, groups like the Committee for Economic Development, an organization of prominent business leaders and financial interests, have begun to tackle the problem of business executives who focus on short-term capital gains instead of the long-term goal of public trust and economic growth.

Interest groups also play a positive role within the electorate, as they help to provide significant benefits for democratic citizens. The primary benefits offered by these groups come in the form of purposive benefits (helping organize and mobilize groups of people to become successful in achieving their political goals), informational benefits (arranging and disseminating information to constituents, government officials, media, and others), selective and public forms of material benefits (goods and services acquired for both members and nonmembers), and solidarity benefits (social capital built up between members making networks of connection and support). Likewise, interest group activities are an important part of maintaining an active and vibrant civil society, which can provide both important aid and critical opposition to governmental actions within a democratic system.[13]

To be clear, the goals of interest groups are not being placed under scrutiny for threatening the process and institutions of democracy. Instead, the concern is with the tactics that enable interest groups to cultivate a disproportionate level of access to public officials to influence policy and the public agenda, as well as the rampant manipulation of information and attempts to pollute democratic dialogue to further their specific interests. The locus of debate about the potentially harmful effects of interest group activity in politics must be how to maintain the positive role that these groups play in informing, organizing, mobilizing, and representing interests in American democracy, while guarding against the potential corrupting influence these groups may have on the democratic deliberation.

So, what checks can be set in place that will allow for the free and fair competition of interests, while protecting the essence of democracy? In 1971, the U.S. government attempted to rein in the corrupting influence of pressure groups with the passage of the Federal Election Campaign Act (FECA). The goal of FECA was to increase public disclosure of receipts and expenditures by campaigns. In 1974, FECA was amended to impose regulatory limits on the amount of hard money contributions (money donated directly to a candidate), as well as to establish a voluntary adherence to spending limits by candidates who wished to receive federal matching funds. In 1976, the FECA regulations were challenged. In *Buckley v. Valeo* the Supreme Court of the United States upheld the regulations, but also decided that candidates may spend on their campaigns from their personal funds. The *Buckley* decision also affirmed voluntary spending limits for candidates wishing to receive matching funds, as well as key disclosure provisions. At the turn of the millennium, the debate about the potentially corruptive nature of money in the political process was reignited in deliberations about the proposed Bipartisan Campaign Reform Act (BCRA), which was passed in 2002. Outlawing many forms of soft money contributions (money donated to political parties for non-campaign purposes, but which is sometimes used to influence elections), the BCRA broadened donation disclosure laws, limited the times during which groups could place issue advertisements, and raised contribution limits to allow them to be indexed with inflation. Like the FECA laws, these efforts were designed to prevent undue influence and corruption of moneyed interests, and they were largely upheld by the Supreme Court as being constitutional.[14]

Although the FECA and BCRA regulations only target the potentially corruptive influence of money in elections, they serve as a model for other potential interest group reforms. For example, in the 2006 political comedy *Man of the Year,* Robin Williams plays a presidential candidate who jokes that politicians "representing special interest groups . . . should be like NASCAR with the little patches on the back: 'Enron: We take your money and run.'" Although delivered as a punch line, such a recommendation is not too far from what other observers are calling for in terms of transparency and public accountability between moneyed interests and governmental officials. Recently, Republican Tom Coburn and Democrat Barack Obama initiated a bipartisan effort in the Senate to increase transparency by creating a federal Web site that would list the names of every group that was set to receive earmarked funds from the federal government and the amount received. Likewise, Birnbaum calls for "über-disclosure," meaning that there should be a full public accounting for all receipts and donations immediately available through the Internet during and after campaign and election cycles. Full and open disclosure would help citizens become more aware of which politicians are in league with which special interests, thereby helping to increase public accountability.[15]

Accountability can also come through the proliferation of watchdog organizations designed to hold groups accountable for the information they put out for public consideration. For example, the Annenberg Public Policy Center at the University of Pennsylvania sponsors The Annenberg Political Fact Check project, which hosts a Web site known as "FactCheck. org." This nonprofit, nonpartisan site is designed to review the accuracy of public claims in order to "reduce the level of deception and confusion in U.S. politics." Sites like these can help reduce the harmful effect of misleading information proliferated by groups, and they may help voters see through demagogic appeals and sophistry that might otherwise work against the long-term interests of a democratic community. The solution to preserve democracy, therefore, may lie in part with more democracy.[16]

One Last Puff on Pluralism

In an interview on The Filmlot, Jason Reitman was asked what he wanted people to take away from his film version of *Thank You for Smoking.* Reitman responded, "I'd like people to laugh—it's a comedy. If people take away a libertarian message as well, there's nothing wrong with that." Likewise, Reitman viewed the film as a forum for people to, as he mentioned in an ABC interview, "think about ideas of personal responsibility and choice." He indicated that the focus on smoking was an ideal foundation for such a conversation, because he felt cigarettes offered a "look into this idea of why we feel the need to tell each other how to live and why we can't take personal responsibility for our own actions when we fall ill from things that we know are dangerous." Ironically, his film, and Buckley's novel, actually helps illustrate how political pressure groups and special interests can work to undermine the ability of members of a democratic community to make informed decisions because of obfuscation and deceit. Far from being a message of libertarianism, *Thank You for Smoking* is a demonstration of why government regulations to counteract the disproportionate effects of special interest groups are needed now more than ever.[17]

Although this analysis began with *Federalist* No. 10, perhaps the more appropriate analysis with which to conclude is provided in *Federalist* No. 51. Here, Madison wrote, "What is government itself but the greatest of all reflections on human nature? If men were angels, no government would be necessary." Human nature, according to Madison, is flawed, thereby giving rise to the need for government to administer protection of those natural rights articulated by the likes of John Locke and Thomas Jefferson. However, it is this skepticism about the nature of man that led Madison to also argue, "If angels were to govern men, neither external nor internal controls on government would be necessary. In framing a government which is to be administered by men over men, the great difficulty lies in this: You must first enable the government to control the governed; and in the next place oblige it to control itself." The same might be said for the politics of pluralism. If the actions of groups were the actions of angels, no regulation of interests would be necessary. But, as *Thank You for Smoking* illustrates, this is not often the case.[18]

Notes

1. Christopher Buckley, *Thank You for Smoking* (New York: HarperCollins Publishers, 1994); David O. Sacks (Producer) and Jason Reitman (Writer/Director), *Thank You for Smoking*, Motion Picture (Los Angeles, Calif.: Room 9 Entertainment, 2006).

2. For a comprehensive listing of nationally registered lobbyist groups, please see

the "Political Advocacy Groups" site updated and maintained by Kathi Carlisle Fountain at the Meriam Library at California State University, Chico (http://www.vancouver.wsu. edu/fac/kfountain/ [accessed March 4, 2008]); Clinton Rossiter, ed., *The Federalist Papers* (New York: New American Library, 1961).

3. See Robert Dahl, *Democracy and Its Critics* (New Haven: Yale Univ. Press, 1989); and Robert Dahl, *Who Governs? Democracy and Power in the American City* (New Haven, Conn.: Yale Univ. Press, 1961).

4. *Congressional Quarterly,* "Political Moneyline," http://moneyline.cq.com/pml/ home.do (accessed March 4, 2008); Center for Responsive Politics, "Money in Politics Data," http://www.opensecrets.org (accessed May 16, 2007); E. E Schattschneider, *The Semisovereign People* (New York: Rinehart and Winston, 1960), 35.

5. Jeffrey H. Birnbaum, *The Lobbyists: How Influence Peddlers Work Their Way into Washington* (New York: Three Rivers Press, 1993), and Jeffrey H. Birnbaum, *The Money Men: The Real Story of Fund-Raising's Influence on Political Power in America* (New York: Crown, 2000).

6. Paul Blumberg, *The Predatory Society: Deception in the American Marketplace* (New York: Oxford Univ. Press, 1990).

7. Buckley, *Thank You for Smoking,* 76.

8. David Stratton interview with Jason Reitman, ABC TV, "At the Movies," http:// www.abc.net.au/atthemovies/txt/s1714051.htm (accessed June 1, 2007).

9. Christopher Mooney, *The Republican War on Science* (New York: Basic Books, 2005); Associated Press, "Group: ExxonMobil Paid to Mislead Public," *USA Today,* January 3, 2007 (updated January 5, 2007), http://www.usatoday.com/money/industries/ energy/2007-01-03-global-warming_x.htm (accessed March 4, 2008).

10. Mooney, *The Republican War on Science,* 87.

11. Paul M. Fischer, Meyer P. Schwartz, John W. Richards Jr., Adam O. Goldstein, and Tina H. Rojas, "Brand Logo Recognition by Children Aged 3 to 6 Years. Mickey Mouse and Old Joe the Camel," *Journal of the American Medical Association* 266, no. 22 (December 11, 1991): 3145–3148; BBC World News, "Camel Shown to Target Child Smokers," *BBC News* (January 16, 1998), http://news.bbc.co.uk/1/hi/world/47858.stm (accessed May 16, 2007).

12. PETA Comics, *Your Mommy Kills Animals,* Issue No. 1 (November 2003); PETA Comics, *Your Daddy Kills Animals,* Issue No. 2 (September 2005).

13. For additional information about the benefits offered by interest groups, see Mancur Olson, *The Logic of Collective Action: Public Goods and the Theory of Groups* (Cambridge, Mass.: Harvard Univ. Press, 1965).

14. *Buckley v. Valeo,* 424 U.S. 1 (1976); *McConnell v. Federal Election Commission,* 540 U.S. 93 (2003).

15. James G. Robinson, Robert N. Fried, and Desmond Mason (Producers) and Barry Levinson (Writer/Director), *Man of the Year,* Motion Picture (Hollywood, Calif.: Universal Pictures, 2006); Chris Edwards, "Reducing Federal Corruption," CATO In-

stitute, *Tax and Budget Bulletin* 34 (May 2006): 1–2; Jeffrey Birnbaum, "PTK Satellite Seminar #3, 'Money Talks': Lobbyists and the Power of Money in Washington," University of Wisconsin–Waukesha Library, Temporary Reserves (April 2, 2007).

16. FactCheck.org, Annenberg Political Fact Check, http://www.factcheck.org (accessed March 4, 2008).

17. Stratton interview with Reitman; The Filmlot, "Interview: Jason Reitman, Director of *Thank You for Smoking*," http://www.thefilmlot.com/interviews/INTreitman.php (accessed March 4, 2008); Beth Gottfried interview with Jason Reitman, "The Trades," May 2, 2006, http://www.the-trades.com/article.php?id=4289 (accessed March 4, 2008).

18. Rossiter, *The Federalist Papers.*

8

ENTERTAINMENT MEDIA AND POLITICAL KNOWLEDGE

Do People Get Any Truth out of Truthiness?

Christopher A. Cooper and Mandi Bates Bailey

When asked about the impact of the entertainment media in shaping America's perception of the president, Jon Stewart (of *The Daily Show with Jon Stewart*) seemed skeptical. "In terms of what I do? On a scale of zero to 10, I'd go with a zero, not very important. I don't know how else to put it." Stephen Colbert (host of *The Colbert Report*) expressed similar sentiments, claiming, "I'm not a political person, and I certainly don't have the answers." Despite Colbert's confession of being apolitical and Stewart's assertion of unimportance, most observers of media and politics believe that entertainment programs are increasingly important in shaping citizens' opinions of politics and political leaders.[1]

Whereas many other chapters in this book examine one form of popular culture in detail, in this chapter, we evaluate the political effects of entertainment media more generally. The paper proceeds as follows. First, we review the literature on media effects and media consumption, then evaluate the debate over entertainment media (often called soft news), highlighting our expectations about the relationship between entertainment media and political information. Next, we review our data, present our analysis, and conclude with a discussion of what the rise in entertainment media means for American democracy.

Media Consumption and Media Effects

Debates over entertainment media assume that the media affect public opinion and political behavior. After all, if the media do not affect the ways we think and act, then there is little reason to debate the differences between various types of media. After years of finding minimal effects, most scholars now agree that the media do affect what we think and how we act—at least at the margins.[2] The most prominent theories of media effects are agenda setting, priming, and framing.

Theories of agenda setting posit that the media "may not be successful much of the time in telling people what to think, but it is stunningly successful in telling its readers what to think about."[3] While early work referred specifically to print media, more recent work demonstrates similar tendencies with televised media. There is also some evidence that stories that come earlier in the broadcast are more likely to influence what people think and believe. Viewers seem to understand the journalistic norm that the most important stories are carried early in the broadcast, and thus tend to "tune out" news stories at the end of the broadcast. Shanto Iyengar and Donald Kinder also find that people with little political knowledge more easily accept the priorities suggested by the media and are thus more susceptible to agenda setting. Of course, the flip side of this effect suggests that political knowledge can combat the agenda-setting effect.[4]

The priming hypothesis, a second, highly influential examination of media effects, holds that Americans are overloaded with information and cannot possibly take into account every piece of information when they evaluate politicians and political candidates. People are therefore forced to use limited information when making political choices. Most people take in enough information that they consider themselves adequately informed and make their decisions on this basis. This process is called "satisficing." People rely upon information that is most accessible in their memory, which comes to mind quickly and easily. Priming relies on this notion of availability and suggests that by covering certain stories at the exclusion of others, the media "prime" certain aspects of political and social life. When citizens evaluate candidates and make voting decisions, it is these primed topics that are immediately available to them, and thus most important. For example, when primed by television news stories on national defense, citizens are more likely to judge the president based upon his defense policy. When primed on stories about inflation, citizens are more likely to judge the president by his economic policy.[5]

Those affected by priming are not the same as those affected by agenda setting. Because priming requires people to make the connection between the issue and the president's involvement with the issue, the politically unsophisticated are not as susceptible to the effects of priming. Priming suggests that the politically sophisticated (those who are politically informed and often politically involved) are also susceptible to the sway of the media's agenda.

While both agenda-setting and priming suggest that media impact on individuals is due to frequency of stories, framing suggests that the way in which the story is covered affects how people will perceive and respond to that particular issue. Simply stated, "Framing is the process by which a communication source constructs and defines a social or political issue for its audience."[6]

One influential study of framing showed that episodic frames (frames that focus on individual cases) cause the viewer to blame individuals rather than society for the problem or issue in question. Thematic frames, on the other hand (frames that focus on social, political, and economic forces), cause individuals to see the incident or concept as socially induced, where uncontrollable social forces are to blame. Needless to say, the way individuals view these issues drastically alters the evaluations of candidates who are elected to solve these problems.[7]

Nelson, Clawson, and Oxley added to the growing body of framing literature through their study of media framing of a civil liberties conflict. They conclude that the frame or angle the media takes on controversy directly affects citizens' perceptions, opinions, and actions.[8]

Types of Media

As the previous discussion highlights, there is a rich tradition of work examining the influence of the media on political attitudes and behaviors. Of equal importance to our study are examinations of the differences between types of media. Debates over the merits of various forms of media are not new, but until recently the debate has asked whether print media or televised media make better citizens. One traditional viewpoint argues that print media (newspapers, magazines, etc.) are inherently better sources of political information than television. For instance, Bennett et al. argue that "the more time Americans spend reading, the more attentive they are to public affairs."[9] Noted academic and public intellectual Robert Putnam also sings the praises of newspapers and print media: "Those who read the news are more engaged and knowledgeable about the world than those who only watch the news. Compared to demographically identical nonreaders, regular newspaper readers belong to more organizations, participate more actively in clubs and civic associations, attend local meetings more frequently, vote more regularly, volunteer and work on community projects more often, and even visit with friends more frequently and trust their neighbors more."[10]

Many of these scholars don't just praise print media, but also levy some heavy criticism against television. Putnam argues that television has transformed leisure time. Whereas people once got together in groups, visited with neighbors, and participated in local bowling leagues, Putnam believes that television has made us more self-centered, and less community oriented—changes that have led to a decline in civic engagement and social capital. Television has also been accused of leading to cynicism about politics and of telling us "what to feel, when to feel it, and how and why as well." In perhaps the most damning critique of television, Neil Postman suggests that television may cause us to amuse ourselves to death.[11]

Don't throw out your television yet, however. A growing group of scholars argues that television has some inherent advantages. First among these is television's visual format, which may increase information recall of certain dramatic events. The terrorist attacks of 9/11 are a perfect example. While reading about these attacks may have given people some necessary information, television was able to convey the horror and human emotion of that day in a much more direct way. It is the vision of the plane hitting the building that is replayed in our minds, not the quotes from the newspaper. In short, television has the ability to make faraway events seem close and immediate. From time to time, this can be a good thing.[12]

The 9/11 attacks also point to another advantage of television—speed of delivery. Few people would have wanted to wait until September 12 to find out what was happening in New York. We wanted to turn on our televisions and know what was happening immediately. Television is clearly an extremely fast and efficient way for us to learn about political events.

Although the debate between television and newspapers has produced some important insights, we believe that the television/newspaper dichotomy is losing its relevance for two reasons. First, "there is no evidence of consistent significant differences in the ability of different media to persuade, inform, or even to instill an emotional response in audience members." More importantly, television and newspaper content are increasingly similar. For instance, *USA Today* was created with the goal of bringing the news to millions of Americans by mimicking television's brief, visual format. Even *USA Today's* newspaper stands were made to look like television sets. On the other hand, C-SPAN was created with the opposite goal—to make television less dramatic, less visual, and more context driven—more like a newspaper. These lines are becoming even more blurry with the advent of the Internet. The same company may own many media Web sites, a number of newspapers, and a television station or two.[13]

Soft News v. Hard News

As the distinction between print and visual media is becoming less important, we believe that the more politically relevant and salient debate is moving toward the impact of "soft news" and entertainment media that have proliferated in recent years. These media outlets, characterized by shows such as *The Tonight Show with Jay Leno, The Daily Show with Jon Stewart, The Colbert Report, Real Time with Bill Maher,* and *Late Show with David Letterman,* are primarily meant to entertain, not to inform. Nonetheless, many Americans now get much of their political information from these trained comedians and entertainers.

Jon Stewart, host of Comedy Central's *The Daily Show,* uses his sharp wit and brilliant comedic skills to take on politicians, pundits, pop stars, and the press to give America a humorous slant on current events. (Moviegoods)

Whereas people previously learned about politics from a few "hard" news channels, entertainment media, like *The Daily Show with Jon Stewart,* and *The Colbert Report* are becoming preferred news sources for many citizens. Recent studies by the Pew Center for the People and the Press find that the percentage of people who regularly watch the nightly news dropped from 58 percent in 1993 to 28 percent by 2006 and the percentage of people who regularly read a daily newspaper dropped from 71 percent in 1992 to 52 percent in 2006. See Figure 1 for graphic evidence of these trends. At the same time that the hard news audience is shrinking, people are less likely to believe the media now than at anytime in recent history.[14]

Politicians have not ignored the rising market share of entertainment media. *Washington Post* columnist Howard Kurtz notes, "The irreverent *Daily Show* is no joke for politicians trying to connect with a younger crowd that doesn't watch the Sunday morning gabfests. That's why North Carolina Sen. John Edwards, a likely presidential candidate, did the show during its stint in Washington last week, joining such previous guests as John McCain (who recently hosted *Saturday Night Live*), Joe Lieberman, Michael Bloomberg, Chuck Schumer, Bob Dole, Bob Kerry and Mary Bono."[15]

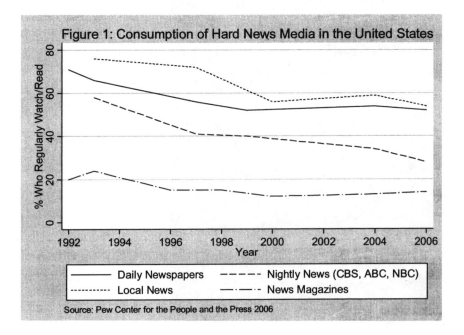

Figure 1: Consumption of Hard News Media in the United States

Source: Pew Center for the People and the Press 2006

Serious politicians used to avoid entertainment shows, but they now seek them out. For instance, a recent advertisement for *Real Time with Bill Maher* bragged that Maher was interviewing guests ranging from actor Sean Penn to presidential candidate Tommy Thompson. Clearly this is a different political environment than the one experienced just a few decades ago, when candidates rarely strayed away from such stalwarts as *Meet the Press*. Matthew Baum finds that appearing on talk shows is a good opportunity for politicians to become more likeable—particularly in the eyes of the opposing party.[16]

What does the scholarly literature lead us to believe about the effects of soft news? For a while, almost all of the scholarly research and commentary criticized the rise of soft news and entertainment media as sources of political information. For instance, Thomas Patterson argued in 2000 that soft news consumption ultimately leads to decreased interest in public affairs as well as a decline in trust in government. Markus Prior, writing in 2003, also found little evidence that people learn from soft news.[17]

Other scholars have come to believe that the rise of soft news and entertainment media as sources of political information may not be all bad. Although people may not tune into entertainment media to learn about politics, the entertainment programming they watch may present political information implicitly or explicitly. Citizens today learn about politics from a variety of sources—fiction and nonfiction, entertainment driven and information driven. For example, in 1999, viewers of the television show *Beverly Hills 90210* watched an episode in which a character had a scare with skin cancer due to excessive exposure to the sun. This storyline was suggested by the Centers for Disease Control because they recognized that "television dramas are a major source of health information for large numbers of Americans."

Children's programming, such as *Sesame Street,* has long used this approach to learning—getting children to pay attention because of entertainment, but sneaking in educational information. This practice is now common in adult shows as well as those meant for children. A few people even posit that some entertainment and soft news media are able to compensate for the shortcomings of typical horse race political coverage by providing relevant information and a dialogue between candidates and voters that traditional news media typically overlook.[18] Below we survey what we know about soft news in three sections—audience characteristics, political attention, and political information.

The Soft News Audience and Political Attention

Citizens who get their information from soft news media differ significantly from those who consume traditional hard news sources. Hard news consumers tend to be more educated, more interested in politics, older, and more likely to be males than soft news consumers. Because of these trends, it is often difficult to determine whether the effects of entertainment media consumption are due to the influence of soft news, or are merely because of the less educated and less politically interested audience. In our analysis, we control for these demographic factors to isolate the impact of entertainment media consumption on political knowledge and participation. Nonetheless, the causal mechanism is difficult to isolate, and as a result our study (like many survey-based studies of political behavior) focuses on correlation rather than causation. We return to this issue in the conclusion.[19]

Soft news consumers are expected to be less interested in politics than those who consume traditional media. This is the primary assumption of this chapter. Citizens who generally pay a lot of attention to politics are likely to get their news from the daily newspaper, the nightly news, news magazines, and the like. To reach politically active voters, politicians still haunt the Sunday talk show circuit, talk politics with media personalities, and court reporters from major papers such as the *New York Times*. Citizens who are not as interested in politics, however, may receive their political information as a byproduct of being entertained. To reach these citizens, politicians have begun to make appearances on entertainment shows such as *Saturday Night Live*.[20]

Soft News and Political Information

Conventional wisdom suggests that consuming soft news leads to lower levels of political knowledge and that consuming traditional, hard news leads to more political knowledge. After all, if citizens get their information from a source aimed at providing entertainment, rather than information, it stands to reason that the reduced political content would produce lower levels of information. Recently, however, the literature on soft news and political information has begun to suggest that soft news may in some cases increase the political information of certain citizens—namely politically inattentive ones. In the most thorough discussion of this phenomenon, Baum argues

Hail to the cheese? Stephen Colbert's short-lived presidential bid for the 2008 election cycle may have failed to get him on any ballots, but his unique brand of "truthiness" is having a lasting impact on a wide audience. (Photofest)

that soft news provides politically relevant information for people who are not normally interested in politics.[21]

Although Baum's work would lead us to expect that soft news consumption is not a hindrance to learning, his study is based only on information levels about foreign policy. Baum is not alone in his focus on foreign policy. The vast majority of the previous research that highlights the positive effects of entertainment and soft news media examines foreign policy attitudes and knowledge. While foreign policy is no doubt important, it is different than most other political issues. Citizen knowledge of foreign policy is quite low, and we know that it is easier for the media to set the agenda when knowledge is low. Consequently, we might expect very different results from other issue areas. Russell Neuman, Marion Just, and Ann Crigler also lead us to question whether this assertion applies to other cases. They suggest that "a great deal more creativity is required in the presentation of less salient news stories." In sum, although we would expect that soft news does not negatively impact learning, we do believe that the question needs to be empirically tested in another context. The 2000 election provides such a test case.[22]

What Is Soft News?

We have established that soft news is important, but what constitutes soft news? Unfortunately, there is no straightforward answer. Baum explains that soft news employs "a set of story characteristics, including the absence of a public policy component, sensationalized presentation, human-interest themes, and emphasis on dramatic subject matter, such as crime and disaster." Although this paints a broad picture, it is far from precise. Doris Graber, in *Mass Media and American Politics,* suggests that *U.S. News and World Report, Newsweek, Time,* and other weekly news magazines contain many qualities of soft news, but Baum includes weekly news magazines in his hard news index. As Thomas Patterson points out, defining soft news reminds us of Justice Potter Stewart's famous disclaimer about pornography, that "I know it when I see it."[23]

No matter how one defines soft news, almost all observers agree that comedy shows such as *The Tonight Show with Jay Leno* and *The Daily Show with Jon Stewart* constitute soft news. *Saturday Night Live,* MTV, and (the now defunct) *Politically Incorrect* are likewise primarily concerned with entertainment, rather than traditional journalistic standards of good reporting. In constructing our soft news index, we include only the unquestionably entertainment-oriented sources listed above. As a result, from this point on we opt for the more limited term *entertainment* media, rather than the more controversial term *soft* news.

Hard Data on Entertainment Media

Guided by the literature discussed above, we seek to learn more about the political influence of entertainment media. We rely on the media interest telephone survey of 1,090 people conducted by the Pew Research Center for the People and the Press prior to the 2000 election. We believe that the 2000 election is an ideal case study to examine the influence of entertainment media. Although entertainment media are not new, the 2000 election was the first major election where Jon Stewart was considered a major player and perhaps the first election where most political operatives realized the importance of entertainment media for persuading voters. If we find effects in the 2000 election, it is likely that a survey of voters in subsequent elections would only produce greater effects.[24]

Our research question asks whether entertainment media consumption influences political knowledge. We expect that consuming entertainment media will help bring knowledge to citizens who are not generally interested in politics. To address this question, we estimate an ordered logistic regression where the variable we are attempting to explain (campaign knowledge) ranges from 0 to 3 and measures how many of the following three questions the respondent answered correctly:

(1) Do you happen to know which of the presidential candidates is now governor of Texas?
(2) Do you happen to know which of the presidential candidates was formerly a senator from New Jersey?
(3) Do you happen to know which of the presidential candidates co-sponsored a campaign finance reform bill in Congress?

This was the only measure of political knowledge available on the survey, and although it is not a perfect measure, we believe that it does capture an important component of knowledge. After all, representative democracy requires that citizens have knowledge of the candidates running for office. At the time of this survey, George W. Bush, Bill Bradley, and John McCain were all serious candidates for their respective parties' nomination for president. Knowledge of these basic facts was certainly necessary for an informed vote. As a result, we believe that these are important components of political knowledge.[25]

In this model we include independent variables for entertainment media consumption, daily newspaper consumption, and political attention. To test whether the effect of entertainment media is different for interested and uninterested publics, we include an interaction term in which we multiply entertainment media consumption by how closely the individual indicated that he or she followed the 2000 presidential election. We also include independent variables for other factors traditionally associated with political knowledge—age, education, income, race (1=white), and sex (1=male). We expect all of these control variables to be positively related to the dependent variable.

To determine whether entertainment media consumption influences political knowledge, we ask whether those who get their news from entertainment media are less likely to know basic information about three major presidential candidates (George W. Bush, Bill Bradley, and John McCain). The results are presented in Table 1.

Each of the control variables (age, education, income, race, sex) is strongly and positively related to political knowledge. This means that older, more educated, more wealthy, white, and male respondents were more likely to be able to identify Bush, Bradley, and McCain than their counterparts. We also find that daily newspaper consumption ($p<.05$) is related to political knowledge, suggesting that people who frequently read the daily newspaper display higher levels of political knowledge than those who do not. This is consistent with early works that find that reading of any sort is highly associated with political knowledge. This also supports Putnam's claim that "newspaper readership remains a mark of substantial civic engagement."[26]

Of more theoretical interest, entertainment media also appear to be a significant predictor ($p<.01$) of political knowledge. Among people with very little political interest, entertainment media do *not* have a negative impact on political knowledge. Our findings actually suggest the reverse—*the more people with little political interest consume entertainment media for political content, the more they know about politics.* Despite frequent critiques from journalists and political pundits, some citizens are able to learn from entertainment media.[27]

In order to parse out the relationship between entertainment media consumption and political knowledge further, we now examine the interaction term (frequency with which the respondent claims he or she follows the 2000 election × entertainment media consumption). The interaction term is negative and highly significant ($p<.01$), indicating that entertainment media affect political learning in different ways for those who claim

Table 1. Ordered Logit Results for Political Knowledge	
Entertainment Media	.205** (.082)
Daily Newspaper	.117* (.054)
Political Attention	.916** (.165)
Entertainment Media × Political Attention	−.085** (.030)
Age	.035** (.004)
Education	.555** (.044)
Income	.157** (.034)
Male	.739* (.121)
White	.384* (.187)
Model Chi Square	500.374*
Cox and Snell R^2	.377
N	1402

* indicates significance at the .05 level; one-tailed test
** indicates significance at the .01 level; one-tailed test
Notes: Dependent variable ranges from 0 to 3 and measures how many of the following three questions the respondent answered correctly. "Do you happen to know which of the presidential candidates is now governor of Texas?" "Do you happen to know which of the presidential candidates was formerly a senator from New Jersey?" "Do you happen to know which of the presidential candidates co-sponsored a campaign finance reform bill in Congress?"
We do not report the intercepts for the different levels of the ordinal dependent variable.

to follow politics frequently compared to those who follow politics rarely or never. Specifically, those who rarely follow news about the presidential election are more likely to learn from entertainment media than those who are more interested in politics.

In sum, we find that *entertainment media bring political knowledge to the politically disinterested*—a group that is unlikely to consume political information from traditional media sources. Given recent concerns over the levels of voter turnout and political engagement among young people and the young audience of most entertainment media, politicians who wish to engage young people and other politically disinterested groups would be well-advised to seek out appearances on entertainment media.[28]

And Now, Your Moment of Zen

Citizens are increasingly reliant on entertainment media for political information. Appearances on *Jay Leno* and *David Letterman* are now nearly as important to a political campaign as taking on the gauntlet of Sunday morning political talk shows. The increasing importance of entertainment media has been under frequent fire from political commentators from across the political spectrum. Scholars have also cited our increasing reliance on entertainment media as an indication of the declining norms of citizenship in the United States. Unfortunately, few have bothered to empirically evaluate the impact of entertainment media on democratic citizenship. Our findings suggest that entertainment media are able to inform politically disinterested people. Although learning about politics is not the primary goal of watching entertainment media, it can be a positive byproduct.

Every study has limitations, and ours is no different. As is the case in much of the literature on political behavior, our study speaks more to correlation than causation. Nonetheless, this does not imply that our findings are not important. This paper adds to a growing literature on the impact of nontraditional media on political knowledge, and participation. Scholars should move from these primarily survey-based findings and conduct experiments that are more apt to identify causal mechanisms. Further, our measure of political knowledge (name recognition) is one that is most likely to result from entertainment media consumption. Name recognition is a necessary—but not a sufficient—condition of educated vote choice and democratic citizenship. Future studies should examine other "deeper" measures of political knowledge and continue to investigate the degree to which entertainment media can inform. In addition, the media environment continues to shift. As more Americans are beginning to get their news on portable devices like cell phones and PDAs, scholars and political observers have not even begun to determine the effects of gaining snippets of information on the go.[29]

Together, these findings suggest that political reformers should not make entertainment media the scapegoat for all of the declining norms of citizenship. Entertainment media bring political knowledge to a group that is often disinterested in politics. The challenge for those interested in reversing the recent decline in citizen participation is to find out how to translate this knowledge into participation. If nontraditional media are able to inform this group, maybe nontraditional appeals to participation can drive them to become more active in the political system.

We should note that there are a host of potential effects of entertainment media and we have only discussed one (political information) in this paper. Other work finds that although entertainment media may help inform politically disinterested people, entertainment media consumption may also decrease institutional confidence and lower evaluations of politicians. In addition, providing people with the choice to be informed through entertainment media can increase political inequality and political polarization.[30]

Despite some good news about entertainment media, our findings still clearly support the notion that reading the daily newspaper is a strong predictor of habits of good citizenship. Those who make a habit of reading the daily newspaper are likely to be politically knowledgeable and politically active. In sum, although entertainment media have positive attributes, we agree with Bennett et al. that "reading is the core of civic literacy."[31]

Notes

1. The Stewart quote is from ABCNews.com, http://abcnews.go.com/sections/nightline/DailyNews/100days_ stewart.html (accessed December 4, 2002), and the Colbert quote is from Adam Stenbergh, "Stephen Colbert Has America by the Ballots," *New York Magazine* (October 16, 2006), http://nymag.com/news/politics/22322 (accessed June 22, 2007).

2. For early studies on minimal effects, see Dilihu Katz and Paul F. Lazarsfeld, *Personal Influence* (Glencoe, Ill.: Free Press, 1955); Joseph T. Klapper, *The Effects of Mass Communications* (New York: Free Press, 1960). For more recent scholarship finding substantial media effects, see John Zaller, "The Myth of Massive Media Impact Revived: New Support for a Discredited Idea," in *Political Persuasion and Attitude Change*, ed. Diana C. Mutz, Paul Sniderman, and Richard A. Brody, 17–78 (Ann Arbor: Univ. of Michigan Press, 1996); and Steven E. Finkel, "Reexamining the 'Minimal Effects' Model in Recent Presidential Elections," *Journal of Politics* 55 (1993): 1–21.

3. Bernard Cohen, *The Press and Foreign Policy* (Princeton: Princeton Univ. Press, 1963), 13.

4. For early work on print media, see Maxwell McCombs and Donald Shaw, "The Agenda Setting Function of the Mass Media," *Public Opinion Quarterly* 36 (1972): 176–85. For work on televised media, see Shanto Iyengar and Donald Kinder, *News That Matters* (Chicago: Univ. of Chicago Press, 1987).

5. For early work on satisficing, see Herbert A. Simon, *Models of Man* (New York: Wiley, 1957). For work on accessibility and the psychology of recall, see Amos Tversky and Daniel Kahneman, "The Framing of Decisions and the Psychology of Choice," *Science* 211 (1981): 453–58. For evidence on priming, see Jon A. Krosnick and Donald Kinder, "Altering the Foundations of Support for the President through Priming," *American Political Science Review* 84 (1990): 497–512.

6. Thomas E., Nelson, Rosalee A. Clawson, and Zoe M. Oxley, "Media Framing of a Civil Liberties Conflict and Its Effect on Tolerance," *American Political Science Review* 91 (1997): 567–83; Thomas E. Nelson, Zoe M. Oxley, and Rosalee A. Clawson, "Toward a Psychology of Framing Effects," *Political Behavior* 19 (1997): 221–46.

7. Shanto Iyengar, *Is Anyone Responsible?* (Chicago: Univ. of Chicago Press, 1994).

8. Nelson, Clawson, and Oxley, "Media Framing of a Civil Liberties Conflict and Its Effect on Tolerance," 576.

9. Stephen Earl Bennett, Staci L. Rhine, and Richard S. Flickinger, "Reading's Impact on Democratic Citizenship in America," *Political Behavior* 22 (2000): 167–95, quote from page 175.

10. Robert Putnam, *Bowling Alone: The Collapse and Revival of American Community* (New York: Simon and Schuster, 2000), 218.

11. Putnam, *Bowling Alone*; Roderick Hart, *Seducing America: How Television Charms the Modern Voter* (New York: Oxford Univ. Press, 1999), vii; Neil Postman, *Amusing Ourselves to Death: Discourse in the Age of Show Business* (New York: Penguin, 1985).

12. Doris A. Graber, *Processing Politics: Learning From Television in the Internet Age* (Chicago: Univ. of Chicago Press, 2001).

13. W. Russell Neuman, *The Future of the Mass Audience* (New York: Cambridge Univ. Press, 1991), 99, quoted in Doris A. Graber, *Mass Media and American Politics*, 6th ed. (Washington, D.C.: CQ Press, 2002), 197. For an excellent and detailed treatment of C-SPAN, see Stephen Frantzich and John Sullivan, *The C-SPAN Revolution* (Norman: Univ. of Oklahoma Press, 1996).

14. Matthew Baum, *Soft News Goes to War* (Princeton: Princeton Univ. Press, 2002). Data on media usage are from the Pew Research Center for the People and the Press, "News Consumption and Media Believability Study," 2006, people-press.org/reports/pdf/282.pdf (accessed June 22, 2007).

15. Howard Kurtz, "Mr. Stewart Goes to Washington," *Washington Post* (November 4, 2002), C01.

16. Matthew Baum, "Talking the Vote: What Happens When Presidential Politics Hits the Talk Show Circuit?" *American Journal of Political Science* 49 (2005): 213–34.

17. Thomas E. Patterson, "Doing Well and Doing Good: How Soft News and Critical Journalism Are Shrinking the News Audience and Weakening Democracy—And What News Outlets Can Do About It," Joan Shorenstein Center, Harvard University (2000); Markus Prior, "Any Good News in Soft News? The Impact of Soft News Preference on Political Knowledge," *Political Communication* 20 (2003): 149–71.

18. Graber, *Mass Media and American Politics,* 195; Silvo Lenart and Kathleen M. McGraw, "America Watches 'Amerika': Television Docudrama and Political Attitudes," *Journal of Politics* 51 (1989): 697–712; Michael X. Delli Carpini and Bruce Williams, "Constructing Public Opinion: The Uses of Fictional and Nonfictional Television in Conversations about the Environment," in *The Psychology of Political Communication,* ed. Ann N. Crigler, 149–66 (Ann Arbor: Univ. of Michigan Press, 1998); Stanley Feldman and Lee Sigelman, "The Political Impact of Television: 'The Day After,'" *Journal of Politics* 47 (1985): 556–78; Christine F. Ridout, "News Coverage and Talk Shows in the 1992 Presidential Campaign," *PS: Political Science and Politics* 26 (1993): 712–16; Doris A. Graber, "The 'New' Media and Politics: What Does the Future Hold?" *PS: Political Science and Politics* 29 (1996): 33–36.

19. For characteristics of new media users, see Richard Davis and Diana Owen, *New Media and American Politics* (New York: Oxford Univ. Press, 1998); Patterson, "Doing Well and Doing Good"; Andrew Kohut, "News Consumption and Media Believability Study," 2006, http://people-press.org/reports/pdf/282.pdf (accessed June 22, 2007).

20. For evidence on political interest and soft news, see Baum, *Soft News Goes to War.*

21. Baum, *Soft News Goes to War.* Baum does not include measures of attentiveness to political issues other than foreign policy.

22. For work on entertainment media and foreign policy, see Lenart and McGraw, "America Watches 'Amerika'"; Feldman and Sigelman, "The Political Impact of Television." For work on citizen knowledge see Michael X. Delli Carpini and Scott Keeter, *What Americans Know about Politics and Why It Matters* (New Haven, Conn.: Yale Univ. Press, 1996). For evidence on agenda setting, see Iyengar and Kinder, *News That Matters;* W. Russell Neuman, Marion R. Just, and Ann N. Crigler, *Common Knowledge: News and the Construction of Political Meaning* (Chicago: Univ. of Chicago Press, 1992), 121.

23. Baum, *Soft News Goes to War,* 92; Patterson, "Doing Well and Doing Good."

24. In each of our models, we use the weights provided by Pew. Because we use weighted data, our sample size often exceeds the actual sample size for the survey. These weights are based on the Census Bureau's Current Population Survey. For more detail on the survey methodology, see http://people-press.org/reports/methodology.php3. Baum, "Talking the Vote," discusses the importance of the 2000 election for entertainment media.

25. See Delli Carpini and Keeter, *What Americans Know about Politics and Why It Matters,* for a thorough discussion of the limitations of fact-based measures of political information.

26. All of the control variables are significant at p<.01 except white and male, which are significant at p<.05. There is multicollinearity between the education, income, and race variables. For instance, education and income are correlated at .33 (Kendall's tau-b). We keep all three variables in our model for three reasons, however. First, the presence of multicollinearity results in a larger coefficient, and thus makes it more difficult to obtain significance—in essence providing a more stringent test of the hypothesis. Next, we are treating these as control variables. Although interesting, they are not central to this investigation. Third, despite the collinearity, income, education, and race are theoretically distinct variables and previous research suggests that they should be included in models predicting political knowledge (Bennett et al., "Reading's Impact"; Putnam, *Bowling Alone,* 218).

27. Because this is a constituent term, later used in an interaction, we must be careful in interpreting this variable. It represents the value for entertainment media consumption when political attention=0.

28. For work on political engagement and young people, see Martin P. Wattenberg, *Is Voting for Young People?* (New York: Pearson Longman, 2007).

29. Pew Research Center for the People and the Press, "News Consumption and Media Believability Study" (2006), 117, available at people-press.org/reports/pdf/282.pdf (accessed June 22, 2007).

30. Jody Baumgartner and Jonathan S. Morris, "The Daily Show Effect: Candidate Evaluations, Efficacy, and American Youth," *American Politics Research* 34 (2006): 341–67; Markus Prior, *Post-Broadcast Democracy: How Media Choice Increases Inequality in Political Involvement and Polarizes Elections* (New York: Cambridge Univ. Press, 2007).

31. Bennett et al., "Reading's Impact," 186.

9

BROADCAST NEWS AND THE MOVIES

Wagging Somebody's Dog

Dick Flannery

As America's adventure in Iraq stalled, and the country faced another third world quagmire with lengthening casualty lists, nightly pictures began appearing on TV of mayhem, explosions, and stretcher-bearers. A familiar climate of hand-wringing, recrimination, and blame began to be felt, and a small film appeared that struck a chord among some moviegoers. *Good Night, and Good Luck* is an off-beat, black-and-white retelling of the fifty-year-old confrontation between the odious Senator Joseph McCarthy and the paradigmatic broadcaster Ed Murrow, featuring a dead-on portrayal of Murrow by David Straithairn, and George Clooney as Murrow's "Sancho Panza," Fred Friendly. There is Murrow on the screen amid clouds of cigarette smoke carefully planning and orchestrating the destruction of McCarthy by showing his audience that the senator is a reckless man doing un-American things in his crusade against Communism. Murrow reveals the baseless nature of McCarthy's charges and shows him playing the bully in his televised hearings. Preparing all along for McCarthy's inevitable counterattack that he and his friends are disloyal, Murrow delivers the final coup by giving Mc-Carthy time on his show for a reply. McCarthy, however, can't stop ranting and revealing himself as exactly the person Murrow has been saying he is. Revealing the power of television, Murrow wins, America wins, and broadcasting does its job of telling truth about power whatever the result.

Probably only a few moviegoers were interested in the fifties any longer when *Good Night* appeared, even though (as the film reminds us in little breaks) the music may have been much cooler then and maybe people had more style, but people remain fascinated by broadcast news. In the film, Murrow represents everything TV news was not during the Iraq controversy. He was not "embedded" with the government, he reported on it. He was not afraid of controversy, he had his job to do. People relied on him, and he tried to be honest with them.

The message is as black and white as the film. The contemporary "millennial media" have betrayed their profession out of fear of those in power and fear of losing favor with any of their audience. Our modern media are cowards and sycophants pretending to be Murrow but betraying him and his legacy in search of more dollars for themselves and their networks. If they had done their job in 2002 and 2003, it is unlikely that the United States would currently be in Iraq, which the 2006 Baker-Hamilton Commission referred to as a situation of high violence and "great suffering" that is deteriorating, because the Bush administration would not have been able to convince the people that Saddam had weapons of mass destruction with incomplete, inaccurate "evidence."[1]

The "historical" setting of *Good Night* tells us something about the position of journalism in the pop culture today. George Clooney and his associates had to look back fifty years to Ed Murrow to find a paradigm. There has not been a heroic Hollywood film about journalism since the 1976 Robert Redford and Dustin Hoffman movie *All the President's Men,* and the most common movies about broadcast news have portrayed the reporters as shallow buffoons. Murrow is lionized in *Good Night,* but the film shows that Murrow, too, participated in his own form of McCarthyism. He purges his own staff so that McCarthy and his minions will not have any targets. He does nothing to help a CBS colleague who is being hounded by the pro-McCarthy press, and the man eventually commits suicide. Murrow does a nice obit for him then. Murrow and Friendly manage to keep the support of CBS boss William Paley (Frank Langella), but Paley chafes at the cost of it all. When the controversy ends, Murrow loses his prime-time slot and is exiled to Sunday afternoons. Paley tells Murrow and Friendly that viewers want to relax when they come home after work, they don't want to be bothered.[2]

The beginning and end of *Good Night* features a speech delivered by Murrow at a broadcast award dinner some time after the McCarthy episode. Murrow raises issues about the impact of broadcasting on the public good that still preoccupy us. Why can't we use the marvels of the new electric technology to revive democracy, not subvert it? Why can't TV show us more often at our best rather than at our worst? Why does the whole realm of TV seem to be mostly a drug to distract us from the realities around us, even those listed among the so-called ranks of "reality" TV? Murrow disdains structural and cultural explanations for our less-than-stellar electric information environment. History is what we make of it, he says. If we turn marvelous technologies into wires and lights in boxes for amusement and escape, *we* will have done it, not some vague "they" or "it."

Early social science evaluations of the impact of broadcast media on politics reached "minimalist" conclusions. Radio and TV were like newspapers with sound and moving pictures. They didn't really change anything, especially people's partisan identification, perhaps the most respected variable of postwar political science. That began to change with the televised Kennedy/Nixon debate of the 1960 campaign and the great national trauma and catharsis of the Kennedy assassination three years later.[3] Soon the media was seen as the cause of some fundamental shifts in our political universe. Some even went so far as to declare that the late twentieth-century United States was the world's first media state.

Most of the assessments of the broadcast media were negative. Broadcasting was creating a new sense of what was normal; it made people think they knew what was happening. But the "normalcy" and the news on TV were misleading, limited, and shallow. Books and good newspapers remained superior sources. Radio and TV were something politicians and advertisers used to "stroke" people and keep them from thinking clearly. Many of these attitudes persist in 2007. Is this evaluation of broadcasting just elitist snobbery? Social scientists, after all, are part of the overeducated demographic. Are the scholarly and privileged elite who dominate cultural criticism linear print dinosaurs in a digital age?[4]

It can be helpful to think of a modern democracy as resting on a triangle of relationships between politicians, the media, and the people. Each group needs the other two to do its democratic business, but in practice the relationships are less symbiotic and more adversarial, or at least filled with suspicion and resentment. Citizens fear that the politicians and the media are keeping them from the truth and information they need to make decisions, that popular sovereignty has been usurped. It would be helpful to citizens if the media and the politicians kept each other more honest, forthright, and open, but manipulative games between politicians and the media can create more confusion than transparency. Two famous Hollywood movies illustrate some common problems.

Paddy Chayevsky's 1976 film *Network* shows the fall from grace of the old Ed Murrow principles of broadcasting, represented in the film by Max Schumacher (William Holden). Schumacher loses both control of the news and his old friend and colleague Howard Beale (Peter Finch) to the corporate weasel Frank Hackett (Robert Duvall) and the evil programming director Diana Christensen (Faye Dunaway). These people are perfectly ready to sacrifice traditional standards for commercial and career success. TV is about getting viewers and selling more advertising. The viewers are going to watch TV shows that make them feel good—or at least resonate with their feelings. (Christensen says of one of Finch's rants, "He's articulating the popular rage.") The point is to be entertaining and sympathetic while delivering some information that doesn't bore the viewers. Chayevsky proceeds to portray and lampoon the whole infotainment universe that has become familiar to all of us with uncanny foresight in the rest of the film. As with *Good Night, and Good Luck,* the good guys and bad guys are clearly identified. The difference is that the bad guys are winning. They are winning because the money motive has prevailed over the democracy and information motives inside the networks.

The bad guys in *Network* are the corporate careerists who put dollar signs ahead of responsible journalism. But are the corporate execs to blame if they're just "giving the people what they want"? It's the viewers who make infotainment a hit, after all; Hackett and Christensen would have lost their jobs if people ignored their new version of the news. Many social critics put the blame on the people, not the media. Probably the most famous example of this analysis is Neil Postman's *Amusing Ourselves to Death.* The title tells the story. It's the citizens who are shirking their responsibility. They can't be bothered to uphold any critical standard when it comes to TV news; they want it to be like other TV shows they watch. And these same citizens are less and less likely to bother with reading the news in the old print media. For example, in 1994, the percentage of Americans that indicated they "read a newspaper yesterday" was 58 percent. By 2006, that number had dropped 18 points to 40 percent. Even when factoring in the boost newspaper readership receives from online newspaper readers, the number increases to only 43 percent. So the citizens turn away from print and toward TV because it's easier, and then they look for the simplest version of the news they can find. Many ignore news altogether. The audience for traditional evening news just keeps on shrinking.[5]

America is "dumbed-down" and our politics follow suit. It's all bumper sticker slogans, images, and hokum. Political parties become gigantic fund-raising machines producing dollars to buy thirty-second commercials for politicians who get elected and spend their time doing everything they can to grease public policy for the good of the people who can give them the money to buy even more commercials to get themselves re-elected. And so it goes.

The idea that the people can't really be trusted with popular government lies deep in the heart of American political theory. Madison's *Federalist* No. 10, for example, identifies liberty as essential for America. However, Madison warns that the same liberty leads to faction because people's passions for different ideas and interests, based on their differing position in life and various levels of talent, are "sown into the nature of man." Faction threatens popular government with both mischief and tyranny. It overwhelmed the old classical democracies in Athens and Rome. But, the Founding Fathers have created not a democracy, but an "extensive republic." This republic will actually be operated by a select few (like Madison), with the masses just doing the voting and choosing the representatives. These people, the elites we would call them, are more trustworthy and experienced and better able to maintain the system of liberty. Furthermore, Madison and the other Founders have constructed an institutional maze in the Constitution that will make it difficult for any powerful faction, especially a "majority faction," to form or to get its way. Thus, we have popular government, but the people are going to have a hard time messing it up because they are not going to be directly in charge.[6]

Has television, advertising, and the whole ethos of the mass society and the mass media trashed the careful design of the Founders and put us on the road back to the "pure" democracies of olden times that ended in passion, tyranny, and empire? Well, look at what the people do when they get to "choose" what's on TV and the news. For 2006–2007 (through July 15, 2007), the top ten shows and their market share and total viewers were: 1. *American Idol,* Wednesday (17.5/27 with 30,640,000 viewers); 2. *American Idol,* Tuesday (17.1/26 with 30,156,000 viewers); 3. *Dancing with the Stars,* Tuesday (13.5/20 with 20,692,000 viewers); 4. *Dancing with the Stars,* Monday (13.0/20 with 19,956,000 viewers); 5. *Dancing with the Stars* Results Show, Wednesday (12.7/20 with 19,123,000 viewers); 6. *Dancing with the Stars* Results Show, Tuesday (12.0/18 with 18,336,000 viewers); 7. *CSI* (11.7/18 with 18,821,000 viewers); 8. *Grey's Anatomy* (11.4/17 with 17,707,000 viewers); 9. *NBC Sunday Night Football* (10.9/17 with 17,016,000 viewers); 10. *CSI: Miami* (10.3/17 with 15,742,000 viewers) and *House* (10.3/16 with

17,357,000 viewers). Doesn't such escapist rejection of information confirm Madison's worst fears?[7]

In 1998 Warren Beatty portrayed Jay Bulworth, a California senator whose life has not turned out the way he wanted. Once he thought to change the world with Bobby Seale and Bobby Kennedy; now he's a hack. So, he decides to end it all by putting out a contract on himself and collecting for his family on a huge policy arranged by his political buddies and money-men in the insurance business. Liberated from the realities of the campaign process, Bulworth proceeds to an orgy of truth-telling in the weekend before the California primary, telling various Democratic constituency groups and the press everything he really thinks and explaining to them how government policy depends on campaign money and how those who can deliver the cash get what they want. (His reply to a black Angelino inquiring why he hasn't done much to get a bill passed that would help the poor with their insurance problems: "Because, you really haven't contributed any money to my campaign.") He also reminds the reporters questioning him that these same moneymen pay the reporters to put together the "news." Thus, Bulworth blames the moneybag elites while *Federalist* No. 10 fears the masses, but the outcome is the same for popular government.

The addiction of citizens to the boob tube means the decline and fall of just about everything. It's easy to understand why Hollywood would take a jaundiced view of broadcasting. After all, TV devastated the movie business back in the 1950s and 1960s when it became everybody's favorite entertainment and people stopped flocking to the movies as they had in the past. A famous joke of that era was: A man calls the movie theater to find out when the show begins, and the theater manager asks him, "When can you get here?"

That was bad news for some moviemakers, but many moved into television production and made their money there. Later, in the 1980s, technology rescued the movie makers with videotapes. Movies could get on TV and collect money from viewers one household at a time, sort of like the old days. Of course, this meant that the viewers had more choices as to what to do with their TV viewing time. Unsurprisingly, viewers chose to watch less "hard" news and the audience for the regular news shows shrank. Pretty soon TV viewers had many more channels to watch than they had had in the old days, in addition to their videotape libraries. Broadcast news became what it is today: one of the fragments of the mass TV audience serviced by special all-news-all-the-time cable channels. The network news operations have turned softer and softer to try and retain audience share. The viewing audience for the hardest newscasts has become older and older, and the shows are sponsored by drug companies hawking the latest pain relievers, sex rejuvenators, and financial planning services to a geriatric audience. Once in a while, a mass event like Oklahoma City, 9/11, Columbine, or Virginia Tech recreates the mass audience for a brief period. In the meantime, broadcasters try to hype anything they can find to keep people tuned in, from O. J. to Anna Nicole to Paris Hilton. Broadcasters are reduced to hoping for hurricanes and paralyzing snowstorms, events that still generate mass interest.

Our contemporary media news situation was best portrayed in the 1997 dark comedy *Wag the Dog*. This movie was written by two people most well-known for Broadway plays, Hilary Henkin and David Mamet. In this movie the villain is neither the greedy media nor the lazy citizens; it's the politicians who exploit the media environment and use it to further their own ambitions. The villain-in-chief is a political "spin doctor," Conrad Brean (Robert DeNiro). Shortly before a presidential election, a sex scandal involving the president and a "Firefly Girl" threatens the incumbent president's big lead in the polls. Brean is called in by the White House staff to find a way out of the danger. Since a presidential sex scandal is a mighty compelling story, it's going to take a lot to distract the media "jackals" from ruining the president's reelection. But Brean is up to the task; he decides to start a war. Well, not a "real" war, but rather the appearance of a war, a "pageant."

It's appearances that matter, the movie tells us time and again. What people think is real is what they see on TV. People may not seek out much news on television, but they believe in TV. They, the folks, believe TV tells them what's going on. What goes on television can be manipulated by people in power if they understand how the media works. Brean turns to Hollywood producer Stanley Motss (Dustin Hoffman). Motss and his Scooby gang, including Fad King (Denis Leary) and Johnny Dean (Willie Nelson), then create the sound bytes, visuals, and patriotic songs of a contemporary American war. They even make T-shirts and "back end" deals with shoe companies. This war is with Albania, chosen by Brean because nobody knows anything about Albania. (The movie was made just before the Kosovo crisis in 1996.) Albania is a threat because of what else? Weapons of Mass Destruction, suitcase nukes in *Wag the Dog*. Through it all, Brean keeps on reassuring worried White House staffers that it's all been done before. He cites the Reagan administration's distracting people from the Lebanon

Films like *Wag the Dog* (above), *Goodnight and Good Luck,* and *Network* reveal the power of the media to shape public opinion. Through framing, priming, and agenda setting, the media can serve as either a watchdog or a facilitator of politicians looking to capture public support. (Jerry Ohlinger's Movie Material Store)

disaster with the Grenada invasion, calling upon the mantra "change the story, change the lead."

The big threat to the spin doctors is that the truth, or some dangerous version of it, will get out and spoil the plan. And the CIA, apparently in cahoots with the president's election opponent, leaks a story that the war is over to put an end to Brean's distraction. But Motss is undaunted. "They" can't end his story. So there's a twist, a chapter two. A hero has been left behind in enemy hands and must be rescued, a great American hero: Sergeant William Schumann (Woody Harrelson), "good old Shoe." Motss and Brean must produce an actual person to play the part, and they do find one. Unfortunately, he's in a military prison under heavy medication, but the plan is finally saved with a certain amount of collateral damage.

In a zany parody of the blurring of fact and fiction in modern pop culture, *Wag the Dog* was released just as the Bill and Monica story broke into the headlines. Probably because of this, the film never got the broader attention it deserved. My colleague Dave Louzecky and I show the film each fall to undergraduate students in a political philosophy class. Dave argues that the film is a "documentary," and the students invariably agree with him in spite of my arguments that maybe it's not quite so easy for politicians to manipulate the media or for the media to manipulate the public. Students seem to agree that political reality is whatever is on TV, but that what's on TV is most likely a fraud cooked up by some Conrad Brean. Thus, there really isn't any political "reality." My students do not seem to have much trouble believing this; nor do they appear to be either frightened or alarmed by it, but I am.

How can there possibly be any real democracy when the information the citizens have is often fraudulent? Whether you condemn the greed and shallowness of the broadcasters, the cynical, manipulative image-making of the politicians and their hired guns, or the slothful citizens who can't be bothered to inform themselves, the end result is the same. The old theoretical democratic standard of one person, one vote is contrasted with the reality of "pluralist" democracy where elite groups use their money and education to over-represent themselves and continue to rule just as their forebears did in olden times. *The Irony of Democracy,* a classic text by Marian Irish and James Prothro, describes how the people were sold on an illusion of democracy most of the time. This made it easier to control them without any need for an oppressive police state. Political scientists differed among themselves as to how bad the situation really was. Many thought that at least there was some consolation that the people got to make certain choices among competing elites.

Modern views of the media suggest that whatever the extent of popular choice there is in modern democracies, it rests on information gathered from a mass media news business filled with distortion and fraud. Why? The answer suggested in both *Network* and *Wag the Dog* is that the people watching prefer their information in packages that are reassuring and familiar. The viewers in Chayevsky's film want a news show that responds to their feelings and makes them feel a little better. They can go to the window and shout along with Howard Beale that they're mad as hell and they're not taking it anymore. Things won't change any when they sit down again, but at least they've "had their say" or—more precisely—Howard said what they were thinking.

Motss and his movie makers in *Wag the Dog* have no doubts what the mass audience wants to see when they dream up their pageant of an American war. They want a war that's righteous. They want an enemy who threatens "the American way of life." They want to rescue other innocent people along with themselves, to save the cheerleaders. They want to feel united with their fellow citizens in the face of danger. And they want heroes who illustrate America, heroes drawn from the ranks of ordinary people that send coded messages from captivity, "Courage, Mom." They want to hear once again a story they've already been told about America and about themselves because they are fond of that story.

This suggests that what people want from the media above all is reassurance, a sense of continuity as part of the "news." Stories that threaten continuity and upset people are dismissed, filtered out. Most of the criticism we hear and see and read about the mass media seems to fit this analysis. Critics argue that the content of the media messages needs to be changed. The two most famous versions of this criticism are that the media are leaving something out or that the information is "slanted" in some particular direction (or what is known in the common vernacular as "spin"). Blacks, women, Latinos, homosexuals, rednecks, immigrants, hard-hats, and so on have all complained that they and their views and their situation are ignored and excluded from the mass media or that they are only presented as narrow stereotypes. People want TV to show people who are like themselves and they want to be portrayed in a positive light.

Other people condemn the media because their views and ideas are not included or they are not taken seriously enough. "Family values" gurus such as David Wildmon want television to portray "decency" and avoid indecency. Wildmon and his followers must think that TV has some impact on what people do. Then there is the famous criticism that goes back to William F. Buckley and Barry Goldwater that the media have a "liberal" bias. Oceans of ink have been spilled on analyzing this claim, and you can turn your radio on any day and hear it repeated by Rush Limbaugh and other conservative talk show hosts every hour of every day. Clearly the nonliberals believe it's true, and one of the results is Fox News. Rupert Murdoch and the employees at Fox made a canny decision about how to attract news viewers to their fledgling network. Give the conservatives a news show they like, where their ideas about things are endlessly repeated, where the politicians they like are lionized and those they dislike are pilloried, where all the information is processed through familiar ideological filters by reporters and analysts friendly to their views. It worked. Lots of heavy news viewers became Fox viewers, presumably many of the same people who listen to and call in to conservative talk radio shows, where a persistent comment is "ditto."[8]

Lest people think that it's only conservatives who are so sheep-like, MSNBC saved itself (at least for a while) from cancellation by turning to an anti-Fox, anti-Bush stance in the Democratic year of 2006. All this suggests that the Hackett and Motss characters had a certain grasp on the reality of what people want from broadcast media. It's not enlightenment; it's a ritual of reinforcing existing viewpoints and updating them for whatever new is happening. Way back when, in the 1800s, most American newspapers were militantly partisan. That came to an end, we're told, with the move toward mass circulation newspapers beginning around 1900. Have we moved back to the past in television news?

Can the broadcast media news be fixed by becoming more Murrow-like, or more multicultural, or more family-friendly, or more "red state," or more "blue state"? All these different remedies suggest that changing the content will change the outcome; broadcast news will be saved for the good if they change what they're saying.

This version of media criticism and analysis is more than a bit like the theory of pluralist group democracy; each group wants it own slice of the TV news pie. If an organization or group is represented somewhat the way it wants to be, then it will be somewhat mollified. This seems to be what the producers of the mainstream news media (now known as MSM to anti-Iraq Internet critics) think they are supposed to be doing if we look at their shows and their op-ed pages these days. Perhaps, then, things aren't so bad?

For all the complaining, is what's going on in broadcast news today just the usual group conflict endemic to contemporary democracy? If so, then maybe there's not so much to worry about. What's going on *is* democracy; it's messy, but it's working. There is even a seat at the table for media critics and intellectual hand-wringing about the future of democracy. While this may not be the best of all possible worlds, it has some benefits. There's something for most viewers, and isn't it better than any of the alternatives from other kinds of societies? Movies such as *Network* and *Wag the Dog* show us that the modern media is robustly self-critical, which is another important sign of real democracy. Editors, publishers, producers, and reporters of mainstream news frequently defend themselves along these same lines. They say that since they are making everybody mad at them, they must be doing something right. So, not to worry, all is well. The critics are exaggerating. You might call this the establishment view of all the criticism. It seems sort of smug and self-satisfied to me.

There is another way to think about the electronic media, which focuses less on specific content issues and the question of bias that dominate our usual discussions of politics and the media. Instead, the emphasis is on the structure of mass media news. Professor Lance Bennett argues that the news will inevitably be personalized and dramatized so public affairs are stories people can follow. People everywhere love stories, and they want their stories to be about characters, not institutions and statistics. And good stories have a beginning and an end, just like horse races. The news will be fragmented because the stories need to be short enough to hold public attention. And the news will be routinized. This concept of Bennett's is a bit more recondite than the other three, but it means that TV news will come to resemble other TV programming so it can be a familiar and predictable part of the viewer's day and the viewer's life. Maybe this concept is suggested by the famous parody of a local TV news teaser: "World comes to an end, film at 11." There is reassurance in routine.[9]

Let's illustrate Bennett's point. Political scientists, editorial writers, and other "serious" people may despair that so many voters choose among presidential candidates as if they were making a casting decision about a game show host, but that is the result of these structural biases. The president is a person who is on TV a lot for years on end. Why not pick someone who's likeable, since you are going to have to watch him? Bruce Miroff wrote a groundbreaking article on the contemporary presidency back during the Reagan years. Presidents still do all the things they always did, making choices among policy alternatives and trying to assemble winning coalitions to put those policies into effect, Miroff wrote, but the presidency has been transformed by the central role the president plays in the mass media.[10]

For most not-very-political people, the presidency is a spectacle. It's more like professional wrestling on TV than it is like a boxing match. People watch prizefights because the outcome is uncertain, the champ might lose tonight. In a spectacle the champ can't lose. What's interesting to the audience is how he shows that he's the champ, something like the *Rocky* movies.

Citizens are judging presidents (and potential presidents in campaigns) based on how well they match viewers' expectations about the presidential spectacle. People expect presidents to be take-charge leaders who get things done, and they expect them to represent and explain and embody traditional American values. The president reassures and unifies us by being presidential, not so much by choosing policy x, y, or z. When a president starts being indecisive, when he can't get things done, the spectacle is ruined. The viewers will turn against the poor individual who has spoiled their presidential show. Gary Cooper can ride off into the sunset with his new Quaker bride Grace Kelly to a life of peace, but not before he takes on the bad guys at *High Noon*.

Miroff points out those spectacles are not "interactive." The audience watches, it does not participate except to cheer and weep at the appropriate places. The mass media has been single-mindedly focused on the White House and campaigns for the presidency for two generations now. Is it any wonder that most people have lost the feeling that the country and its politics are theirs and they are responsible for maintaining liberty and democracy? Ben Franklin told the people outside the Philadelphia Convention that the Founders had put together "a Republic, if you can keep it." Now every four years and most of the time in between we're mesmerized with the idea that if we can just find that one perfect person who can pull the presidential sword from the stone, all will be well. We have been waiting around for this Mr. Goodbar for thirty years of deadlock, drift, and disappointment in our politics since Watergate times. Nobody seems to get the message that our problems are bigger than the presidents; we are stuck in a storyline that lets the rest of us off the hook.

Is there a path out of the swamp and its quagmires? Some people think there is, but it is unlikely to happen unless we change the way the media is organized so that democracy can begin to flourish again in a new information environment. Robert McChesney of the University of Illinois is the leading academic spokesman for this movement. You can follow their ideas and activities online at "freepress.net." McChesney's first academic work studied the history of government regulation of radio, which was greeted back in the 1920s with the same "wow" expectations we all had for the Internet back in the 1990s. What happened to radio back then, McChesney argues, has kept on happening ever since and is happening to the Internet right now. The public interest, and specifically the interests of citizen-driven democracy, is systematically minimized in favor of commercial and profit interests of the owners of broadcast stations and companies.[11]

The way to change the media, he and the reformers argue, is to change government media policy. It won't be easy because the politicians, the advertising business, and the media corporations are in bed with each other. They have been making cozy backroom deals with laws and regulations since the 1930s, just like the mobsters and the Cuban politician cutting up the Cuban-shaped cake in the opening of *The Godfather, Part II*. It's tough to get reform in this policy area, but it's the only way to get lasting change.

McChesney argues that most people are hypnotized by one or more of four myths about media policy:

1. Our media system is The American Way. The truth is that government policies have protected the public interest from excessive commercialism and media monopolies at times in the past and can today.
2. Professional journalism (such as Murrow's) can protect the public interest. Journalists have simply never been that powerful. Even though Murrow-like professionalism is much better than the alternatives, the William S. Paleys of the industry have always had too much control over what they do.
3. Like it or not, the media gives the public what it wants. McChesney argues at length in his *The Problem of the Media* that the system of producer sovereignty (NOT consumer sovereignty) now in place gives consumers limited choices within a narrow framework of producer interests. You have a choice as a viewer, but not really a choice for a different kind of media environment for the whole society. That's the choice we need.
4. The Internet will set us free. As marvelous as the web is, take a look this morning at Yahoo, AOL, Google—the sites which ARE the Internet for most users. Notice how much they look like your TV set and how much your TV set looks like them.

For these reformers, the fight is on. It's about licenses, it's about media monopolies and anti-trust policy, it's about appointments to the FCC, it's about bandwidth regulation, it's about some sensible limits on copyrights, it's about building a robust nonprofit media sector citizens can use, and so on.

The media reformers are different from all the reformers who want to change the content of the news; they want to change the structure of how news is produced and delivered. The media reformers are committed to the deep reform of the whole society in a direction of more democracy, more discussion of the public interest by more people all the time. This kind of politics looks beyond the issues of the moment and the next election. That's the politics of which dog is going to win tomorrow. A more fundamental question is which kinds of dogs are running, how the race is organized, who makes the rules.

Are the reformers dreaming? Lots of people like dogs, some people like races, some people like to put their money down. But dog racing is far removed from our everyday concerns, too far removed for much chance that the people will organize to demand change. The reformers answer that what our everyday concerns are is a byproduct of how society is organized. It makes some sense that democracy would be an everyday concern in a democratic society, but that's clearly not true of American society, where democracy is an occasional concern at best for most citizens.

Why is it that we don't see that much democracy very often? The people have lots of potential power, but they are mostly indifferent to politics and content to be spectators. This is certainly a question raised in all the textbooks. We can answer that this kind of behavior is "sown into the nature of man," but apparently so was building cathedrals at one time and stealing slaves at another, so the nature arguments seem incomplete and unfulfilling. Is the massive pop culture/entertainment/media culture we live in essentially a huge distraction from doing the things that need to be done, a way of "de-politicizing" the folks so the powers that be can get on with their business?[12]

The films considered here differ some in their judgment of which tail it is exactly that is wagging the dog. Maybe it's the greedy media moguls and careerist journalists, maybe it's the power-hungry politicians who only care about power and winning, maybe it's the lazy and smug and self-involved audience that wants to be coddled. Whatever the tail is, there is some unanimity about whose dog is getting wagged. The victim, the loser, is the public interest, the common good, democracy. McChesney and the media reformers have a powerful faith that democracy and the common good are not illusions. Murrow shared that confidence.

Do we, the people, deserve that faith? The answer to that question depends on what we do. Politics is us, not them. Nobody is going to stop you from ending your inertia and becoming politically active. The "system" is just what everybody does every day. When people start doing things differently, the system changes, too.

Notes

1. James A. Baker and Lee H. Hamilton (Co-Chairs), with Lawrence S. Eagleburger, Vernon E. Jordan Jr., Edwin Meese III, Sandra Day O'Connor, Leon E. Panetta, William J. Perry, Charles S. Robb, Alan K. Simpson, *The Iraq Study Group Report: The Way Forward—A New Approach* (New York: Vintage Books, 2006), xiv, 1; Dan Plesh and Richard Norton-Taylor, "Straw, Powell Had Serious Doubts over Their Iraqi Weapons Claims," *The Guardian,* May 31, 2003, http://www.guardian.co.uk/Iraq/Story/0,2763,967548,00.html (accessed June 22, 2007); ABC News Online, "Powell Regrets UN Speech on Iraq WMDs," ABC News (September 9, 2005), http://www.abc.net.au/news/newsitems/200509/s1456650.htm (accessed June 22, 2007).

2. The public affairs ghetto is now Sunday morning; of course, Murrow was active before the networks went to pro football on Sunday afternoons.

3. Doris A. Graber, *Mass Media and American Politics,* 7th ed. (Washington, D.C.: CQ Press: 2006), 12–14, for "minimal effects." This text contains a summary of much of the social science on the broadcast media.

4. It's important to remember that the media is not a monolith even though we often speak that way. Broadcast news is different than book publishing, fashion, sports, Internet blogs, and so on. The audience for each is also different. It has been true in recent times that all parts of the media tend to spill over into each other.

5. Pew Research Center for the People and the Press, "Online Papers Boost Newspaper Readership: Maturing Internet News Audience Broader than Deep," July 30, 2006, http://people-press.org/reports/display.php3?ReportID=282 (accessed June 22, 2007).

6. James Madison, "Federalist No. 10: The Same Subject Continued: The Union as a Safeguard Against Domestic Faction and Insurrection," *New York Daily Advertiser,* November 22, 1787, General Records of the Department of Justice, Record Group 60, National Archives Building, Washington, D.C.

7. Nielsen Media Research, "Season-to-Date by Total Households," July 18, 2007.

8. Studies have shown that Fox News claims the largest market share of regular viewers. Journalism.Org, "The State of the News Media, 2006," Annual Report on

American Journalism (2006), http://www.stateofthenewsmedia.org/2006/narrative_
cabletv_audience.asp?cat=3&media=6 (accessed June 22, 2007).

9. Lance Bennett, *News: The Politics of Illusion,* 5th ed. (New York: Longman, 2003).

10. Bruce Miroff, "The Presidential Spectacle," in Michael Nelson, *The Presidency and the Political System,* 7th ed. (Washington, D.C.: CQ Press, 2003), 278–304, has an updated version of this famous piece.

11. Robert McChesney, Russell Newman, and Ben Scott, *The Future of Media* (New York: Seven Stories Press, 2005), 9, for the part of McChesney's views reviewed here. See also his "The Power of the Producers," in the widely available reader *Debating Democracy* by Bruce Miroff, Raymond Seidelman, and Todd Swanstrom, 5th ed. (Boston: Houghton Mifflin, 2005), 196. *Rich Media, Poor Democracy* is probably McChesney's key book-length work for these questions.

12. See Michael Parenti, *Inventing Reality* (Boston: St. Martin's Press, 1984), 20–24, for a classic brief explanation of how this happens.

Part 3

LIGHTS, CAMERA, POLITICS

CONTEMPORARY ISSUES IN AMERICAN GOVERNMENT

10

TORTURE, TERRORISM, AND *24*

What Would Jack Bauer Do?

Timothy Dunn

In June 2006, the Heritage Foundation, a conservative think tank, hosted a two-hour symposium on fighting terrorism. After opening remarks from Homeland Security Secretary Michael Chertoff, the symposium turned to a more jocular panel discussion, moderated by talk radio host Rush Limbaugh. Members of the panel included experts on terrorism and homeland security policy as well as producers and cast members of the popular counterterrorism drama *24*. During the discussion, panelists were asked to comment on *24*'s frequent, sometimes graphic depiction and apparent endorsement of torture, for which the show has often been criticized. In defense of the series, the Heritage Foundation's own homeland security scholar, Jim Carafano, expressed the commonsense view that the dramatic events and scenarios depicted on *24* are highly unrealistic and bear little resemblance to the often mundane work necessary to win the real war on terror. Thus, *24* should not be taken so seriously. As *24*'s co-creator Howard Gordon later said, "I think people can differentiate between a television show and reality."[1]

Unfortunately, not everyone shares Gordon's optimism. In November 2006, Brigadier General Patrick Finnegan, the dean of the U.S. Military Academy at West Point, accompanied by three experienced military and FBI interrogators, flew to Hollywood to implore the show's producers and writers to scale down the torture scenes, on the grounds that *24*—popular among soldiers and cadets—might encourage future interrogators and soldiers in the field to mimic Jack Bauer's (Kiefer Sutherland) methods. According to

Jane Mayer, Finnegan and his colleagues were worried that "the show promoted unethical and illegal behavior and had adversely affected the training
and performance of real American soldiers." And in May 2007, at the GOP
primary debate, moderator Brit Hume asked candidates to describe how
far they would go in preventing a hypothetical terrorist attack. Colorado
Republican Representative Tom Tancredo responded by saying, "I'm looking for Jack Bauer at that time, let me tell you." The crowd responded with
thunderous applause.[2]

These and other references to *24* and its hero Jack Bauer are surface
indicators of a deeper debate in this country regarding the proper use of
torture in the war on terror. Under what circumstances, if any, is torture
justified? Should U.S. law be altered to allow for the torture of suspected
terrorists or other nonlawful combatants? Although *24* is only a TV show, it
is not a bad place to begin a discussion of these questions, because attending
to the differences between *24* and reality will help us understand just what
is at stake in this debate.

Jack Bauer and the Ticking Bomb Case

Suppose there is a nuclear bomb somewhere in New York City, set to go off at
any moment. Suppose further that you are a counterterrorist official and you
have in custody one of the terrorists thought to be responsible for planting
the bomb. Naturally, he won't reveal its location. Wouldn't you be justified in
doing anything to prevent the bomb from going off, including torturing the
suspect, if that were the only way to get him to talk? Given what's at stake,
this is presumably a no-brainer—of course it's morally acceptable for you
to torture the terrorist. Indeed, not only is torture *acceptable,* it is morally
required—not to do everything possible to protect the public in such a case
would be an unforgivable dereliction of duty.

The above scenario is a common variation on the so-called ticking bomb
case. Ticking bomb cases are a staple on *24.* The premise of the show is that
Jack Bauer, who works for a fictional government agency known as the
Counter Terrorist Unit (CTU), has just twenty-four hours to prevent some
catastrophic terrorist attack. With the exception of the first season, the terrorist threats always involve weapons of mass destruction and a potential death
toll of hundreds of thousands. Jack's modus operandi is clear: he will stop
at (almost) nothing to prevent the catastrophe. Here are a few examples. In
season three, Jack threatens to infect villain Stephen Saunders's (Paul Black-

thorne) daughter with a deadly virus unless Saunders calls off an impending virus attack. In season four, Jack tortures his girlfriend Audrey's (Kim Raver) estranged husband with electric shocks. In season six, Jack finds it necessary to torture his own brother—in this case, suffocating him with a plastic bag. And if killing a terrorist suspect, or even an innocent person, proves necessary, Jack is willing to do what it takes. In season two, for example, in order to gain the confidence of someone who might have information relevant to an impending nuclear attack, Jack first shoots then decapitates a protected criminal witness (this is made more palatable by the fact that the witness is guilty of sexually assaulting children). In season three, in a desperate attempt to buy time, Jack complies with Saunders's order to shoot his colleague Ryan Chappelle (Paul Schulze). In season four, with Audrey's husband in critical condition, Jack orders the doctor to cease operating on him and save the life of a terrorist suspect instead, in the hope that the suspect will be able to provide crucial information. As a result, Audrey's husband dies. These are, of course, merely a few of Jack's career highlights.

Jack is not the only one on *24* willing to resort to torture. Even President David Palmer (Dennis Haysbert) gets his hands dirty when he orders a secret service agent to torture Roger Stanton (Harris Yulin), the head of the National Security Agency, whom he suspects of involvement in the plot to blow up Los Angeles. The case of David Palmer is particularly interesting, since his character more than any other is supposed to reflect American values and ideals. Palmer himself possesses great wisdom, intelligence, and probity. But if he has a flaw, it is that he is not always willing to do what it takes to achieve the objective (this is ostensibly the reason why his vice president and chief of staff conspire against him). In season two, for instance, Jack asks the president to authorize threatening Syed Ali (Francesco Quinn) with the serial execution of members of his family in order to get him to talk. Palmer refuses, but Jack disobeys the order, apparently executing one of the terrorist's sons. To save the rest of his family, Ali does talk, and as events unfold it is pretty clear that without that information Jack would not have been able to stop the bomb from going off. Clearly, Jack's ruthlessness is vindicated, though the show's writers can be accused of waffling after we learn that the execution was staged. Still, Jack's actions would qualify as torture under existing law.[3]

For Jack Bauer, torture is simply a necessary means to a justifiable end, no different in principle from any other means. The attack must be prevented, the conspirators must be exposed, and so on—if not at absolutely any cost,

Jack Bauer (Keifer Sutherland), known for his ruthless and controversial methods for extracting information, is a symbol for the divisive debate about America's tactics in the war on terrorism. (Jerry Ohlinger's Movie Material Store)

then at any reasonable cost, including self-sacrifice. One of the reasons Jack is such a hero is that he is nearly always willing to sacrifice his own interests for the sake of the cause. In season two, for example, Jack insists on flying the plane carrying the nuclear bomb to safety—even though he will certainly die in the process (he escapes just in time, but only because George Mason [Xander Berkeley], who conveniently is dying anyway, takes over). In season three, Jack volunteers for a mission that will make him an enemy of the state, unable ever to return to his country. And the back story between seasons two and three has Jack becoming a heroin addict in order to gain the confidence of a drug lord with terrorist connections. There seems to be nothing he won't do to save the country. We are inclined to think that if Jack tortures someone, even an innocent person, it's okay because he himself is willing to suffer and be tortured if necessary. And, of course, he is frequently severely tortured, though curiously he never breaks.

That is not to say that Jack is always right. In season three, for instance, he shoots his nemesis, Nina Myers (Sarah Clarke), at least arguably in cold blood. In season five, he does the same to Christopher Henderson (Peter Weller). In season three, he engages in a possibly treasonous conspiracy with Tony Almeida (Carlos Bernard) and Gael Ortega (Jesse Borrego) in an effort to foil a terrorist plot. Ironically, this may in fact simply reinforce Jack's heroism—he is willing to face execution for treason if doing so is necessary for the cause. In any case, it should be clear by now that the show portrays Jack's actions by and large as morally justified.

From Ticking Bomb to Torture

The ticking bomb case is the stock in trade of torture advocates. One strategy for defending torture is simple: begin with a ticking bomb case. Your opponent is now in a bind: how can she deny that torture is acceptable in such a case without coming across as morally naive? But once one admits that torture is acceptable in a hypothetical case, it becomes harder to deny that it is acceptable in at least a few real cases. To oppose the use of torture categorically then appears at best misguided and at worst morally pernicious, and the remaining question is simply where to draw the line. Charles Krauthammer, for example, adopts this strategy. In a December 2005 article in the *Weekly Standard*, Krauthammer argues that the ticking bomb case proves that "however rare the cases, there are circumstances in which, by any rational moral calculus, torture not only would be permissible but would be required (to acquire life-saving information). And once you've established the principle, to paraphrase George Bernard Shaw, all that's left to haggle about is the price." Krauthammer himself draws the line at ticking bomb cases and the "slower-fuse high-level terrorist." By this he means, roughly, terrorists who are at the top of the organizational hierarchy or who otherwise possess valuable information about ongoing or future operations. Osama bin Laden and Ayman al-Zawahiri, for instance, would clearly qualify as high-level terrorists, as would many lesser figures (Krauthammer does not say exactly how high-level they must be to qualify for torture).[4]

One way to respond to such arguments is to argue that torture is never justified, even in ticking bomb cases. This can be done on several different grounds. Pacifists, for example, would simply reject the use of coercion and violence, even in pursuit of a just cause. On this view, even if torture is effective, it should never be used, not even to save the lives of thousands of innocent people. In response, torture advocates would insist, with some plausibility, that such a view is morally unacceptable. It is worth remarking in this connection that torture, under any circumstances, is officially illegal in this country. Article Two of the United Nations Convention Against Torture and Other Cruel, Inhuman, or Degrading Treatment or Punishment, ratified by the U.S. Senate in 1990 (though not taking full effect until later), expressly states that "no exceptional circumstances whatsoever, whether a state of war or threat of war, internal political instability or any other public emergency, may be invoked as a justification of torture." The proper interpretation of U.S. law is of course a very complicated matter, but even if it clearly prohibits torture under any circumstances, torture advocates would respond by arguing that U.S. law ought to be changed.[5]

Whatever the merits of such a strategy, there is another way to deal with the ticking bomb argument for torture. In order for the argument to work, ticking bomb cases must resemble real-life cases in relevant respects; otherwise, whatever moral intuitions we have about the former would be irrelevant to our intuitions about the latter. In other words, if ticking bomb cases have little to do with reality, then they cannot be invoked to justify torture in the real world. Torture advocates want us to think that if torture is acceptable in a hypothetical case, then it is likely to be acceptable in real cases as well. But if ticking bomb cases are highly unrealistic, then this argument falls apart (though there remains the possibility of justifying torture on other grounds).

Ticking Bombs, *24*, and Reality

How realistic are ticking bomb cases? There are at least seven key differences or disanalogies between the typical ticking bomb case and reality. Since ticking bomb cases can be described in different ways, and some of the differences between them and reality are matters of degree, it would be incorrect to say that they have no bearing whatsoever on the real world. However, when considered together, the seven differences outlined below make a strong case against the use of ticking bomb cases as part of a defense of torture.[6]

To see this, let us turn once again to *24*. As we have seen, Jack Bauer regularly faces ticking bomb scenarios. How does the world of *24*, and thus the ticking bomb case, differ from reality? The first key difference is this: in *24*, the threat is imminent—the bomb will explode today, the virus will be released in six hours, missiles containing the nerve gas are about to be launched from the submarine, and so on. The ominous ticking clock, present before and after commercial breaks and at the end of each episode, consistently reminds us of this fact. When, as in *24*, time is short, the case for using "harsh interrogation methods" may appear stronger. In real life, however, the time for preventive action is usually much more open-ended. Take, for example, the 9/11 attacks. The now infamous President's Daily Brief of August 6, 2001, entitled "Bin Ladin Determined to Strike in U.S.," offered some clues as to the possible method of attack (hijacking planes), but the details—dates, times, identities of the hijackers, and so on—were still largely unknown. The attack could have been planned, for all we knew, for February 11, 2002. As of August 2001, intelligence officials had sketchy knowledge of an indeterminate plot to attack the United States sometime in the future. By all means, threats like this need to be taken very seriously, but the information available to intelligence officials in August 2001 made the threat a slow-fuse case at best.

Here is another real case. In 2003, U.S. intelligence officials learned of a possible al Qaeda plot to release anthrax. The time frame and exact location of the attack, however, were unknown. Computer hard drives confiscated from former al Qaeda safe houses in Pakistan revealed detailed casing photos of various locations in New York City, including hotels, banks, and Grand Central Terminal. An attack was probably being planned, or at least considered. But when? Where, exactly? There was no indication that the attack was imminent—we just didn't know. Again, this case belongs in the slow-fuse category.[7]

The second key difference is this: in *24*, the available courses of action are artificially and unrealistically limited. For instance, if Jack doesn't threaten to kill Syed Ali's family, the bomb almost certainly will go off. There really is only one viable alternative: torture. In real life, however, we almost always have multiple options. Prior to the 9/11 attacks, for example, the FBI had the option of sharing intelligence data with the CIA—not the stuff, perhaps, that TV shows are made of, but something that could have prevented the actual attacks. Better sharing of information among law enforcement and intelligence gathering agencies is one of the principal recommendations of the 9/11 Commission, one that so far has been poorly implemented. Regarding interrogation methods, most experts claim that establishing trust, weakening the suspect's identification with the cause, using simple deception or trickery (such as giving him a postcard to mail to his family, and thereby learning his home address), and other techniques are more effective than torture in most cases. These alternative forms of questioning do sometimes take time. Thus the case for torture once again depends on our regarding the threat as imminent (i.e., we do not have the luxury of employing more humane interrogation techniques). Torture seems justifiable in *24* in part because all other acceptable options have been written out of the script. But real life does not always follow the script.[8]

The third and fourth differences are as follows: in *24* torture is almost always successful, and it rarely has any harmful side effects or consequences. In real life, torture is usually unsuccessful, and it often has harmful side effects. When Bauer threatens to kill Syed Ali's family unless he reveals the location of the bomb, Ali resists at first. But after Bauer apparently has his son killed, he relents. Good thing Jack tortured him, we are inclined to think. But according to terrorism experts, this is not what typically happens. Most torture victims do eventually talk, of course, but the information they reveal is often false. According to most experts, in order to escape torture, a subject will usually reveal what he thinks the interrogators want to hear. As a method of arriving at the truth, torture is pretty unreliable. Moreover, the consequences of acting on false information can be devastating.[9]

Consider the case of Abu Zubaydah. Captured in Pakistan in March 2002, Zubaydah was initially believed to be a top al Qaeda operative. In a press conference announcing his capture held on April 9, 2002, President Bush described him as "one of the top operatives plotting and planning death and destruction in the United States." In fact, as al Qaeda expert Dan Coleman quickly realized, he was a relatively low-level al Qaeda operative, with little knowledge of operational affairs. Worse, he was "insane," "certifiable," and had a "split personality." This did not prevent the CIA from subjecting him to waterboarding, beatings, and death threats. His medication was withheld and he was constantly bombarded with harsh lights and deafening noise. Eventually, Zubaydah divulged al Qaeda plans to target shopping malls, banks, supermarkets, nuclear facilities, water systems, and apartment buildings. Resources were diverted to investigate these plots, but in each case the threats were spurious.[10]

Finally, a thoughtful CIA interrogator employed a different method. Relying on Zubaydah's belief that things happen for a reason and his own familiarity with the Koran, the interrogator argued that since he was not killed in the raid that led to his capture, he must have been predestined to cooperate with his captors. Eventually Zubaydah gave up two pieces of information: the name of Jose Padilla and the identity of a man known as Mukthar, now known as Khalid Sheikh Mohammed. Padilla was convicted on August 17, 2007, on charges of aiding terrorist organizations and conspiracy to commit murder, while Khalid Sheikh Mohammed (usually referred to as K.S.M.) was al Qaeda's most senior tactical operative. K.S.M was eventually captured, severely tortured, and finally sentenced to life in prison in 2006.[11]

What lessons can we learn from this episode? Admittedly, it is hard to tell. For some members of the intelligence community, it was clearly a victory for the so-called softer methods of interrogation. But others offered the following counterpoint: did the softer methods work only because he was tortured first? It is impossible to know for sure, and one must be careful not to draw conclusions from just one case, but there is considerable evidence that torture in general does not work. In the world of *24,* torture is a regrettable, though necessary and effective, means of combating terror. But if in the real world it is neither necessary nor effective, then it appears to be just regrettable (or worse).

But perhaps these experts are wrong. Suppose that torture does sometimes work—might this not justify its use, even if it sometimes leads us astray? Any responsible policy must take into account, as much as possible, foreseeable side effects of its implementation. The problem with torture in the real world is not only its general lack of effectiveness, but also the unwelcome consequences that may result from it. For example, there is little question that America's reputation has suffered, and continues to suffer, not only because of the war in Iraq in general, but specifically because of Abu Ghraib and Guantánamo Bay, as well as extraordinary rendition. Our loss of credibility, both politically and morally, is a significant and predictable result of our policies. The damage done to our reputation, in turn, leads to further problems. Out of opposition to our counterproductive policies, other nations, even our allies, may be less willing to share intelligence, allow access to suspects, and so on—activities that are essential to preventing another terrorist attack. Even more importantly, by employing torture, we expose ourselves to the charge of moral hypocrisy and lend credibility to the claims of bin Laden and others. Torture is an effective recruiting device for terrorists.

There are other potential side effects as well. The psychological damage done to those who have been tortured often lasts years, even decades. This is particularly important because, in the real world, some of those tortured are almost certain to be innocent. In fact, such cases have already been documented. The harm done to those who inflict torture must also be taken into account. Interestingly, *24*'s producers argued that torture does take a psychological toll on Jack Bauer. As Howard Gordon put it, "Jack is basically damned." I wonder whether *24*'s fans see it that way. Real-world interrogators, on the other hand, are all-too-familiar with the psychological effects of witnessing others experience excruciating pain. Joe Navarro, one of the FBI's leading interrogation experts, put it this way: "Only a psychopath can torture and be unaffected. You don't want people like that [Bauer] in your organization. They are untrustworthy, and they tend to have grotesque other problems."[12]

Moreover, as John McCain and others have argued, if we torture our enemies, our enemies may be more likely to torture us. Proponents of torture sometimes respond by insisting that our enemies are barbarians, that they will torture us anyway, and so on. But even if our enemies are more likely to use inhumane methods against us no matter what we do, it is plausible to suppose that they will be even more inhumane if we are inhumane to them.

These are just a few of the likely side effects. Again, the fact that torture has unwelcome side effects is not a conclusive argument against it, but it serves as a reminder that even if torture does work, it may not be worth the political and moral costs associated with it.

The fifth key difference is as follows: in *24*, the motives and intentions of the good guys are almost always beyond reproach: when they torture someone, it is always with good reason, and only as much as is necessary to achieve the objective. Jack is no sadist, he just wants the information. Even the rather disagreeable Ryan Chappelle tortures Gael Ortega for a good reason: he has evidence that Gael is working with the terrorists (oops—not so, as we learn an episode or two later). Moreover, because the threat is imminent, torture is almost always done on the fly, so to speak, with little supervision or oversight. This is rarely the case in reality. In fact, one of the leading advocates of torture, Alan Dershowitz, insists that any acceptable policy of torture must include proper legal oversight—the standards for the acceptability of torture have to be clearly defined, the permission of a judge must be given, and so on. No doubt Dershowitz is concerned with potential abuses. But the good guys almost never abuse their power in *24*. The potential for abuse in real life, however, is quite clear. The Abu Ghraib case is just one example of what could happen if there is little guidance or oversight regarding what is acceptable and what is not.[13]

The claim that sanctioning torture will result in abuse is a type of slippery slope argument. The idea is that a practice that might be justified in isolation should not be made policy because of the potential for abuse. In the case of torture, there is good reason to believe that its use would not be restricted to ticking bomb cases or slow-fuse, high-level targets. Moreover, as Michael Kinsley has argued, there is a deeper problem not only with Krauthammer's argument, but also with any strategy that relies on ticking bomb cases. The problem is that the moral rationale underlying ticking bomb cases—a kind of "emergency defense"—can easily be extended to other cases. Krautham-mer, for instance, insists that torture should not be used against military personnel, presumably because they are lawful combatants and should be treated according to the Geneva Conventions. But it does not take much imagination to construct a ticking bomb case involving a lawful combatant. If there really were a ticking bomb case, and torture was necessary to prevent a catastrophe, what difference does it make if the person being tortured is a lawful combatant?[14]

Torture advocates could try to find other ways of drawing an accept-able line. Alan Dershowitz's insistence on legal safeguards, for instance, is an attempt to prevent ourselves from sliding down the slope, but it is far from clear that such restrictions would work in practice, and his way of drawing the line seems arbitrary (and would not help in ticking bomb cases anyway, where there is no time for warrants). Whether a policy of torture can be crafted in such a way as to be effective (assuming torture is effective to begin with) without being subject to misuse is an open question. One of the main problems with torture as it is now practiced in the war on terror is that few of the safeguards are in place, no clear, acceptable policy has been formulated to deal with the issue, and worst of all, we rely all too heavily on the morally disingenuous policy of extraordinary rendition—as if we could evade moral responsibility for torture by asking someone else to do it. In this respect, *24* does echo reality—recall the opening scene of season two, in which the torture takes place in South Korea. The point is that in *24*, the safeguards are never presented as necessary—if Jack tortures someone, there must be a good reason.

The sixth difference is this: the terrorist plots in *24* lack context. Little is known about how we got to this point—how is it possible, for example, that terrorists should have succeeded in smuggling a nuclear bomb into the country? The show does sometimes provide some context. In season two, for example, we learn later (after Roger Stanton is tortured) that some officials in the government knew about the bomb and allowed it to enter the country, with the intention of seizing it just in time, in order to force the president into adopting a more muscular foreign policy. In real life, it matters a great deal what happened (or did not happen) a month, a year, or even a decade earlier. In *24*, CTU is the only major player, but in real life our economic and political policies, among other factors, play a much larger role in causing or preventing terrorism. Ignoring historical and political context enables *24* to present torture as a more plausible option—what else could we do? But critics of torture as a weapon in the war on terror can rightly ask how we got to this point, and whether other policies might have been more effective. The 9/11 Commission report, for example, did not include more torture as one of its recommendations. In other words, context matters because it helps us focus on how best to prevent another terrorist attack. Even if torture were effective, it is incumbent on us morally to seek alternative methods of achieving our objectives, if such methods are possible, for the simple reason that torture is, in itself, bad. By largely ignoring context, *24* gives us the false impression that we often face a choice of last resort, when in fact we do not.

The final difference is in many ways the most difficult for many of us to admit. In *24* the cause is unambiguously just. Whatever our nation may have done (note that the terrorists almost always want to punish us for our allegedly unjust policies), there clearly is no justification for detonating a nuclear bomb over Los Angeles. When Jack tries to make that argument to arch villain Habib Marwan (Arnold Vosloo), it is of no use—Marwan simply insists that it is pointless for either side to try to persuade the other. There, we heard it from the terrorists themselves: there is no reasoning with them, so all that is left is force. Aside from embodying an all-or-nothing mentality, this way of thinking reinforces our unwillingness to understand our enemies' point of view. I am not arguing that all causes are equally just (they are not), nor am I arguing that the crimes of the U.S. government are as bad as those of, say, Nazi Germany (they are not), nor am I arguing that our crimes are bad enough to justify terrorism (they are not). The point is that even if in some abstract sense our cause is just, particular policies may not be just, and even if a just cause justifies ruthless means, an unjust cause clearly does not. If the war on terror as it is currently being practiced is itself unjust, then using torture as a means of furthering that cause is also unjust.

Conclusion

I have argued that ticking bomb cases, so common in *24*, are highly unlikely to occur in real life. But I am not arguing that they cannot ever occur, or even that they have never occurred. Such a conclusion would be unwarranted. Indeed, David Luban has argued that the conditions necessary to produce real-life ticking bomb cases might in fact sometimes exist in countries like Israel. But even if there are, or could be, real-life ticking bomb cases, they are highly unlikely, and are far less common than Krauthammer's slow-fuse, high-profile case. It is this type of case that ought to concern us. Whether torture, suitably restricted to limit abuse, should be included in the list of approved interrogation techniques is, for all I have said here, an open question. But in trying to decide what our policy regarding torture should be, it is helpful to remember that some of the arguments against torture in ticking bomb scenarios apply just as forcefully to slow-fuse cases, or indeed any torture case. For example, the potential for abuse, the harm to our reputation, the unreliability of torture itself—these concerns remain regardless of how imminent or severe the terrorist threat is. Most importantly, we must never allow unrealistic scenarios to serve as the foundation for public policy.[15]

Notes

1. A video recording of the symposium can be found on the Heritage Foundation's Web site, http://www.heritage.org/Press/Events/ev062306.cfm (accessed August 16, 2007). The Howard Gordon quote is from Jane Mayer, "Whatever It Takes," *New Yorker,* February 19 and 26, 2007, 66–82.

2. The Finnegan quote is from Mayer, "Whatever It Takes," 72. The Tancredo quote

is from Rosa Brooks, "Don't Tell These Guys Torture's Wrong; The GOP Debate Was a Jack Bauer Impersonation Contest," *L.A. Times,* May 18, 2007.

3. Mayer, "Whatever It Takes," 70.

4. Charles Krauthammer, "The Truth about Torture," *The Weekly Standard,* December 5, 2005, 21–25. For a response to Krauthammer's argument, see Michael Kinsley, "Torture for Dummies," *Slate,* December 13, 2005, http://www.slate.com/toolbar .aspx?action=print&id=2132195 (accessed July 25, 2007).

5. A copy of the Convention can be found at http://www.hrweb.org/legal/cat.html (accessed August 18, 2007). Others have argued that torture simply doesn't work, even in ticking bomb cases.

6. An excellent discussion of these and related issues can be found in David Luban, "Liberalism, Torture, and the Ticking Bomb," in *The Torture Debate in America,* ed. Karen Greenberg, 35–83 (New York: Cambridge Univ. Press, 2006).

7. The plot is described in Ron Suskind, *The One Percent Doctrine* (New York: Simon and Schuster, 2006), 249–57.

8. The postcard example is given in Mayer, "Whatever It Takes," 72.

9. A helpful summary of some the relevant research on torture can be found in Mark Costanzo, Ellen Gerrity, and M. Brinton Lykes, "Psychologists and the Use of Torture in Interrogations," *Analyses of Social Issues and Public Policy* 7, no. 1 (December 2007): 7–20. Among other points, the authors indicate that most alleged evidence of torture's effectiveness is anecdotal and unsubstantiated, while there is irrefutable evidence that coercive techniques in criminal cases yield a high rate of false confessions. Their implicit conclusion is that torture is even more likely to yield bad information. I would like to thank Joe Foy for referring me to this paper.

10. Suskind, *The One Percent Doctrine,* 87–89, 99–100, 115–18.

11. An exciting account of K.S.M.'s capture can be found in Suskind, *The One Percent Doctrine,* 203–6. For an account of his torture, see Suskind, *The One Percent Doctrine,* and also Jane Mayer, "The Black Sites," *New Yorker,* August 13, 2007, 46–57.

12. The quote is from Mayer, "Whatever It Takes," 72. The case of Khaled el-Masri, a German car salesman subjected to torture based on false intelligence, is discussed in Mayer, "The Black Sites," 54.

13. David Luban gives several historical examples in which torturers regularly crossed the line and argues that such abuse is not surprising, given human psychology and the fact that decisions regarding torture are subject to bureaucratic pressures. See Luban, "Liberalism, Torture, and the Ticking Bomb," 48–49. Heather MacDonald has argued that the abuses at Abu Ghraib were the result of poor war planning and a breakdown in military order, not a policy, official or unofficial, of torture. See Heather MacDonald, "How to Interrogate Terrorists," in Greenberg, ed., *The Torture Debate in America,* 93–94.

14. Kinsley, "Torture for Dummies."

15. Luban, "Liberalism, Torture, and the Ticking Bomb," 76 (fn).

11

CIVIL LIBERTIES V. LAW AND ORDER

Exploring Responses to Terrorism in *The Siege*

Nathan Zook

Dramatically portraying incidents of terrorism by extremist Muslims in New York City followed by the profiling of Arabs and the sacrificing of basic civil liberties in order to achieve law and order, *The Siege* may seem to provide an interesting historical account of post-9/11 America. However, it was released in 1998 and largely reviewed as a cynical "can't happen here" type of film. Nevertheless, it is an effective medium for understanding counterterrorism programs in post-9/11 America. It also vividly illustrates numerous conceptual themes in American politics, including origins and causes of terrorism, prevention of terrorism, and responses to acts of terrorism.

Counterterrorism and *The Siege*

The Siege features U.S. Army, CIA, and FBI representatives attempting to fight terrorism without a coordinated offense due to bureaucratic rivalries. The breakdown in communication leads to successful terror operations by cells of young Arab men. In order to track down the cells and ward off the birth of new cells, the U.S. Army representative, General William Devereaux (Bruce Willis), determines that martial law combined with the use of torture may be necessary to secure the nation. His counterterrorism rival, FBI agent Anthony Hubbard (Denzel Washington), argues that engaging in racial profiling and placing all suspicious young Arab males into holding prisons reminiscent of Japanese American internment camps simply provides a victory for those engaging in terrorism since these governmental actions trample the U.S. Bill of Rights. Meanwhile, the CIA representative, Elise Kraft (Annette Bening), is struggling with the results of "blowback," where previous covert operations abroad, such as providing weapons and training to dissident Iraqi groups, have resulted in the use of these resources against the United States.

The core debate of the film is mirrored in real life. Must civil liberties necessarily be sacrificed in order to provide a stable, orderly society? This theme can be useful in analyzing actual congressional debate in the United States prior to the authorization of the USA PATRIOT Act. Can law and order be achieved within the bounds of constitutionality? Is the Constitution flexible enough to fight terrorism and at the same time allow for the exercise of liberty by all citizens regardless of ethnicity or creed?

Origins and Causes of Terrorism

Debates over definitions of terrorism and what causes terrorism have been waged ever since the concept was first introduced during the French Revolution. Over one hundred different definitions of terrorism have been proposed by different governmental and nongovernmental bodies.[1] One working definition used by the U.S. government has been "premeditated, politically motivated violence perpetrated against noncombatant targets by subnational groups or clandestine agents, usually intended to influence an audience."[2] A definition originating in academia declares terrorism to be: "A synthesis of war and theater, a dramatization of the most proscribed kind of violence—that which is perpetuated on innocent victims—played before an audience in the hope of creating a mood of fear, for political purposes." A basic component of both definitions of terrorism is the desire to publicize the threat of violence to a large audience.[3]

The "amplification effect" refers to the media's ability to exponentially increase the message that those engaging in terrorism are trying to convey.[4] The September 11 attacks occurred on high-profile institutions near major media centers, providing an immediate opportunity for the terror to be viewed globally. In the film, prior to a bus explosion that kills numerous innocent passengers, Elise Kraft watches from a distance and ponders why the terrorists are holding the passengers hostage for so long without engaging in negotiations with law enforcement. Suddenly she exclaims to Agent Hubbard that "they're not here to negotiate, they were waiting for the cameras!" As soon as the media is in place, the bus bombers set off the explosion.

Later, during a fourth incident of terrorism, when Hubbard's agents are surrounding a schoolroom where children are being held hostage, Hubbard is informed that helicopters containing news reporters are beginning to circle the building. Recalling the bus explosion, Hubbard decides he has just enough time to dive into the room and rescue the children while the terrorist waits for the media to get into place.[5]

Without specifically addressing social science theories on causes of terrorism, *The Siege* presents numerous scenarios that reflect the range of debate in this field. The terms "Islamic fascists" and "Islamofascism" were used by politicians, including President George W. Bush, following September 11. Such individuals view Islamic radicalism as a major cause for concern and a leading force behind modern terrorism. When the film was released, it was vehemently protested by members of the Islamic community because of its portrayal of radical Islam as a violent influence and cause of terrorism. In particular, many protesters were worried that the film "basically links terrorism to Islam."[6] Although some academics during the late 1990s felt it "almost taboo to discuss terrorism in the Islamic context," others noted "that in the contemporary world most of the violent conflicts, internal and external, happened and continue to happen in Muslim countries or in those with active Muslim minorities."[7] Such theories received much more publicity when al Qaeda, a group with a radical Islamic philosophy promoting violence, was found to be instrumental in the 9/11 attacks.

Throughout the film, Islamic radicalism is viewed as the primary motivation for the five tragic acts of terror. One of the suicide bombers during the bus explosion was discovered to have been wearing an Egyptian cotton shroud that was believed to have been part of his ritual of self-purification prior to his death. At one point, Elise expresses frustration with the legal obstacles to pursuing potential terrorists. She argues that Hubbard should not have to wait for a warrant to search an apartment. Since the terrorists believe they "have a warrant from G-d," the United States' "quaint laws don't mean shit to these people." Later, prior to a key strategic maneuver, Elise reminds Hubbard of the religious zeal of those they are pursuing when she declares, "If things get hairy, remember the most committed wins."

While radical Islam is the general cause of terrorism in the film, other factors help to explain why individuals made the decision to engage in acts of violence. Elise points out that violence begets violence when she tells a group of policy-makers that "each cell operates independent of the others. . . . Cut off one head and another will rise up to take its place." By violently engaging in counterterrorism activities, law enforcement agents may be creating new causes for acts of terrorism. Acts of violence against terrorists may incite others to take their place in a "cycle of violence."[8] At the same time, acts of violence by terrorists may inspire others to follow their lead. Samir Nazhde (Sami Bouajila), a seemingly nonreligious professor of Arab Studies in New York City, ponders giving his life to the cause after contemplating the futility of his life in contrast with that of his brother, who had been a Palestinian suicide bomber, destroying a crowded Israeli movie theater.

Terrorism typically involves the death of seemingly random, innocent people, unlike guerrilla warfare, which seeks to strategically target military outposts or a clearly defined enemy. Threats against the lives of innocent civilians reflect another cause of terrorism: the desire to strike fear into the hearts of a wide audience due to a belief that people will only pay attention if those dying are considered innocent. If a military official dies, civilians may explain away the official's death as being a result of his/her position in the military and not feel threatened. However, if another civilian dies while going about day-to-day life under ordinary circumstances, civilians may worry about their own lives and pay more attention to the goals of those engaging in terrorism.

The third incident of terrorism in *The Siege* takes place at a Broadway theater on opening night. Present are a "veritable who's who" of New York's cultural elite. However, ordinary New Yorkers were sufficiently scared by this seemingly random attack on innocent people. Later, the film portrays a city bus having trouble with its muffler. The resulting loud noises cause pedestrians to dive to the ground for cover. While Agent Hubbard argues the city needs to go on as normal, the underlying symbolism reveals that the terrorists have the attention of the populace that they so desire.

The most dramatic illustration of an individual seeking to engage in terrorism out of a desire to gain immediate attention occurs near the end of the film. A large coalition of New Yorkers have come together to protest against violations of civil liberties by military troops. Samir marvels over the beauty of "Christians and Muslims, Arabs and Jews, blacks and whites" marching together in unity. As he shares these insights with Elise, it slowly dawns on her that the next attempt of terrorism will be against the marchers. Samir explains the value of such an attempt by asking, "Can you imagine anything more tragic?" The desire to continually raise the level of fear and gain more attention can be one of the very basic causes of terrorism.

Blowback

Blowback is the concept that actions taken by government agencies may come back to haunt them. While originally coined by the Central Intelligence Agency, this concept has gradually gained more widespread usage as awareness has grown of results of the history of various U.S. foreign operations. It refers in particular to "the unintended consequences of policies that were kept secret from the American people."[9] During the Reagan era, for example, the United States provided strong support for Saddam Hussein. Think of the infamous picture from December 20, 1983, of special envoy Donald Rumsfeld shaking hands with President Hussein in Baghdad. Later it was alleged that the rekindling of diplomatic ties between the United States and Iraq enabled Hussein to tighten his political and military control over Iraq without outside intervention. Hussein's increased power came back to haunt the United States in the decades that followed.[10]

Another alleged example of blowback is referenced in the film. Immediately following September 11, reports surfaced concerning possible connections between the CIA and Osama bin Laden. On September 13, it was discovered that the CIA may have supported bin Laden's Islamic uprising against Soviet advances in Afghanistan during the 1980s. Was this support and training later useful in September 2001? *The Siege* begins with Sheik Achmed Bin Talal (Ahmed Ben Larby), who bears strong resemblances to Osama bin Laden, being captured by the U.S. military. His followers realize he is in U.S. custody before the FBI has this information. The incidents of terrorism that follow are a series of attempts to gain his release.[11]

While the cause-and-effect relationship between the sheik's capture and the resulting terrorism are immediately evident in the film, other instances of blowback are more complex. Later in the film, numerous historical incidents are revealed that indicate blowback goes much deeper. For example, a rather unreliable informant within the New York Muslim community is revealed to have earlier been a part of the CIA operation to destabilize Saddam Hussein.

A more stunning revelation provides deep personal turmoil for Elise Kraft. After much difficulty in tracking terrorist cells, Elise reveals that in her role as a CIA agent she had trained many of the members of these cell groups in the use of explosives. "The sheik was going to help us overthrow Saddam . . . he was our ally, we were financing him," Elise confesses.

After the sheik and his followers suffered defeats at the hands of Saddam's government, Elise had stepped in to repair the damage. The insurgents the CIA had trained were being slaughtered, so she helped them get visas to escape to the United States. As a result, men who were trained by the CIA to kill Saddam Hussein, following the frustration of their efforts, emerged in Manhattan with the newly acquired training and capability to use explosives on U.S. soil. The film's ironic twist features Elise dying at the hands of one of the individuals she helped empower in the ultimate symbolic representation of blowback.

Preventing Terrorism

The United States has successfully and unsuccessfully engaged in numerous efforts to deal with modern forms of terrorism. In an era when simple tools such as box cutters can cause significant havoc and when individuals are willing to commit suicide rather than negotiate with law enforcement agencies, communications breakdowns due to bureaucratic rivalries and intelligence-gathering shortcuts such as racial profiling are likely to occur.

One major obstacle to preventing terrorism is the lack of communication across bureaucracies and other governmental institutions. The 9/11 Commission report details numerous examples of such bureaucratic rivalries. For example, the FBI and the Criminal Division of the U.S. Justice Department were not cooperating as fully as departmental procedure would allow following the first bombing of the World Trade Center. The FBI and the INS (Immigration and Naturalization Service) were also not sharing information to the extent they were allowed. State and local law enforcement agencies were either not invited to cooperate or chose not to for a variety of reasons. In sum, counterterrorism forces were not as coordinated as they could have been, and President George W. Bush pushed for the creation of the Department of Homeland Security in order to limit such lack of coordination. Whether this flaw in counterterrorism was due to actual rivalry or simple communication breakdown is debatable. However, the film illustrates these bureaucratic flaws as examples of outright rivalry.

The Siege highlights bureaucratic rivalries by portraying three government agencies, the Department of Defense, the CIA, and the FBI, that are obsessed with guarding their own informers and intelligence "turf" and denying access to other agencies. Information and technology are not tools to share with other agencies for the good of the country, but rather resources to acquire for the good of the agency. Nevertheless, the film accurately reflects a trend throughout American history of numerous foreign policy failures resulting from communication breakdowns due to bureaucratic rivalries.[12]

In the film, although the CIA was aware of terrorist cells operating in New York City prior to any incidents of terrorism, this information was withheld from the FBI. In a desperate effort to obtain information, the FBI, represented by Agent Anthony Hubbard, invades a CIA strong house during an interrogation in order to arrest a suspect that the CIA earlier had abducted from the FBI. On the one hand, CIA agent Elise Kraft argues she was engaging in surveillance. On the other hand, Anthony charges her with "kidnapping, obstruction of justice, assault," and even threatens he will seek to have her sentenced to prison on Riker's Island. Meanwhile, Anthony's sidekick, Agent Frank Haddad (Tony Shalhoub), stews about how he can

Although released three years prior to the terrorist attacks of September 11, 2001, *The Siege* highlights the tensions between liberty and security that dominated political discussion in the wake of 9/11. (Jerry Ohlinger's Movie Material Store)

replicate the CIA's technological capacity for intelligence gathering. He notices microwave technology and is only satisfied after he can confiscate similar equipment.

The Army is not above participating in the bureaucratic rivalries between the FBI and CIA. General Devereaux plunges into the fray by capturing and interrogating Tariq Husseini, a suspect Agent Hubbard had arrested for questioning, and by seeking to neutralize the impact of the CIA's counterterrorism operations. While Devereaux withholds information from the FBI and CIA regarding high-profile prisoners that could be useful in negotiations with potential terrorists, he emphasizes his disdain for agencies that are less adept. At one point, he disparages the intelligence-gathering capabilities of the CIA by declaring that the intelligence agency "didn't know the Berlin Wall was coming down until bricks started hitting them in the head." Rather than seeking to share information, the agencies deride one another for their ineptness. It should be noted that this concern about the ineptness of the CIA was investigated and noted by numerous scholars following September 11.[13]

Such bureaucratic rivalries lead to difficulties in protecting the citizenry of New York City and contradictory policies between the three agencies. At one point, as Hubbard expresses his frustration to a presidential staffer regarding the slow filtration of information and inconsistent policies, the staffer sarcastically asks, "What do you think, Hub, our government works as one coherent entity?" The film indicates that this lack of coherence is not just due to bureaucratic boundaries between agencies, but rather to blatant, intentional rivalries.

Decision makers are not omniscient and typically lack certain vital pieces of information in making decisions. When the costs of becoming better informed seem insurmountable, these decision makers may rely on shortcuts to acquire knowledge. For law enforcement agencies seeking to prosecute wrongdoers, it would be too costly to investigate and interrogate an entire population. It may seem simpler to develop a profile of the type of characteristics most likely to be present in a person who commits a crime. While this profile could focus on obvious factors, such as past criminal violations, it may also include more controversial ones, such as race or ethnicity. During World War II, such reasoning led to severe civil liberties violations when many Japanese Americans and even German Americans were thrust into internment camps.

Those supporting racial profiling typically argue that if members of a certain racial group are statistically more likely to engage in a criminal activity, then they should be the primary focus of any criminal investigation. Those opposing racial profiling point out that if law enforcement agents focus the majority of their time on investigations of one particular racial group, then it is no surprise that members of this group will have a higher likelihood of arrest. More surveillance will result in "heavily disproportionate incarceration."[14]

The Siege illustrates the U.S. Army engaging in racial profiling following terrorist incidents in New York City. General Devereaux develops a profile of the person most likely to be part of a terrorist cell group. This person would be an Arab-speaking male between the ages of fourteen and thirty who had been in the U.S. for less than six months. The use of this profile reduces the number of possible suspects from the population of New York City to only twenty individuals. To find these individuals, however, Devereaux argues for the necessity of house-to-house searches in Arab neighborhoods in Brooklyn. All Arab-speaking males are then transported to a holding camp in a stadium in Brooklyn.

The film presents a major emotional argument against racial profiling through the family situation of FBI agent Frank Haddad. Frank's thirteen-year-old son is one of the young Arab-speaking males imprisoned in the stadium. Although Frank had been an American citizen for twenty years and a very loyal FBI agent, representatives of the U.S. Army indicated that even his profile was not flawless since he was of Lebanese, and possible Shi'ite, origin. Frank protests the imprisonment by throwing his FBI badge at Agent Hubbard's feet and declaring that he will not be "their sand-nigger anymore."

The film illustrates the real-life frustration that many practicing Muslims faced following the internment of suspects in holding cells in Guantánamo. Reminiscent of Frank's protest, a Muslim U.S. Army chaplain, James Yee, has provided outspoken criticism of the treatment of Muslim prisoners and even army officers by other U.S. soldiers.[15]

Responding to Acts of Terror

On October 11, 2001, a major debate occurred in the U.S. Senate regarding whether to create powers for the president that would provide greater authority for law enforcement, or to limit such powers in order to protect civil liberties. The resulting USA PATRIOT Act increased the ability of law enforcement agencies to investigate electronic and phone messages, to indefinitely detain and deport immigrants, and to acquire private records of suspected individuals.

The core quandary for law enforcement agents in *The Siege* is whether to protect the civil liberties of the population they are trying to police or to seek to maintain law and order as the ultimate priority. While the characters in *The Siege* may vacillate between the two perspectives, by the end of the film the lines are clearly drawn between those who believe focusing on civil liberties will put law and order at risk and those who believe prioritizing law and order will endanger civil liberties.

Numerous examples are used to convey the idea that protections for civil liberties can be obstacles to law and order. In the very beginning of the film, a possible criminal suspect carrying a large sum of money in a duffle bag is briefly detained. He can be held for questioning according to standard operating procedure if the stacks of cash amount to $20,000. When it is discovered that the actual sum falls $10 short, Agent Frank Haddad openly drops a $10 bill in the bag and the FBI proceeds with interrogations. When the suspect is finally released, Haddad is still not satisfied that the interrogations were sufficiently rigid and complains, "Back home [in Lebanon] security would be up this guy's ass with a poker. . . . What do we do? We let him go." Haddad firmly believes that too much attention to legalities in the name of civil liberties can divert the FBI from the goal of protecting law and order.

While Agent Hubbard and Elise Kraft are debating whether or not to wait for a legal search warrant prior to invading an apartment, Elise argues that the suspected terrorists would not hesitate to engage in their operations. She declares that this operation may call for a decision that may seem to be the lesser of two evils. "It's easy to tell the difference between right and wrong. What's hard is telling the wrong that's more right." Although she acknowledges violating civil liberties may be wrong, Elise firmly believes that in this instance it would be more wrong to sacrifice law and order.

The opposing perspective, that prioritizing law and order may infringe upon civil liberties, is accounted for in the film as well. Rather than solely focusing on bringing hostage-takers to justice, Agent Hubbard exemplifies greater concern for the hostages. He proposes that he become a substitute for the hostages and promises that the police and the FBI would "disappear." Although the hostage-takers are not willing to negotiate on this point, Hubbard's effort is an acknowledgment of the secondary importance that he places upon detaining criminals.

Nevertheless, following an explosion that is the worst attack on U.S. soil since the Oklahoma City bombing, even Hubbard begins to engage in activities that civil libertarians would view as unconscionable. He declares his intentions to "rumble every trap, hole, mosque, community, and community center" in his effort to bring the terrorists to justice. His interrogation of a man who may possess valuable information features threats with a lighted cigarette near the neck of a man that already visibly has cigarette burns.

Hubbard quickly has a change of heart once he sees the degree to which General Devereaux is willing to go in prioritizing law and order. After the general begins a house-to-house search in Arab neighborhoods in an attempt to detain nearly fifteen thousand young Arab-speaking males, Hubbard realizes this approach severely infringes upon civil liberties. When he enters the stadium where Devereaux is holding the detainees, Hubbard stumbles upon a debate between several law enforcement and military officials over whether to engage in Chinese water torture or sleep deprivation in interrogations.

Declaring that "the time has come for one man to suffer to save hundreds of lives," Devereaux argues in favor of torturing a suspected terrorist conspirator named Tariq Husseini (Amro Salama). Hubbard, however, vociferously argues that maybe the goal of those engaging in incidents of terrorism is to have U.S. law enforcement agents "shred the Constitution" by violating civil liberties. He argues that the terrorists have "won" when civil liberties are sacrificed on behalf of law and order.

During the grand finale, a confrontation between the FBI and the Army, Hubbard tries to arrest Devereaux and stop the ongoing violations of civil liberties. As he pulls out his weapon, Hubbard declares, "You have the right to remain silent . . . You have the right not to be tortured, not to be murdered, rights that you took away from Tariq."

Much of the film uncannily portrays aspects of counterterrorism that became reality following September 11, with the exception of the implementation of martial law on U.S. soil. While martial law did not become reality in 2001, the use of the military to fight a war on terror did come to pass. *The Siege* provides several reasons to oppose such an occurrence. First, the film indicates that invoking martial law could lead to injustices due to lack of civilian control over military officers. Second, the film gives the impression that less cumbersome government bureaucratic agencies may wield greater deftness in pursuing a war on terrorism.

In the film, a U.S. senator first suggests using the military as the primary focal point in routing out terrorists. He advocates the use of bombs along with the landing of troops from the U.S. Army or National Guard in Manhattan. During the ensuing debate, General Devereaux actually appears to oppose the use of "his" military in this capacity. He warns the assembled decision makers that the presence of ground troops in New York City "will be noisy, it will be scary, and it will not be mistaken for a VFW parade." He also mentions that the U.S. Army is a "broadsword," not a "scalpel."

Nevertheless, public pressure increases upon the president to invoke martial law against the terror being broadcast on TV screens. One news anchor declares, "How many people have to die before we do bring the army in?" The president's administration eventually yields to the public outcry and pressures Devereaux to carry out martial law by bringing tanks into New York City and sealing off the borough of Brooklyn, where the majority of the Arab-speaking population under suspicion are believed to reside. This reflects earlier scholarly concerns that "desperate societies" will be willing to allow formerly "benign governments" to be transformed into "coldly efficient, centralized tyrannies."[16]

Devereaux's characterization of the Army as a broadsword rather than a scalpel in the war on terror is clearly portrayed following the implementation of martial law. While Agent Hubbard and other FBI agents are seeking to arrest and interrogate Tariq Husseini, an individual who may hold information about existing terrorist cells, army helicopters begin circling Husseini's shop, firing rockets. If the explosives had met their target, these tactics could have eliminated not only any threat posed by Husseini, but also any information he had that could lead to uncovering much larger terrorist operations.

Conclusion

As the film concludes, it becomes clear that its sympathies lie on the side of balancing civil liberties over law and order. But either side of the equation may seem like an all-or-nothing choice. On the one hand, Patrick Henry declared, "Give me liberty or give me death." When popular culture conveys the idea that what makes America great is its freedoms, death may seem a welcome alternative to those who feel their freedoms are eroding. On the other hand, without some attention to national security, death may not be a choice, but a requirement, given the increasing ferocity of terrorism.

Nevertheless, some scholars argue that the pitting of law and order against civil liberties is a fallacious choice. There may be alternatives to discarding one or the other.[17] Perhaps there is a rational middle ground that encompasses both sides of the equation. Hopefully members of Congress will ascertain the right choice, and not copy Elise Kraft's decision to simply settle for "the wrong that's more right."

Notes

1. Alex P. Schmid, Albert J. Jongman, et al., *Political Terrorism: A New Guide to Actors, Authors, Concepts, Data Bases, Theories, and Literature* (New Brunswick, N.J.: Transaction Books, 1988), 5–6.

2. U.S. Department of State, *Patterns of Global Terrorism* (Washington, D.C.: U.S. Department of State, 2001), vi.

3. Cindy Combs, ed., *Terrorism in the Twenty-First Century,* 2nd ed. (Upper Saddle River, N.J.: Prentice Hall, 2000), 7.

4. Ibid., 128.

5. All film quotes in this chapter are taken from: *The Siege,* directed by Edward Zwick (Twentieth Century-Fox, 1998).

6. Tyrone Prather, "'Siege' Meets Protest: Students Upset over Characters," *Stanford Daily* (November 9, 1998).

7. Walter Laqueur, *The New Terrorism: Fanaticism and the Arms of Mass Destruction* (New York: Oxford Univ. Press, 1999), 128.

8. Combs, *Terrorism in the Twenty-First Century,* 24–27.

9. Chalmers Johnson, *Blowback: The Costs and Consequences of American Empire* (New York: Henry Holt, 2000), 8.

10. The George Washington University National Security Archive: http://www.gwu .edu/~nsarchiv/NSAEBB/NSAEBB82/press.htm (accessed August 20, 2007).

11. "Osama bin Laden: From U.S. Friend to Foe," *Seattle Times,* September 13, 2001, http://archives.seattletimes.nwsource.com/cgi-bin/texis.cgi/web/vortex/display?slug= osama13&date=20010913 (accessed August 20, 2007).

12. Mark Riebling, *Wedge: From Pearl Harbor to 9/11—How the Secret War between the FBI and CIA Has Endangered National Security* (New York: Touchstone Press, 2002).

13. Thomas Powers, "The Trouble with the CIA," *New York Review of Books* 49, no. 1 (2002), http://www.nybooks.com/articles/15109 (accessed March 4, 2008).

14. American Civil Liberties Web site: http://www.aclu.org/racialjustice/ racialprofiling/index.html (accessed July 13, 2007).

15. James Yee, *For God and Country: Faith and Patriotism under Fire* (New York: PublicAffairs, 2005).

16. N. C. Livingstone, "Taming Terrorism: In Search of a New U.S. Policy," *International Security Review: Terrorism Report* 7, no. 1 (1982): 20.

17. David Luban, "Eight Fallacies about Liberty and Security," in *Human Rights in the "War on Terror,"* ed. Richard Wilson (New York: Cambridge Univ. Press, 2005), 242–57.

12

INFLUENCING AMERICAN FOREIGN POLICY THROUGH POPULAR MUSIC

All the World's a Stage

Brett S. Sharp

> I'm just a singer of simple songs; I'm not a real political man. I watch CNN
> but I'm not sure I can tell you the difference in Iraq and Iran.
> —Alan Jackson, "Where Were You
> (When the World Stopped Turning)"

The American public has historically paid little attention to foreign affairs. Occasionally, events like Pearl Harbor or the September 11 terrorist attacks shock the public into engaging international events directly as important issues. Even then, the willingness of Americans to devote full attention to the global arena is remarkably short-lived. In America, much of what goes on in the world competes with domestic news for attention. Interest groups and political activists who wish to gain mileage with American public opinion must resort to a variety of methods. Among these strategies is to communicate information or provide a new perspective through music. For example, the tendency of Americans to be so self-involved that they ignore their own government's foreign policy was effectively parodied in Don Henley's 1985 hit, "All She Wants to Do Is Dance." The irony was probably lost on most of the young people out dancing to the tune at nightclubs, blissfully ignorant of the active agenda of American foreign policy. But there was always a portion of the crowd, what political scientists term the "active public," who closely listened to the lyrics and heard its political message.

Music provides the soundtrack for American politics. The "Star Spangled Banner" and other patriotic songs have become a primary means to voice allegiance to the nation. Politicians routinely use songs to thematically reinforce their campaigns. Songs also have a long and enduring tradition of alerting the public to international issues and mobilizing public opinion with calls to action.

Music-based political movements have been forceful in protesting unpopular wars, providing debt-relief for third world nations, promoting human rights around the globe, coordinating famine relief, responding to national disasters, and informing listeners about the global consequences of destructive environmental policies. Music even provided solace for Americans enduring the pain of the terrorist attacks of September 11. Through songs, musicians express the hopes and concerns of American policies played out in the wider global arena.

War—What Is It Good For?

The most pressing issue for a government—above all other policies domestic or foreign—is maintaining the security and safety of its citizenry. A strong defensive posture backed by credible military force is often essential. Music has long been closely intertwined with the exercise of America's military might. From signals by drums, fifes, and bugles to the extraordinary orchestrations of John Philip Sousa's military marches, musical arrangements have served both strategic and inspirational functions. And yet, the quest for peace against the ever present threat of war also has inspired many of America's most familiar tunes. With few exceptions in the modern political era, voices of protest against war have dominated musical discourse over American international politics.

Two very simple folk songs inaugurated the long era of protest music against the Vietnam War. In 1961, the Kingston Trio recorded a song first arranged by Pete Seeger, "Where Have All the Flowers Gone?" They added a couple of verses with allusions to the growing military involvement in Vietnam: "Where have all the young men gone? Gone to soldiers every one." The song hit the Top 40 the following year.[1]

Within months, Peter, Paul and Mary took Bob Dylan's "Blowin' in the Wind" near the top of the charts. It quickly became the quintessential American protest song. The song asks in musical metaphor the enduring question about the necessity of war, "How many times must the cannon balls fly before they're forever banned?" A subsequent verse, "how many deaths will it take till . . . too many people have died," foreshadowed the famous question asked by a soldier just returning from Vietnam. Young John Kerry, the future senator and presidential candidate, challenged members of the Senate Foreign Relations Committee in April 1971 when he asked, "How do you ask a man to be the last man to die in Vietnam?"

Barry McGuire's "Eve of Destruction" topped the charts in 1965 with the first explicit mainstream protest of the Vietnam War. The song signaled a growing resistance among an emerging generation not yet old enough to vote. Its politically laden lyrics express the troubling incongruity: "The eastern world, it is explodin' . . . you're old enough to kill, but not for votin.'" At the end of that same year, the Byrds took another Seeger song to #1 on the charts with their folk rock rendition of "Turn! Turn! Turn! (To Everything There Is a Season)." Elaborating beyond its base of Ecclesiastical verse, the song closes with the claim that there is a "time for peace" and "it's not too late." If there was an opportunity for peace, then the "Masters of War"—as folksinger Bob Dylan termed American foreign policy makers—did not see fit to take advantage. The increasingly unpopular war continued. It eventually took down President Lyndon Johnson, who realized he wouldn't be able to successfully seek another four years in office. The Doors sang wistfully for the mounting war dead with their "Unknown Soldier."

At the end of the decade, the most popular songs began to evoke the pains and strains of war on relationships. Jimmy Webb's beautiful love song "Galveston," sung by Glen Campbell, hit #4 on the pop charts and became the #1 country music hit. It paints the melancholy picture of a soldier longing for the girl he left back home. Kenny Rogers and the First Edition shook the public with the vividly bitter imagery of a wounded soldier in "Ruby, Don't Take Your Love to Town." In the song, a soldier having returned from war paralyzed and dying is forced to endure the further pain of his love stepping out in the evenings to seek the romance she can no longer find at home. Years later, Bruce Springsteen would sing his signature song "Born in the USA," which is also about the hardships faced by a veteran of Vietnam returning home.

In that summer of '69, the musical protest movement got even edgier. One song was considered so provocative that it bounced around Motown's catalog in search of a performing artist who would not be overly hurt by the ensuing controversy. Ultimately, Edwin Starr took his rendition of Motown's "War" to the top of the charts. The song points out that the "war has caused unrest among the younger generation" and then asks those facing the draft, "Who wants to die?" In "Fortunate Son," Creedence Clearwater Revival empathizes with a soldier drafted because he "ain't no senator's son." Speaking specifically about President Dwight Eisenhower's son David getting married to Richard Nixon's daughter Tricia during a time when other young men were being sent to war, songwriter John Fogerty remarked, "You got the impression that these people got preferential treatment, and the whole idea of being born wealthy or being born powerful seemed to really be coming to the fore in the late-sixties confrontation of cultures." John Lennon softened the protest a bit with his plaintive cry to "Give Peace a Chance." As the decade closed, country singer Merle Haggard was one of the few remaining popular singers to express any pro-establishment sentiments. In his "Okie From Muskogee," Haggard observes, "We don't burn no draft cards down on Main Street."[2]

The seventies arrived with little evidence of President Richard Nixon's living up to his campaign promise to implement a secret plan to end the Vietnam War. Hope did not die among musical activists still anxious to influence American foreign policy. Crosby, Stills, Nash, and Young waxed poetic with their cover of Joni Mitchell's ode to the most famous music festival of all time. In "Woodstock," the singers speak of a dream in which "bomber death planes riding shotgun in the sky" turn "into butterflies above our nation." Mitchell explains, "Suddenly, as performers, we were in the position of having so many people look to us for leadership." Even musicians from other countries took advantage of their prominence to send Americans a political message. For example, the Canadian rock band Guess Who, in their song "American Woman," bluntly proclaim to the American military-industrial complex that they "don't need your war machines."[3]

With lyrical reference to Barry McGuire's "Eve of Destruction," the Temptations, a wildly popular Motown group, powerfully describe the world of 1970 as a "Ball of Confusion." Among its rapid-fire references to the various problems of the late sixties and early seventies, they point out that "people all over the world are shouting" to end the Vietnam War. The following year, another Motown star asked, "What's Going On?" Marvin Gaye delivers what is arguably the most beautiful song in the pantheon of anti–Vietnam War music. He advises in poetic fashion, "We don't need to escalate. You see, war is not the answer."

As the Vietnam War finally began to wind down, a retrospective theme began to creep into much of the popular music scene. America was about to enter a long era in which it grappled with the ghosts of Vietnam. Elton John's hit song "Daniel" criticized the war in more oblique fashion. Bernie Taupin, the song's lyricist, explains, "I forget now if it was *Time* or *Newsweek*—it was about this guy who'd been wounded in the Vietnam War and had gone back to his hometown just wanting to forget it all and get on with his life. But the people there wanted him to be a hero and wouldn't leave him alone," so he "decided the only way out was to leave America altogether." The song is described from the point of view of Daniel's little brother. The younger sibling watches his big brother's plane leave for Spain. He asks poignantly, "Daniel my brother you are older than me. Do you still feel the pain of the scars that won't heal."[4]

Cat Stevens in his devotional "Peace Train" sounded one of the first notes of optimism that the Vietnam War was nearing its end. He admits to being happy and "smiling lately, dreaming about the world as one." He invites everyone to "jump upon the peace train." About that same time, ex-Beatle John Lennon offered his most powerful and most challenging war protest song. In fact, "Imagine" is considered one of the greatest songs of all time. He enjoins his listeners to "Imagine there's no countries . . . nothing to kill or die for and . . . all the people living life in peace." He describes a utopian "brotherhood of man." After agreement was reached in the Paris peace talks in 1973, the United States began its withdrawal of military personnel from Vietnam. A new generation of Americans bound together by music learned to flex their political muscles for the first time and effect real change in the world.[5]

The Vietnam War was in many respects a manifestation of the wider Cold War. This broader struggle between the East and West was described as "cold" because the risk of nuclear war forced the conflict to be played out in more manageable arenas. Preventing major escalation of hostilities became imperative. American foreign policy makers and their adversaries—most notably the Soviet Union—had to reinvent the rules of war. The U.S. defense planners deliberately followed a multi-pronged strategy that (1) emphasized competition in nonmilitary matters, (2) attempted to limit communist expansion through a policy of containment, (3) allowed only skirmishes to take place on a small scale and often through proxy states, and (4) followed somewhat counterintuitive strategies, such as the MAD (mutually assured destruction) doctrine, in which a nuclear strike by one side would be met with immediate and utter destruction by the other side. That perspective encouraged an arms race in which each side built up weaponry that would destroy all life on planet earth several times over if ever deployed.

The ever-present dread of nuclear annihilation instilled a feeling of helplessness. Songs that dealt directly with Cold War issues probably faced great difficulty getting airplay. Perhaps the listening audience used music more as escapist entertainment and producers responded in kind. The Beatles offered a tongue-in-cheek commentary on the emergence of this bipolar world with its "Back in the USSR." The song was an obvious take-off of Chuck Berry's "Back in the USA," performed in the style of the Beach Boys with parallels to their "California Girls." The Beatles may have been the very heart of the sixties zeitgeist, but explicit Cold War references are nonexistent in the fab four catalog. "Back in the USSR" was about the closest they ever came. Even so, the Beatles likely played a crucial role in the ultimate resolution to the Cold War. "Beatlemania, along with the Beatles themselves, may have contributed in a significant way to the collapse of the communist regimes in Eastern Europe," explains sociologist Vessela Misheva, who grew up behind the Iron Curtain. "The real dissidents were those young East Europeans who grew up in minds without 'walls,' and who in large numbers failed to learn early in childhood how to fear and hate the political enemy of the communist system."[6]

Criticism of the tightrope walk inherent in the MAD doctrine came out in the international hit "99 Luftballons" ("99 Red Balloons" in English). German singer Nena sang this memorable new wave hit. It tells the story of a computer malfunction that inaccurately identifies a cluster of floating balloons as a military threat. One side issues a red alert and scrambles its weapons systems. "The war machine springs to life" and turns cities to dust. This song is one of the very few that played out the apocalyptic vision so common in literary and cinematic genres of that same time period.

Elton John's "Nikita" tells of love unconsummated because the Soviet Union placed artificial barriers to separate the peoples of its satellite countries from direct contact with the West. The Berlin Wall that divided the east and west sides of the city became symbolic of what Winston Churchill called the "Iron Curtain." Elton John's song simultaneously sounds a note of both hope and despair. He sings, "Oh Nikita, you will never know anything about my home." But in a later verse, he imagines another possibility: "And if there comes a time guns and gates no longer hold you in and if you're free to make a choice, just look towards the west and find a friend." Within four years, the Berlin Wall came down, marking the official end of the Cold War.

Not Ready to Make Nice

A series of regulatory and legislative changes occurred during the 1980s and 1990s, most notably the 1996 Telecommunications Act, easing restrictions on the ownership of broadcast stations. The net result was that a smaller number of corporate entities were acquiring a greater number of radio stations. Some fans noticed more limited and more sanitized playlists. In other words, appealing to the most customers meant minimizing political controversy. On the eve of the Iraq war in 2003, some analysts were decrying a noticeable absence of musical activism over the airwaves. After witnessing a local folksinger belt out "one more rendition" of Bob Dylan's "The Times They Are A-Changin'" at a 2002 peace rally in Seattle, Ann Powers observed, "Political songs rarely make it onto mainstream radio, and when it's time to focus on an anthem, too often what we all know is vintage 1968." Brent Staples in a *New York Times* editorial claimed, "A [protest] song about George W. Bush's rush to war in Iraq would have no chance at all today. There are plenty of angry people, many with prime music-buying demographics. But independent radio stations that once would have played edgy, political music have been gobbled up by corporations that control hundreds of stations and have no wish to rock the boat."[7]

Political events and social forces inside and outside the music community were creating fertile ground for the reemergence of protest music in the American mainstream. Rage Against the Machine set the stage with the release of its Grammy Award–winning "Guerrilla Radio." The song argued for the power of radio to influence politics—"the weapon of sound above the ground"—which had become the "guerrilla radio" to counter the "vultures who thirst for blood and oil." The dramatically close presidential election of 2000 hardened the positions of the political extremes and heightened the polarization of an already divided American electorate.

The September 11, 2001, terrorist attacks temporarily masked the division among American political elites, and the American public began to recover from the immediate shock of the fall of the World Trade Center towers through such old standards as Billy Joel's "New York State of Mind" and Frank Sinatra's rendition of "New York, New York." Rock music responded to the tragedies with Bruce Springsteen's empathetic album, "The Rising." Country music star Alan Jackson offered the definitive song capturing the emotional spirit of that moment in history with his eloquent "Where Were You (When the World Stopped Turning)." Country musicians Toby Keith and Darryl Worley took their songs "Courtesy of the Red White and Blue (The Angry American)" and "Have You Forgotten?" to the top of the country music charts. Both songs were ostensibly written in support of America's invasion of Afghanistan, but were subsequently used to encourage extending military intervention to oust Saddam Hussein during the buildup toward the war in Iraq.

Remarkably, numerous peace organizations worldwide coordinated a massive protest against the looming war on February 15, 2003. MTV played a powerful video of "Boom!" a song by the alternative rock band System of a Down. The video was directed by Academy Award–winning activist Michael Moore and portrayed many of the activities of the peace rallies in various countries. It communicated to a specific segment of American society that millions of people had enough reservations about the American drive to war to protest in the streets.[8]

The Beastie Boys released one of the first major protest songs against the war in Iraq in the spring of 2003. Its unconventional release as a free mp3 file on the band's Web site increased its popularity but kept the song under the radar of the rest of the music industry. The song portended many of the issues of controversy about American involvement in Iraq. This hip-hop song aims directly at President Bush: "All you want to do is take control. Now put that axis of evil bullshit on hold." A host of other musical artists also skipped the traditional music industry process for releasing anti-war material, including John Mellencamp, Sonic Youth, R.E.M., and George Michael. Music critic Larry Katz asks, "But will anyone's mind be changed by listening to a song? It's doubtful. Those who go to the trouble to download a song will likely be predisposed to agree with what they hear." If he's right, such songs are merely singing to the choir. The key then for music to have much chance to actually influence political opinion is to embed the message in a song that makes it to the pop charts.[9]

Another hip-hop group, the Black Eyed Peas, with Fergie as their new vocalist and with some uncredited assistance from Justin Timberlake, delivered their first breakthrough single, "Where Is the Love?" Here, for the first time in a generation, a clear anti-war protest song made it near the top of the pop charts. This funky call for pacifism echos the spirit of Marvin Gaye's "What's Goin' On?" Beyond the obvious similarity of their questioning titles, both songs employ a prayerful style and speak in a more universal tone. "Where Is the Love?" is a bit more bound by its historical context, with its references to stopping terrorism overseas. Even though both songs are primarily anti-war anthems, each references multiple issues. Moreover, both songs have a timeless quality that will ensure their place in the medley of protest anthems for generations to come.

Within the span of just a few months, a new era of American protest music was reborn. The war in Iraq rekindled an American tradition of musical activism arguably as intense as during the height of the Vietnam War. New technologies such as the iPod and YouTube facilitated these insurgent musical performances' going viral, but corporate radio has obviously sensed an untapped market and has entered the business enthusiastically. Numerous protest songs have climbed the popular music charts, including Green Day's "Holiday," System of a Down's "BYOB (Bring Your Own Bombs)," Barbra Streisand and Barry Gibbs's "Stranger in a Strange Land," Pink's "Dear Mr. President," Pearl Jam's "World Wide Suicide," and John Mayer's "Waiting on the World to Change." In addition, there is now a parallel universe to the standard music industry. Rapper Eminem released "Mosh" as a free download, including a well-produced animated video that still makes the rounds on YouTube. Measuring the popularity of songs released in this fashion is problematic without the ability to track all sales, but no doubt this song and others like it are getting widespread play across the Internet.

The most high-profile drama to unfold in the world of politics and music was between the Dixie Chicks and their base of country music fans. While playing a concert in London just days before the U.S. military invaded Iraq, lead singer Natalie Maines made an off-the-cuff remark, "Just so you know, we're ashamed the president of the United States is from Texas." While receiving little attention right away, their remark eventually made it Stateside. Country music fans, however, tend to be more conservative and were generally supportive of the president, especially during the run-up to the war in Iraq. They were especially offended that Maines delivered her criticism overseas during a time of imminent hostilities. Bonfires were held to burn Dixie Chicks CDs. The phrase "Dixie-Chicked" was coined, meaning to loose radio airplay and to experience plummeting CD sales due to unpopular political stances taken by a popular performer.[10]

In an unsuccessful attempt at damage control, Maines issued a semi-apologetic explanation, "As a concerned American citizen, I apologize to President Bush because my remark was disrespectful. I feel that whoever holds that office should be treated with the utmost respect. We are currently in Europe and witnessing a huge anti-American sentiment as a result of the perceived rush to war. While war may remain a viable option, as a mother, I just want to see every possible alternative exhausted before children and

The Dixie Chicks saw a temporary decline in album sales and airplay following an anti-Bush statement in 2003. The voracity of the attacks against the country music trio was likened to a modern-day witch hunt. (Photofest)

American soldiers' lives are lost. I love my country. I am a proud American." She would later not only take back her apology, but responded powerfully in song form that she was "Not Ready to Make Nice." Through verse she asks, "How in the world can the words that I said send somebody so over the edge that they'd write me a letter sayin' that I better shut up and sing or my life will be over?" The Dixie Chicks may have alienated many of their original fans, but the new song climbed the charts and they were ultimately rewarded with five Grammy Awards in 2007. At the same time, public support for the war in Iraq had plummeted and George W. Bush was experiencing historically low presidential approval poll numbers. The jury is still out as to whether or not George W. Bush will be considered by future historians more like the heroic but unpopular-in-his-time President Harry S Truman or the still disgraced Vietnam War promoters, Presidents Lyndon Johnson and Richard Nixon. In either case, the popular music industry already has delivered its verdict.[11]

We Are the World

Live Earth is the most recent in a series of large-scale musical attempts to influence world opinion as well as to bring public attention and aid to pressing international issues. These events seem to struggle self-consciously to recreate the spirit, style, and mythical presence of the famous Woodstock festival of August 1969. Held on a dairy farm in upstate New York, Woodstock was never intended to be anything more than a profit-making event. Attendance at Woodstock far outstripped actual ticket sales. As Joni Mitchell stated in her commemorative song, "By the time we got to Woodstock, we were half a million strong." It quickly became the iconic event for a politically active generation just then coming of age.

Three years later, famed Beatles guitarist George Harrison organized an event loosely using Woodstock as the template—The Concert for Bangladesh. He gathered several notable rock stars of the time, including Eric Clapton, Bob Dylan, Leon Russell, Billy Preston, and even his fellow Beatle Ringo Starr. They played two concerts at Madison Square Garden in New York City, raising funds for South Asian refugees still reeling from the massive flooding of the 1970 Bhola cyclone and the country's subsequent civil war to gain independence from Pakistan. Later album and video releases supplemented their initial donations to the United Nations Children's Fund (UNICEF). Similarly, the Bee Gees and other major stars helped mark 1976 as the International Year of the Child with "A Gift of Song: The Music for UNICEF Concert."

The United States, mostly through its Central Intelligence Agency, had invested heavily in creating conditions that ultimately led to the overthrow of Chile's socialist leader, Salvador Allende, in 1973. Folksingers Arlo Guthrie and Phil Ochs subsequently played various commemorative concerts, most notably "An Evening with Salvador Allende" at New York's Madison Square Garden, to provide financial support for Chilean refugees and moral support for Chilean forces rebelling against the new U.S.-backed leader of Chile, General Augusto Pinochet.

Folksinger and songwriter Harry Chapin became impassioned about world hunger and used his musical talents to highlight the issue. In 1977, he along with John Denver, James Taylor, and Gordon Lightfoot gave a benefit concert in Detroit to help fight against world hunger. Likewise, Jackson Browne organized several benefit concerts joined by the likes of Linda Ronstadt, Bob Dylan, Stevie Wonder, Bette Midler, Jimmy Buffett, and others to champion the nuclear freeze movement. Browne became particularly vocal against American involvement in El Salvador and Nicaragua in the 1980s and "played concerts, donated money, wrote songs on his albums, and gave media interviews to combat Reagan's war against social change in Central America."[12]

Bob Geldof, the lead singer for the new wave Boomtown Rats, perfected the supergroup charity concept. He initially experienced the promise of these lavish entertainment projects to do good in the world with his participation in one of the early Secret Policeman's Balls sponsored by the human rights group Amnesty International. He built on this previous success to form Band Aid, a supergroup composed mostly of British and Irish musicians to aid in the relief of a famine in Ethiopia. They issued a best-selling single, "Do They Know It's Christmas." The superstar ensemble included members of famed rock groups such as Genesis, Spandau Ballet, Duran Duran, U2, Kool and the Gang, Bananarama, Culture Club, and Frankie Goes to Hollywood. Former Beatle Paul McCartney and avant-garde David Bowie even sent in contributions from afar. Geldof also participated in a similar American effort, USA for Africa, which released a benefit album and music video with the song "We Are the World." It featured most of the top musical acts of 1985, including Michael Jackson, Paul Simon, Lionel Richie, Kenny Rogers, Billy Joel, Diana Ross, Dionne Warwick, Willie Nelson, Kenny Loggins, Daryl Hall, John Oates, Bruce Springsteen, Al Jarreau, Huey Lewis, Cyndi Lauper, and Kim Carnes. Bob Geldof was uniquely situated to organize an even grander project.

A news report about the severe famine in Ethiopia inspired Geldof to gather together several of his music colleagues to launch a major benefit show that became known as Live Aid. The event was staged mostly at London's Wembley Stadium and Philadelphia's JFK Stadium, but also included performances in Moscow and Sydney. Satellite technology made the performances available in over 150 countries, and nearly 2 billion people watched or heard some portion of the event. It generated almost $50 million in proceeds for people starving in Africa. Hundreds of musicians from the most popular music acts in the world participated.[13]

Live Aid became the template for several successor projects addressing other domestic and international issues. For example, Steven van Zandt (most recently of *Sopranos* fame), who cut his musical teeth performing with Bruce Springsteen and the E Street Band, formed Artists United Against Apartheid, which released the well-renowned *Sun City* album to challenge the then still existing South African policy of apartheid, an entrenched system of racial segregation. A host of other imitations ensued, including Willie Nelson's Farm Aid and Geldof's own Sport Aid. Geldof returned to the form with Live 8 in 2005 in order to place public pressure on leaders attending the summit meeting of the G8 (a group of the eight leading industrialized economies: Canada, France, Germany, Italy, Japan, Russia, the United Kingdom, and the United States) to provide debt relief for impoverished nations in Africa. And of course, Live Earth, with its goal to champion against global warming, is the most recent incarnation of the global super-charity concert event. These events often come across as cheesy, preachy affairs, and they often do not represent the height of musical quality. However, to see these large groups of prima donna personalities temporarily shed their egos to share a stage in common cause still sends chills down the spines of most fans. As new international issues intensify, musical artists will surely respond with the tried and true strategy of charitable collaboration.

It's Not Easy Being Green

Live Earth was a seminal event in getting the American public's attention on global warming. Another notable effort was Al Gore's Academy Award–winning documentary *An Inconvenient Truth*. It is the only documentary to ever win an Oscar for Best Original Song. The film features Melissa Etheridge's "I Need to Wake Up." It was an extremely effective call to action, but it's only the latest in a number of musical efforts to champion environmental causes. One of the unofficial anthems for the United States is "America the Beautiful." The natural beauty of America's wilderness directly inspired Katharine Lee Bates to write the song's poetic verses, even though it would take a few generations for Americans to become environmentally conscious to any degree. In fact, before the 1960s, few songs explicitly advocated addressing environmental concerns.

Two successive events in particular marked the sudden birth of the modern environmental protection movement. The first was the 1962 publication of Rachel Carson's *Silent Spring*, which warned that indiscriminate use of the highly effective insecticide DDT was causing—as one of its side effects—the dangerous thinning of bird egg shells. She warned about the potential mass extinction of several bird species, the most symbolic of which was the national bird of the United States, the bald eagle. Domestically, the United States would pass wildlife protection laws and eventually ban the manufacture and use of DDT. The United States then led worldwide efforts to control the application of DDT except for limited disease control purposes under various international agreements.

The second signal event in the environmental movement was the release of the photograph known as "Earthrise," taken by the Apollo 8 mission as it came back around its orbit from the dark side of the moon in 1968. Suddenly, the Disney tune "It's a Small World After All" took on a whole new meaning. As seen from space, the earth is obviously a finite sphere. No distinct lines or differently colored geographical areas mark the borders between nation-states. The Gaia principle that the earth is really one complex and interrelated biological system began to gain prominence. Ecology became a universal concern.

Songs of green immediately appeared. First out was "Big Yellow Taxi," written by Joni Mitchell and first performed by the group Neighborhood. It reached the Top 40 in 1970 with its memorable lyric line, "They paved paradise and put up a parking lot." The song continues with "Hey farmer, farmer put away your DDT now. Give me spots on my apples but leave me the birds and the bees, please." The song is so appealing that numerous music groups over the past few decades have covered it, including Amy Grant and more recently Counting Crows. The granddaddy of all environmental songs is "Mercy Mercy Me (The Ecology Song)," written and performed by the legendary Marvin Gaye. The song's mesmerizing musical progression masks its disturbing images of poison wind, oil spills, mercury-tainted fish, and deadly radiation. Gaye asks, "What about this overcrowded land? How much more abuse from man can she stand?"

Another earth song is the hard rock offering by—of all groups—the Osmonds. The title track of their 1972 album *Crazy Horses* appears to speak against automobiles contributing to air pollution with its lyric line, "There they go, what a show, smokin' up the sky, yeah. Crazy horses all got riders, and they're you and I." The next year, John Denver initiated a long list of environmentally conscious songs with his most famous hit, "Rocky Mountain High." Although the song is known for showing some enthusiasm for a certain cannabis plant, its basic appeal is its wonderful imagery of the Colorado mountains and their surrounding wilderness. The inherent environmental message is capped with Denver's concern that developers will "tear the mountains down to bring in a couple more; more people, more scars upon the land." The sad irony is that no other single individual did more to publicize the attractiveness of Colorado. In effect, his own eloquence advanced the state's population growth and development to a great degree. It reveals a major paradox in environmentalism: to get people to care about wilderness areas, they have to experience them, and that experience necessarily involves some level of encroachment. Later, John Denver would sing "Calypso" in honor of Jacques Cousteau's famous research vessel studying ocean habitats.

One of the most effective environmental songs was the "Colors of the Wind," from Disney's *Pocohantas*. Vanessa Williams sang the version that made it to the pop charts in 1995. In the song, the naturalistic lifestyle of Native Americans is contrasted with the Western mind-set of exploiting natural resources. "You think you own whatever land you land on; the Earth is just a dead thing you can claim." Then the song asks, "How high will the sycamore grow? If you cut it down, then you'll never know."

Keep on Rockin' in the Free World

On the whole, musicians are a smart bunch—not that they always make smart choices. But it takes some brain capacity to write and perform appealing music. Street cred might sell albums, but there's no denying that mastering a musical instrument demands enormous discipline and focus. Even natural talent must be cultivated by hard work. What's more is that the very life of a popular musician demands travel around the world. They become aware of problems and issues of which their fans may not yet be aware. The music industry has certainly been an accommodating platform for political activism. Smart, civically engaged musicians are bound to use their natural soapbox to stand and espouse their views. Of course, many are tempted by opportunities for self-aggrandizement, and being politically conscious may just be the latest in-thing to do. Fortunately, others want to selflessly bring about real change for the betterment of the world. The archetype for the latter is Bono, the lead singer for the Irish rock group U2. He has demonstrated that he is extremely knowledgeable about the issues he advocates. His humanitarian work has earned him an honorary knighthood from British royalty, a Nobel Peace Prize nomination, and designation as Person of the Year by *Time* magazine. Even Laura Ingraham, the conservative radio host, praises Bono in her book *Shut Up and Sing,* a work sharply critical of most performers who dabble in politics. She writes, "There are a few entertainers out there who are liberal, and yet, unusually, have the credibility to back up their views. Bono . . . spent years learning about AIDS prevention and Third World debt relief. The merits of his views aside, at least he is intelligent and informed and has some firsthand experience with these matters." He works hard and he's good at what he does. When Bono discovered that getting a president's commitment to foreign policy change was not sufficient in the American system, he set out to lobby Congress. He explains, "I found myself inside the body politic, trying to figure out how it lived and breathed, how

Bono, the legendary front man of U2, has transcended traditional assumptions about rock stars and politics, as he has championed causes for peace, global debt and poverty, the environment, AIDS, and more, winning the respect of politicians, pundits, and even the Pope. (Photofest)

it behaved—a rock star wandering around the corridors of power rather than placarding at the gates outside." Bono has set the standard for future musical activists to emulate.[14]

Music is the proverbial universal language. It engages the human mind at a fundamental level. "In the 1950s, music theorist Leonard Meyer of the University of Pennsylvania proposed the now widely accepted notion that the enjoyment of music comes from a subtle interweaving of expectation and surprise. If there is too much surprise in a musical piece, a listener gets lost; if there is too little surprise, the listener becomes bored." In a political context, an interesting piece of music can focus attention on a message that a listener might otherwise choose not to hear. It is a gentle, but powerful way to expose listeners to ideas that challenge presuppositions. The political music analyzed here represents a rich genre, and there are limits to what can be covered in a single chapter. Hopefully, the songs highlighted here will spark further interest.[15]

Notes

1. All references to chart rankings are taken from Joel Whitburn, *The Billboard Top 40 Hits*, 8th ed. (New York: Billboard Books, 2004).

2. Tim Morse, *Classic Rock: The Stories behind the Greatest Songs of All Time* (New York: St. Martin's Press, 1998), 134.

3. Ibid., 90.

4. Ibid., 80.

5. Bill Crandall, "500 Greatest Songs of All Times," *Rolling Stone,* no. 963 (December 9, 2004): 65–163.

6. Vessela Misheva, "The Beatles, the Beatles Generation, and the End of the Cold War," *Public Voices* 9, no. 1 (2007): 15.

7. Ann Powers, "The Power of Music," *The Nation* (January 13, 2003): http://www.thenation.com/doc/20030113/powers (accessed March 4, 2008); Brent Staples, "The Trouble with Corporate Radio: The Day the Protest Music Died," *New York Times,* February 20, 2003, 30.

8. Neil Strauss, "The Pop Life: MTV Is Wary of Videos on War," *New York Times,* March 26, 2003, Sec. Arts/Cultural Desk, 1.

9. Neva Chonin, "Musicians Make Peace with the Net: Anti-War Songs Change Online Music Industry," *San Francisco Chronicle,* April 9, 2003, D1; Larry Katz, "Notes of Conflict: Internet Fuels Boom of Songs about U.S. Involvement in Iraq," *Boston Herald,* April 2, 2003, Sec. Arts and Lifestyle.

10. Betty Clarke, "Pop—The Dixie Chicks: Shepherd's Bush Empire, London," *The Guardian,* March 12, 2003.

11. Chris Willman, *Rednecks and Bluenecks: The Politics of Country Music* (New York: New Press, 2005), 28.

12. Darrell M. West and John Orman, *Celebrity Politics* (Upper Saddle River, N.J.: Prentice Hall, 2003), 71.

13. Esther B. Fein, "Reports of Concert Aid Range Up to $50 Million," *New York Times,* July 15, 1985, C18.

14. Laura Ingraham, *Shut Up and Sing: How Elites from Hollywood, Politics, and the Media are Subverting America* (Washington, D.C.: Regnery Publishing, 2003), 100–101; Michka Assaya, *Bono: In Conversation with Michka Assaya* (London: Penguin Books, 2005), 100.

15. William F. Allman, "The Musical Brain: Studies of Pitch and Melody Reveal the Inner Workings of the Mind, from Basic Perception to Appreciating Beauty," *U.S. News and World Report* 108, no. 23 (June 11, 1990): 56–62.

13

TWENTIETH-CENTURY AMERICAN FOLK MUSIC AND THE POPULARIZATION OF PROTEST

Three Chords and the Truth

Craig W. Hurst

In addition to entertainment and aesthetic edification and enlightenment, one of the many functions music serves is to unify people. Communally performed or experienced music provides people a sense of belonging, solidarity, and common ground with others. Music also may support common citizenship, membership in an organization or movement, or ownership and support of a belief or ideology. Examples would include the singing of "The Star Spangled Banner" at various public gatherings in the United States, the singing of a school alma mater at a graduation, homecoming, or reunion, or the singing of hymns in a church service. Music has also served as a means of aiding group cohesion by expressing an ideology or attempting to motivate action. Music can bring to light particular personal social conditions or the social condition of a person or groups of persons toward whom one feels empathy or compassion.

Examples of contemporary songs about the working classes or the dispossessed include U2's "Red Hill Mining Town," from their 1987 *Joshua Tree* CD, or Bruce Springsteen's 1995 song "The Ghost of Tom Joad." Springsteen also brought to light the plight of the American Vietnam veteran with his 1984 song "Born in the U.S.A." Other singer/songwriters have satirized the state of society in general while also making critical remarks about politics or leadership in the U.S. government. Neil Young's 1989 "Rockin' in the Free World" details the existence of child abandonment, drug addiction, and general social hopelessness in opposition to ideological statements made by then President of the United States George Herbert Walker Bush and the assumption of abundance for all in American life. Tracy Chapman's 1988 song "Fast Car" details a more personal view of ongoing generational poverty and dreams of escaping urban blight for a more desirable life. Suzanne Vega's 1987 song "Luka" describes the experience of physical abuse from the perspective of an abused child. This song has also been injected into American popular culture through a parody, "Suka," sung by Homer Simpson in the "Reality Bites" episode of the popular television cartoon *The Simpsons.*

Episodes of *The Simpsons* are, themselves, often a source of satire on American culture and have also exemplified through parody the traditional role folk music and music by singer/songwriters working in a folk style has had as an aid in promoting solidarity in social protest. In the episode "Last Exit to Springfield," while Homer Simpson and his coworkers at the Springfield nuclear power plant are walking a picket line on strike, Lisa Simpson sings "They have the plant, but we have the power," accompanying herself on acoustic guitar. Very direct political statements also may be found in music supporting recent American war efforts in Afghanistan and Iraq, such as Toby Keith's 2003 "The Taliban Song," or Darryl Worley's 2003 song "Have You Forgotten?" In opposition to support for the current military action by the United States in Afghanistan and Iraq is Steve Earle's "John Walker's Blues," written in 2003 as a sympathetic remembrance of the twenty-year-old American Taliban John Walker Lindh. Additionally, Neil Young's 2006 CD *Living with War* presents a very strong political statement about America's current foreign wars and negative commentary on segments of society who support the wars. Perhaps the strongest statements are those in regard to the executive leadership of the U.S. government and claims that President George W. Bush should be removed from office.

Regardless of the label (pop, rock, country, blues, jazz, etc.) applied to different types of music, songs of a topical or political nature have been part of the folk heritage of the United States and can be traced back to nineteenth-century labor songs, through the early twentieth-century songs of Joe Hill and the Industrial Workers of the World (IWW), and particularly with the rise of the American Communist Party and organized labor during the 1930s. The songs of the IWW (also known as the Wobblies) exemplify some of the earliest twentieth-century music promoting social change. The

Wobblies' songs would parody well-known hymn tunes with lyrics promoting the solidarity of their labor union. In the face of the challenges of the 1930s brought about by the Great Depression, some American intellectuals were drawn to social programs of the Communist and Socialist parties. Concomitantly, segments of politically radical groups discovered music that addressed issues of social change complimenting a utopian goal to sum up the quality of the land and the lives of its people. To bring to light authentic folk music was to reveal and "valorize" the "real American folk." Perhaps the poor working-class southern textile workers and coal miners were idealized as real American folk. These workers drew upon their Appalachian musical heritage to craft songs detailing the oppression of their social and working conditions and expressing a need to unify in a block of solidarity against those concerned more with the bottom line of profit rather than the welfare and well-being of people.[1]

Topical singer/songwriters have been an important source of American popular music. By the late 1930s, a community of professional folksingers had developed in New York City recognizing that there was an economically viable market for folk songs. While virtually all of the promoters of folk music and record companies recognized the economic value of folk songs, radicals such as Alan Lomax and Charles Seeger were also motivated toward social change via newly written folk-styled music based on traditional folk music.[2] One of the most influential singer/songwriters to come out of the folk tradition was Woody Guthrie, who influenced numerous others, Bob Dylan among them. Dylan began singing in a folk style when he emerged in the early 1960s, and he in turn would influence future singer/songwriters and perhaps influence the course of rock and roll, not only with his topical lyrics but also by becoming a rock musician himself in the mid-1960s. The seriousness of topical expression as exemplified in specific songs and CD releases discussed above is evidence of a continuation of the popularization of protest.

Despite definitions of authentic folk music, common practice and parlance have led to the definition of a folk song as any song written in the style of the folk songs of the past. That is, a song with accessible, straightforward lyrics and simple acoustic instrumental accompaniment delivering a simple and straightforward message. A folk song singer would therefore be one who draws upon the folk song repertoire of the past, but also could be a popular singer/songwriter whose original songs are in a folk song style.[3]

What Is Authentic Folk Music?

Not all music called folk music is by definition authentic folk music. Further, what is or is not folk music is at best ambiguous in that the term may have different meanings or shades of meaning, because there is no universal concept, as such. There is some common agreement on an emphasis on oral transmission as a key component of categorizing music as folk music; however, the International Folk Music Council does not seem able to clearly separate folk music issues from other musical and sociological issues. In regard to authentic folk music of the United States, in attempts to define folk music it is agreed that to flourish, folk music needs to exist in the context of a way of life that fosters community with stable conditions favorable to oral transmission. These are not conditions often found in highly industrialized, urbanized, and mobile America, and it may be there never has existed an authentic American or United States folk music.[4]

Typically, for music to be considered folk music, it must be music that has followed a long oral tradition within a given community. Typical traits of a folk song will be its antiquity, anonymity, simplicity, and variability in performance. These traits are perhaps what make the song accessible and durable, and it is this durability and accessibility that also may define folk songs as songs that have survived over time without the benefit of commercial media. Although various immigrant and native musical traditions have blended into an American musical culture, the music that came to be labeled folk music in the United Sates existed well before the term was popularized.[5]

The label authentic folk was not applied to American music because of distinctive musical style, performance practice, or origination, but rather because of a "cultural need" during the early part of the twentieth century. It was perhaps this cultural need that led folklorists to preserve American folk traditions. This preservation was to counter the possible demise of folk traditions in the face of increased urbanization and the growth of modern society in the United States. Other folk enthusiasts simply sought to bring folk music to the American middle class, and with the growing market for phonographs and records during the 1920s and 1930s, record companies sought out any material that might be salable. With the establishment of the Archive of Folk Song at the Library of Congress in 1928, the U.S. government also invested in folk song preservation.[6]

Music of Union and Solidarity before 1930

By the early twentieth century, in the United States and Europe, in addition to songs common to the international socialist movements such as "The Internationale" and "The Red Flag," various left-wing groups and political organizations all developed their own stock of revolutionary lyrics. The IWW (Wobblies) was important in the history of American protest music. Their ideology involved the creation of one single, big union to take on the labor bosses on behalf of both skilled and unskilled laborers in the context of an anarchist political orientation. The Wobblies were remembered for their effective use of propaganda music, crafting songs to fit hymn tunes played by Salvation Army brass bands that were sent by labor bosses to drown out IWW street corner meetings. The Wobblies wrote most of their own songs grounded firmly in real labor experiences, took great pride in their singing, and published their own songbook, *The IWW Songs,* better known as "The Little Red Songbook," in 1909.[7]

Some of the most famous of the IWW songwriters were Ralph Chaplin, Harry (Mac) McClintock, T-Bone Slim, and Joe Hill. "Solidarity Forever" (sung to the tune of "Johns Brown's Body"), written by Chaplin, is still the most popular union song written in this country. Like other IWW songwriters, Hill put his words to existing well-known popular tunes so they could be learned and used easily; however, other than his song "The Preacher and the Slave," few of Hill's songs are still well known. Joe Hill is probably the best remembered and best known of the IWW songwriters because he became idolized as a martyr after his execution by the state of Utah in 1915. Hill had been convicted of murder; however, the evidence was largely circumstantial, and part of the Joe Hill mythology is that his conviction and execution were influenced by Utah copper barons opposed to Hill and the IWW. Alfred Hayes and Earl Robinson's 1936 song "Joe Hill" has immortalized him, and the song has been recorded frequently by a number of artists, including Paul Robeson and Joan Baez.

Despite their contributions to protest music, it isn't likely Joe Hill or other of the IWW composers or other contemporaries in other socialist movements thought of themselves as folksingers or as creating folk songs as a propaganda medium or that folk music would serve as an aesthetic for the music culture of workers' movements. Likely, more of the music created by the IWW entered folklore than came from it, and the Wobblies created more folklore than any other labor group in American history. Additionally, Wobblies generated various opinions about the role of IWW songs as vehicles for social change.

Articles published in 1915 in *Solidarity,* the IWW newspaper, paralleled Wobblies' songs with broadsides sung by English minstrels to the common people. IWW songs exposed the pretensions and contradictions of capitalist society, expressed ideas of a new class, and presented new thoughts and ideals necessary to the beginning of a new society. Elizabeth Gurley Flynn, also writing in *Solidarity,* referred to Joe Hill's songs as songs that "crystallized the IWW's spirit into songs of the people—folk songs." Flynn's statement was well before the communist movement would gain momentum in the United States; however, she perhaps had caught a glimpse of the future position of the communist movement that would tie traditional folk songs and propaganda music composed mostly in folk style into one collective genre of "the true music of the working masses." Despite Joe Hill's legend and songs, the impact the Wobblies held would eventually diminish. Much of the decline of the IWW occurred because of their opposition to World War I and the rise of the communist movement in 1919, as many Wobblies became communists. After the demise of the Wobblies, music was temporarily disenfranchised as a tool for social change; however, by the time the American communist movement began to be established in the 1920s, the search, study, and preservation of indigenous folk traditions had begun to intensify. It is not surprising then that references to American folk traditions appeared more and more frequently in American communist literature.[8]

Leftist Politics and Folk Music in the 1920s and 1930s

The attraction of the Communist Party during the 1930s is perhaps understandable considering the conditions of society in the United States during the Depression. The farm depression in the mid-1920s, the stock market crash in 1929, and the resultant Great Depression that followed led to extraordinary unemployment levels. In 1932 when Franklin Roosevelt was elected president, the United States was on the verge of total economic disaster. In the Soviet Union, by contrast, there was optimism and a new vision toward total economic equality. This ideology was enormously appealing to intellectuals and artists in America. The economic and social future of the United States was very uncertain, and many joined the Communist Party.

The party encouraged the formation of the Workers Musicians Club, which included a Composers Collective, which was part of the Pierre

Degeyter Club (Degeyter was the composer of the anthem "The Internationale"). The Collective included many prestigious names associated with music, such as Aaron Copland, Henry Cowell, and Charles Louis Seeger. The goal of the Collective was to create new proletarian music that would expand the consciousness of the American working class by marrying politically radical song lyrics to modern compositional techniques. Initially this notion was attractive, but several factors led them to change their minds. The American communist movement's failure to find a unique but broadly based native proletarian music led to the discovery of folklore as people's culture. Since the mid-1920s, the party leadership had sought to Americanize the communist movement by focusing on organizing workers born in the United States. Mike Gold, a communist columnist writing in *New Masses* in 1931, called attention to the fact that there were no new workers' songs, and in a 1933 article Gold complained that American workers don't sing like the Wobblies did years before, and that perhaps what was needed was a communist Joe Hill.[9]

Additionally, there was an active singing tradition in the southern United States, where the Communist Party was involved during the 1920s organizing alternative radical unions in textile mills and coal mines. In 1929, the deplorable conditions in textile mills of long hours, low pay, and poor food led to a walkout that lasted for five months. Amid increasing hysteria, vigilante terrorism, and the jailing of union leaders, the communist press covered the strike very closely, including details on the lives of the textile workers in the area. From this activity several labor minstrels, such as Ella Mae Wiggins, emerged. Wiggins, an organizer for the National Textile Workers Union, addressed public gatherings, helped organize union activities, and composed new songs about the struggle. After her murder in 1929 while organizing textile workers, her song "Mill Mother's Lament" was sung at various rallies in New York supporting unions for southern textile workers. Mill worker Dave McCarn popularized protest and found an audience for his music among those seeking solidarity protesting against their working and living conditions, as he sold thousands of records in mill towns and his songs were actually sung by striking mill workers. Some mill workers, such as Homer "Pappy" Smith, a fiddler and singer, were commercially successful enough with the popularity of their music that they were able to leave the mills and work full time as musicians.[10]

As bad as conditions may have been in the textile mills, they were much worse in the coalfields of the eastern United States. With a decline in the price of coal during the 1920s made worse by the Depression, in the 1930s coal companies passed falling prices in coal on to employees, taking entire communities to the brink of starvation. Like the textile workers, coal miners had a long history of recounting their labors and meager existence in songs. It was in this context that communist organizers began penetrating the coalfields, and once radical organizers committed to agitation in the coalfields of Kentucky, West Virginia, Pennsylvania, and Ohio, it was only a matter of time before they stumbled on the hard-bitten folk poetry of the mining communities and enlisted it in the communist cause.[11]

The coal strikes of the early 1930s received extensive coverage in the radical press, particularly the Kentucky conflicts of 1931. A committee of northern writers led by novelist Theodore Dreiser visited Harlan, Kentucky, to investigate and publicize local mining conditions. A coal miner's wife, Aunt Molly Jackson, also an organizer for the communist-led National Miners Union and a singer/songwriter, was one of those interviewed by the committee. As Jackson answered questions from the committee on infant mortality and malnutrition she had seen in her role as a midwife, she dramatized the desperate conditions of the coal camps by singing one of her own songs, "Ragged Hungry Blues." Like many of the IWW songwriters, Jackson set her lyrics to existing melodies. Instead of using well-known hymns, however, like the Wobblies did, her melodies were southern mountain tunes. As a result of her interview and singing she received considerable mention in the radical press and, along with her stepbrother Jim Garland, accompanied the Dreiser Committee north. Steeped in the traditions of their Appalachian heritage, Jackson and her stepbrother combined the terse language of the folk with the class-conscious slogans of northern organizers, resulting in a body of powerful statements on the struggle of the common laborer. Jackson and Garland spent December 1931 singing and speaking to groups of left-wing intellectuals and workers, and they collected money and goods to send the coal families in need of relief. Her performance of her "Ragged Hungry Blues" for the Composers Collective influenced Charles Seeger to envision a new radical music movement built around traditional American folk music, rather than classical art songs.[12]

Left-Wing Intellectuals and Folk Music

Charles Louis Seeger, a respected musicologist, brought a highly esteemed academic perspective to the role folk music could have in spreading the winds of change in American society. Seeger enjoyed the kind of privileged childhood that would seem to make him an unlikely member in the left-wing movements of his day. After completing his education at Harvard University and studies in Germany for three years, at age twenty-four Seeger accepted a full professorship in music at the University of California at Berkeley (he was the youngest full professor in the history of the institution) and was head of the music department from 1912 to 1919. While at Berkeley, Seeger's outlook on society changed through his exposure to socialists and reformers, including the Wobblies. He attended IWW meetings and, although he never formally joined them, treasured their literature and songs. Meanwhile, because of pacifist statements he had been making since the United States' entry into World War I, Seeger was fired from his professorship at Berkeley.[13]

Seeger later taught at the Institute of Musical Art in New York and lectured at the New School for Social Research. In 1932 he was introduced to hillbilly music through the Missouri muralist Thomas Hart Benton. Benton would also introduce Charles's son Pete Seeger (the legendary folk song singer) to the five-string banjo. From 1935 to 1941, Charles Seeger served as musical technical adviser in Roosevelt's Resettlement Administration and deputy director of the Federal Music Project of the Works Progress Administration. Through these federal cultural programs Seeger became friendly with Alan Lomax, and the two of them created a vision of using folk songs as a tool for radical change. Seeger's thinking, the variety of his work, and his concerns for balance between individual and society made a significant impact on American attitudes toward music and its place in society. Along with Alan Lomax, Charles Seeger became the most powerful influence in the development of protest music and the folk music revival that would follow.[14]

Alan Lomax also attended Harvard University, where his awareness of left-wing issues increased. However, his growing level of activism led to political difficulties with the university's administration. These difficulties, coupled with poor grades, prompted Lomax to leave Harvard. He joined his father (folklorist John Lomax) on folk song collecting expeditions, and while recording and describing folk songs, Lomax's political awareness sensitized him to the manner in which the lower classes voiced their complaints through folk songs. Perhaps this led to his ideas regarding the place of folk song in society and that the folk songs might prove useful in helping to stimulate sociopolitical change in urban centers. Lomax became an advocate for folk music. Using various forms of print and broadcast media, he helped promote and elevate the genre.[15]

Between 1936 and 1941, folk songs in particular enjoyed increasing popularity in left-wing circles. One of the inherent problems in bringing folk music to urban centers to liberate the working classes, however, was that most urban factory workers and union members were consumers of popular music and generally had no background in American folk music. Alan Lomax, sensitive to this situation, realized that singers like Aunt Molly Jackson might be too raw for the average American and instead saw that singers like Woody Guthrie epitomized his vision of the radical songwriter. Also, others such as Pete Seeger, Josh White, and Burl Ives were musicians with a smoother and polished sound that would have greater appeal to the average American. Lomax helped to advance the careers of these and other folk musicians he felt were worthy and talented. He mentored a number of folk song singers, helped them get recording contracts and appearances on radio shows and in nightclubs, and wrote about them in books, magazines, and album liner notes. These performers loosely coalesced into what may be termed the Alan Lomax School of musicians. By the early 1940s these performers would leave an indelible and far-reaching influence on the American musical scene. Whether they came from rural or urban roots, they were guided by Lomax's political spirit and educated in his ideological world view. With his political savvy, strategic positions at the Library of Congress and Office of War Information, and enthusiasm for spreading the gospel of folk songs as the true music of the people, Lomax put himself at the center of the evolving radical approach to folk song style and content. More than any other scholar or performer of the 1930s, Alan Lomax shaped the popular outlook on folk songs that influenced an entire generation of urban folksingers.[16]

The Lomax Singers and Commercial Protest Music

For many years, anyone wanting a recording contract or access to the key marketplace for network radio shows would have to go to New York City. Desiring such, Woody Guthrie, Huddie ("Leadbelly") Ledbetter, Josh White, Pete Seeger, Lee Hays, and many other folk song singers came to Manhattan. In 1941, Millard Lampell, Pete Seeger, and Lee Hays began singing together and soon were joined by Woody Guthrie, Bess Lomax (Alan's sister), Gordon Freisen, and Sis Cunningham. They all moved in together and, along with a number of other singers associated with the group, formed the Almanac Singers. Functioning like an early hippie commune, all the house members shared expenses and communally wrote songs. The Almanacs sang for many radical causes, including the American Communist Party's position against the involvement of the United States in support of Britain and France in World War II. In April of 1941, the Almanacs recorded the album *The Death of John Doe,* which contained six anti-war songs that strongly attacked President Roosevelt. Following Japan's attack on Pearl Harbor the Almanacs' anti-war stance changed considerably. Also, when Germany invaded the Soviet Union on June 22, 1941, violating the Soviet-Axis pact, *The Death of John Doe* was withdrawn from circulation. The first few months of the United States' involvement in World War II were the most successful for the Almanac Singers, especially in terms of media exposure. New venues opened up for the Almanacs, and they began performing for numerous war effort causes, agencies, and programs with more mainstream sponsorship. With greater exposure, the William Morris Agency expressed interest in representing the group and Decca Records offered a recording contract. By early 1942 the Almanac Singers were on the verge of success, if not stardom, in the ordinary capitalist music scene.[17]

This new fame pushed the Almanacs to resolve the apparent contradiction between the capitalist star system and their sociopolitical ideologies. On one hand, the group damned the show business idiom and establishment media, but at the same time they flirted with suggestions of big-time bookings, large fees, and promises to air the Almanacs' songs nationwide. It would all become moot, however, for during the first half of 1942 anticommunist newspaper coverage in the New York press began attacking the group for having sung in support of communist causes before their appearances on various radio programs in support of America's war effort. The William Morris Agency and Decca Records dropped their contract negotiations, essentially ending an eighteen-month roller coaster ride of creativity, friction, and stable financial status in a state of idealistic progressive ideology and social change prompted during the years of World War II.[18]

Among the most famous of the Almanacs was Woody Guthrie, whose long-term appeal has been described as the genius of simplicity. As "America's balladeer," he lifted the lowly spirits of millions of dispossessed people. Guthrie's songs reflected Alan Lomax's beliefs in working people expressing themselves through folk culture and that early folk music provided an embodiment of authenticity of musical genre. Lomax also saw the authentic folk ethos embodied in Woody Guthrie. His appeal may also have been due to his deliberately making himself less sophisticated than he was and forming a persona shaped to meet the fantasies of the Communist Left to be a voice of the people, intelligent without being formally educated, droll but perceptive.[19]

In the lineage of contemporary folk music, there is first and foremost the overwhelming presence of Woody Guthrie. He is a progenitor to everyone who has held an acoustic guitar. Pete Seeger started his career by touring with Guthrie, and Bob Dylan has acknowledged early and often that Guthrie was the better and more important songwriter. Woody Guthrie established the template for what an authentic folk performer has to be. He met the folk and understood their lives, singing not only at concerts but also on the picket line and in the street. Likewise, Guthrie established the precedent of activism that now seems self-evident in folk music, crafting lyrics with sharp anti-government, pro-union, and pro-communist lyrics, all foregrounded with his humanist, radical politics.[20]

The Almanac Singers were not the first group to sing protest songs, but they certainly were important in aligning music and politics. In 1946, Pete Seeger spearheaded a meeting that led to the formation of two organizations. People's Songs was an organization designed to encourage the writing and transmission of radical protest songs, and People's Artists was essentially a booking agency that sought to find jobs for radical performing musicians. The organization published a bulletin and put together a songbook consisting of protest songs called *The People's Songbook*. Despite the organization and tremendous enthusiasm at the beginning, and Pete Seeger as the national director, the organizations were headed toward failure. Political changes in the United States contributed to views of any left-wing sentiment as being identified with communism and disloyalty. This along with internal disagreements led to the demise of both organizations by 1949.[21]

In 1948, Pete Seeger, Lee Hays, Ronnie Gilbert, and Fred Hellerman formed the singing group the Weavers. All had radical folksinging backgrounds. Initially the group sang at People's Songs hootenannies and for radical causes. Hays and Seeger began to collaborate on songs, and their "If I Had a Hammer" became one of the best-known American political folk songs. "Kisses Sweeter than Wine," another eventual hit for the group, was also written by Hays and Seeger. After People's Songs failed, the four turned professional with their first playing gig at New York's Village Vanguard in Greenwich Village. Their Vanguard engagement lasted six months and they were signed to Decca Records in 1950. Decca sold over 4 million Weavers records and they became the first hit pop-folk group. Now that popular success was in their grasp, the Weavers agreed to avoid left-wing associations in order to keep their high commercial profile going for as long as possible. Given the past history of members of the Weavers, it is not surprising that they would run into trouble with people seeking to root out communists in the arts. Eventually Seeger and Hayes were called to testify before the House Un-American Activities Committee. Decca Records would terminate the Weavers' record contract, they were denied television work, and a number of their live appearances were cancelled. The Weavers reunited in 1955 for a concert at Carnegie Hall, but by then new artists were appearing in the pop-folk genre as successful recording artists.[22]

Folk Music as Popular Music and Popularization of Protest

By the 1950s, the music that drew from a long tradition of simple, straight-forward songs about real life, hard times, and personal and public struggles, often with simple acoustic accompaniment, had certainly entered the popular cultural mainstream. Between 1958 and 1965, among number one hits were "Tom Dooley," "Michael Row the Boat Ashore," "The Lion Sleeps Tonight," "Walk Right In," "The House of the Rising Sun," and "Turn, Turn, Turn," a musical setting by Pete Seeger of a biblical text.[23]

In the early 1960s, the times were changing and a commercial market for folk music was flourishing. When Bob Dylan recorded for Columbia Records, he was surprised himself that one of the foremost record labels in the country would see commercial appeal in a music that was largely considered by the record industry as junky and second rate. John Hammond, a talent scout for Columbia, explained that he saw Bob Dylan as someone in the long line of traditions. Dylan very well may have recognized his legacy of popularizing protest, as he divulges his debt to the past: "I didn't compose a song for Joe Hill. I thought about how to do it, but didn't do it. The first song I'd wind up writing of any substantial importance was written for Woody Guthrie."[24]

Prior to the 1960s, topical songs had typically been linked to the labor movement. By the 1960s, however, the inspiration for organizing songs was the civil rights movement. "We Shall Overcome" was introduced in 1960 by Guy Carawan, a music director of the Highlander Folk School in Tennessee, and the song became the anthem of the movement. Soon other songs flourished within the civil rights movement, bringing solidarity and strength to members. The Student Non-Violent Coordinating Committee (SNCC),

Music has long been a vehicle for political statement and public action. As singer/songwriter Bob Dylan once noted, "We live in a political world." (Photofest)

formed in 1960, the Congress of Racial Equality (CORE), and Martin Luther King's Southern Christian Leadership Conference (SCLC) all used songs. The fervor for civil rights led directly into university campuses with the founding of organizations such as Students for a Democratic Society in 1960 and the University of California Berkeley Free Speech movement in 1964. Folk music would also remain a fixture of campus organizing, and in the face of escalating fighting in Southeast Asia, folk music served as a rallying cry for the mounting peace movement and a focus for the enlarging crowds at anti-war rallies.[25]

The 1960s were a roller coaster ride for folk music, with its popularity peaking in 1964. The sounds of folk music, however, would last well into the future, with singer/songwriters led by Bob Dylan, who was the most successful in carrying the folk tradition that dated from Woody Guthrie. By the late 1980s, the subtleties and simplicity that was prime in protest music emerged in songs about domestic violence and economic hardship. During the mid-1980s a swell of singer/songwriters emerged from coffeehouses to national attention and commercial success, cresting in 1996 with the singer Jewel's break to superstardom. The 1990s also saw the success of the 1997 Lilith Fair tour of women singer/songwriters launched by Sarah McLachlan, and there was also a surprising commercial market for traditional folk music evidenced by the enormous sales and numerous Grammy Awards garnered by the reissue of the *Anthology of American Folk Music* in 1997. By the end of the twentieth century, folk music had taken on various identifications and aspects. Protest songs would remain part of folk music, but only as part of a much larger popular/commercial musical scene. Folk music has never been easy to define, but it has always existed and always will in some form or fashion.[26]

Notes

1. Ronald D. Cohen, *Folk Music: The Basics* (New York: Routledge, 2006), 148; Ronald D. Cohen, *Anthology of American Folk Music* (Washington, D.C.: Smithsonian Folkways/Sony Music Special Products, 1997), 23; Dick Weissman, *Which Side Are You On? An Inside History of the Folk Music Revival in America* (New York: Continuum, 2006), 10; Ian Peddie, ed., *The Resisting Muse: Popular Music and Social Protest* (Burlington, Vt.: Ashgate, 2006), 31.

2. Weissman, *Which Side Are You On?* 10, 13.

3. Cohen, *Anthology of American Folk Music*, 5

4. Stanley Sadie, ed., *The New Grove Dictionary of Music and Musicians* (Washington, D.C.: Grove's Dictionaries of Music, 1980), 6:692–93, 19:436.

5. Weissman, *Which Side Are You On?* 17; Cohen, *Anthology of American Folk Music,* 5; Sadie, *New Grove Dictionary of Music and Musicians,* 19:436.

6. Peddie, *The Resisting Muse,* 30–31; Weissman, *Which Side Are You On?* 9–10.

7. Richard A. Reuss, *American Folk Music and Left-Wing Politics, 1927–1957* (Lanham, Md.: Scarecrow Press, 2000), 26; Weissman, *Which Side Are You On?* 38–39.

8. Reuss, *American Folk Music and Left-Wing Politics, 1927–1957,* 27; Weissman, *Which Side Are You On?* 39.

9. Weissman, *Which Side Are You On?* 39–40; Reuss, *American Folk Music and Left-Wing Politics, 1927–1957,* 27, 32–35.

10. Weissman, *Which Side Are You On?* 40–41; Reuss, *American Folk Music and Left-Wing Politics, 1927–1957,* 40, 42.

11. Cohen, *Anthology of American Folk Music,* 23.

12. Weissman, *Which Side Are You On?* 41–42; Reuss, *American Folk Music and Left-Wing Politics, 1927–1957,* 27, 84–85.

13. Reuss, *American Folk Music and Left-Wing Politics, 1927–1957,* 27, 87–88

14. Ibid., 27, 89–90; Weissman, *Which Side Are You On?* 43–44; Cohen, *Anthology of American Folk Music,* 24.

15. Weissman, *Which Side Are You On?* 43–44; Reuss, *American Folk Music and Left-Wing Politics, 1927–1957,* 27, 49–50.

16. Sadie, ed., *New Grove Dictionary of Music and Musicians,* 17:101; Reuss, *American Folk Music and Left-Wing Politics, 1927–1957,* 27, 122–23.

17. Sadie, ed., *New Grove Dictionary of Music and Musicians,* 11:139; Weissman, *Which Side Are You On?* 44–45.

18. Reuss, *American Folk Music and Left-Wing Politics, 1927–1957,* 116–17, 122.

19. Ed Cray, *Ramblin' Man: The Life and Times of Woody Guthrie* (New York: Norton, 2004), 169–71; Studs Terkel, "Forward," in Cray, *Ramblin' Man,* xvii; Peddie, *The Resisting Muse,* 32; Weissman, *Which Side Are You On?* 45–47; Reuss, *American Folk Music and Left-Wing Politics, 1927–1957,* 164–65.

20. Peddie, *The Resisting Muse,* 32–34; Reuss, *American Folk Music and Left-Wing Politics, 1927–1957,* 164, 166, 173, 176; Weissman, *Which Side Are You On?* 48.

21. Weissman, *Which Side Are You On?* 57–58.

22. Ibid., 65–67, 69–70.

23. Cohen, *Anthology of American Folk Music,* 3.

24. Bob Dylan, *Chronicles, Volume One* (New York: Simon and Schuster, 2004), 5, 54.

25. Cohen, *Folk Music: The Basics,* 151–53.

26. Ibid., 166, 176–77, 181, 185–87.

14

REEVALUATING DEMOCRACY IN AMERICA

Profound Disappointment, Profound Hope

Margaret Hankenson

Alexander Payne is considered by many critics to be a defining force in contemporary American film, due in large part to his ability to "def[y] Hollywood by making character-driven films that are sharply observed satires on modern America." As a director and screenwriter, Payne has created four feature-length films, exploring a broad range of topics, from the bitingly satirical look at the absurdly comical and hypocritical battles between pro-life/pro-choice activists to save the once-again pregnant fume-head Ruth Stoops in *Citizen Ruth* (1996) to the hilarious and poignant examination of friendship, love, and wine in the Oscar-nominated *Sideways* (2004). What sets Payne's films apart is his ability to create movies that are clearly successful comedies but that deftly explore subject matter with empathy and insight that one is more likely to find in a film that falls more firmly in the category of drama.[1]

There is little argument regarding the successful use of humor in Payne's films. Take, for example, the use of the letters Warren Schmidt (Jack Nicholson) writes to his Child Reach Tanzanian "foster" child, Ndugu, in *About Schmidt,* or the butt-naked pursuit of Miles (Paul Giamatti) following his retrieval of Jack's (Thomas Hayden Church) wallet that was lifted during the previous night's one-night stand in *Sideways.* These are hilarious scenes that would not be out of place in any of the more conventional Hollywood comedies. What sets Payne's films apart is the way these comedic moments are used with great success to shed light on the more fragile, substantiate, and human aspects of the characters that grace Payne's films. It is through the bizarrely incongruous letters that Warren Schmidt writes that we realize just how incomplete and meaningless he finds his life to be. Likewise, it is via the slapstick adventures (the downing of the wine tasting slop; the brick-powered crashing of Miles's car into a tree) in California wine country that frames Miles's profound disappointments regarding his almost-failed attempts to live a more meaningful live. The impact that Payne's use of comedy has on his films is well captured by *Newsweek* film critic David Ansen. States Ansen: "Alexander Payne has the uncanny ability to wed hilarity, humiliation and heartbreak. But its laughs—and there are many—arise from loss and pain, and you may leave in tears."[2]

Part of what drives the heartbreak that anchors many of Alexander Payne's films is the disappointments that many of the characters experience when they recognize that the reality of their lives fails to live up to their idealized expectation. Alexander Payne's *Election* (1999) provides a double meditation on the disappointments that come from reality failing to live up to ideal. *Election* is a delightful political and social satire that focuses on the campaign for president of the Student Government Association at the ironically named George Washington Carver High, an all-white high school set in the heart of Middle America: Omaha, Nebraska. Alexander Payne was born and raised in Omaha, and as is illustrated by many of his films (three of four are set in Omaha), his representation of the aesthetics, values, and ironies of Middle America are spot-on. This is due in large part to the choices he makes regarding location and casting. The homes of many of the characters that inhabit Payne's films are the homes of real-world residents of the Greater Omaha region. Many of the smaller roles (students and teachers of the fictional Carver High) are cast using actual students and teachers from the Omaha area. (Chris Klein, the actor who plays Paul Metzler in *Election*, was an Omaha high school student at the time of the filming. He auditioned for Payne and got the role.)

However, Payne's ability to capture the texture of Middle America goes beyond set and casting choices. It isn't just that Payne uses "real" people and locations, but it is how he uses these features that really sets the tone of his films. There is a certain level of irony that underpins much of Payne's work, and it is an irony that makes up much of life in America, whether it is recognized or not. As a filmmaker, Payne does an uncanny job of leading viewers to recognize these very real incongruities, whether it be the all-white George Washington Carver High, or the idealized statements of just how wonderful and meaningful the home and work life are of beloved civic teacher Jim McAllister (Matthew Broderick), observations that are contradicted by the banal and pathetic real moments of his life (a silent dinner with his wife of chicken potpie, water, and salad topped with Light Ranch dressing; masturbating in the basement to a hidden stash of porn; having sex with his neighbor on the floor of her living room after clearing her bathroom tub drain of a grotesque clot of her dark brown hair). What makes Payne's films particularly funny but equally heartbreaking is the clash between what many of his characters think and say about the lives they are leading (an insight the audience has full access to due to Payne's clever use of voice-overs, telephone monologues, and letter writing) and the lives that they actually do lead. This is evidenced by the choices and actions the characters make.

The themes developed in *Election* provide insight into the broader themes that are developed in many of Alexander Payne's movies. Taken as a whole, Payne's movies are a meditation on the recognition (to varying degrees) of the failure to live a more ideal, heroic, meaningful, honest life. The characters that inhabit Payne's films come to us at different points on the continuum of recognition of these failures. Some characters, like Jim McAllister, never come close to recognizing the contrast between the ideal and realities of his life. Others, Miles and Warren Schmidt in particular, are more fully aware of their failings. However, despite their failings as well as their inability to recognize these failures, none of these characters are completely pathetic (although McAllister comes closest), and in many ways they offer glimpses of more hopeful versions of themselves and their lives yet to be lived—particularly at the end of the films with Schmidt and Miles (Schmidt's ability to touch someone else's life in a meaningful way and Miles's ability to love both himself and others).

However, as mentioned above, the movie *Election* provides not a single, but a double meditation on the clash between the ideals and realities. *Election* explores the clash between ideals and realities on a personal level and also serves as a microcosm of the clash between the ideals and the realities of the democratic process. On one level the movie is about a meaningless high school election gone awry. But what makes the movie particularly intriguing, and also of importance to the study of democratic governance, is its ability to shed light on the ironies present in advanced democracies such as the United States. The principles of the founding, and those that are still professed in popular rhetoric and political circles, are certainly high and honorable, and yet America lacks a deeply democratic culture. There are low rates of participation, leading to a distortion of what constitutes representative government. Incidents of voter fraud, voter suppression, and negative campaigning call into question just how committed political parties are to popular sovereignty. The general decline in civic participation makes one wonder whether Alexis de Tocqueville downplayed his concerns regarding the threat radical individualism may play in American political culture. Democracy in the United States definitely does, as Agnes Repplier observes, "forever [tease] us with the contrast between its ideals and its realities, between its heroic possibilities and its sorry achievements." Alexander Payne's movie *Election* offers an excellent lens through which to see these contrasts within democracy.[3]

Procedural and Substantial Democracy

When asking how free a country is, one variable that is examined is political participation and the development of democratic processes, as generally embodied by campaigns and elections. Freedom House, a nongovernmental independent organization, is dedicated to spreading democratic institutions throughout the world and, in turn, steadfastly opposes dictatorship both on the left and right of the political spectrum. Key to the promotion of freedom is coming up with criteria for assessing just how free a country is.

Looking at their mission statement, one finds a clear articulation of what constitutes freedom. According to Freedom House, "freedom is possible only in democratic political systems in which the governments are accountable to their own people; the rule of law prevails; and freedoms of expression, association, belief and respect for the rights of minorities and women are guaranteed." One could consider this mission statement to be an expression of the ideal principles of a free and democratic state, ideals that societies concerned with creating a free and democratic government strive to realize.[4]

While there are many different variables that one could and does examine when assessing the level of freedom and presence of democracy within a country, it would be difficult to claim that a country is free without a close examination of the campaigns, elections, and political participation (in all its many forms), as it is these elements that really make up the bedrock of a democratic political system. Likewise, it doesn't seem like it would be that difficult of a task to assess whether or not campaigns, elections, and political participation result in a realization of the ideals outlined in the mission statement. For example, it seems pretty clear whether or not a government is accountable to its people when it comes to the result of an election. If, after the election (which is a fairly straightforward expression of the will of the people), the government is not reorganized, incorporating the newly elected into the different governmental institutions (i.e., if the results of the election are ignored or, more likely, tampered with), one can safely assume the country is not free or democratic—the ideal has not been realized.

Likewise, if citizens, by law, are forbidden to form and join all or any political parties, or are broadly censored when it comes to certain types of political speech, it is easy to conclude that the country is neither free nor democratic. Good examples of a clear contrast between the ideals of democracy and the reality can be found in Iran, where only certain political parties are allowed to form (those of certain religious affiliations are forbidden), and in the one-party system of the People's Republic of China. The failure of the real to live up to the ideal is initially clear only because the country does not embrace the principles of freedom as outlined by Freedom House (although this may not be entirely the case with countries like Cuba, China, or maybe even Iran—it is more a question of interpretation of these ideals). Likewise, there are clear violations of democratic process—fraud, intimidation, and extortion are rampant, as ballots are not counted and voters are threatened with violence. In other words, when there is neither the substance of democracy nor the process of democracy, it is easy to conclude that democratic ideals have not been realized.

But what about countries wherein the ideal regarding the process of democracy is for the most part realized, yet the ideals regarding the substance of democracy have not been met? When attempting to answer the question: "Is this country's government accountable to its people?" we tend to answer by examining the process of democracy—whether elections are free of fraud and whether all voices are included in calls for accountability (i.e., universal suffrage). When attempting to answer the question: "Is the electorate free to express and associate?" we frame this question with our understanding of liberty in the negative—that is, "freedom from" government restrictions on speech and association, rather than in a more positive understanding of freedom, that being that society or government creates the conditions that enable, encourage, and support free and democratic action. This is a concern well articulated by Robert Dahl. States Dahl: "In the actual world . . . 'democracies' are never fully democratic: they invariably fall short of democratic criteria in some respects. Yet our judgment about feasible alternatives depends in part on how well the democratic process functions in practice."[5]

When thinking about adherence to the process of democracy or procedural democracy, the United States, for the most part, ranks high. That is not to say that there have not been legitimate and important concerns regarding procedural democracy in the contemporary political context. The concerns following the last two presidential elections regarding ballots, voting machines, voter fraud, and voter suppression clearly illustrate that problems regarding the procedure of democracy still persist. However, while these problems do persist (and given the size of the electorate, the history of federalism, and the implications that these have for elections, these problems will always exist to a certain degree in the United States), it is fair to assert that the problems with campaigns and elections in the United States as they relate to democracy are not in large part concerns regarding procedure, but rather, and more importantly, concerns regarding substance.

Take, for example, voting rights. Legally and constitutionally, all citizens eighteen years old or older have the right to vote. States and the national government, per constitutional amendment and federal legislation, are forbidden to discriminate against a voter based on age, race, ethnicity, disability, or sex. When it comes to assuring universal suffrage and keeping a check on discrimination, there have been movements in the United States to lower the voting age to sixteen as well as to reform felon disenfranchisement laws. So, when looking at voting rights from the perspective of law and process, the United States is highly democratic—all adults can participate in elections and the process sets the stage for an ideal to be realized—widespread political participation.

But what is the *substance* of democratic participation? In other words, who actually participates in the process? Anyone can participate—but who actually *does* participate? As is well known, the substance of democratic participation falls far short of the ideals allowed by the process. "High" voter turnout in national elections in the United States nowadays is defined as less than two-thirds of the eligible pool of voters. Voter turnout is even lower for state and local elections, often falling below 20 percent of those eligible to vote.[6] Percentage of voter turnout is only one aspect that indicates a lack of democratic substance found in electoral participation. Looking at electoral participation according to socioeconomic indicators, some groups participate at a much higher rate than others. The poorer, younger, and darker-skinned a citizen is, the much less likely that person is to vote, let alone participate in politics more generally. Consider that an average of only 47.2 percent of eligible voters in the United States have turned out to vote in national elections from 1945–2003.[7] Of this group, the vast majority was older, wealthier, and whiter than the population taken as a whole.[8] Breaking this down even further, a person was elected to serve as president of the United States with the active support of less than 25 percent of the total electorate in 2000, and just a little more in 2004. While it is indeed true that the process in place in the United States is highly democratic, it is hard to conclude, at least in the matter of electoral participation, that what results from this process is the same.

Seeing the Contradictions of Democracy through the Lens of *Election*

The movie *Election* provides a good illustration of the tensions between procedural and substantial democracy. When we are first introduced to Tracy Flick (Reese Witherspoon) it is in the context of the procedures of democracy. She is at school nearly at the crack of dawn ("You know what they say, the early bird gets the worm") snapping the legs of the card table that holds her nomination papers into place with a vigor and determination not usually found in the average teenager. As noted by Jim McAllister, Tracy Flick's drive was "so astonishing it was scary." Several legal pads line the table, way more than is needed to hold the requisite number of signatures, each holding a ballpoint pen precisely attached with string and tape, and identically numbered in order to tally up the needed signatures in the most orderly and efficient manner. It is the orderly process necessary for any functioning democracy.[9]

It is when we next see these nomination papers that we begin to get some insight regarding the tensions between the process and substance of democracy. The scene starts with a close up on Tracy Flick's face—shouting out to "Mr. M." (as the kids call him for short) with an intensity normally reserved for an emergency. Running across the parking lot with the same level of intensity, nomination papers in hand, neatly bound in a plastic binder, she stops Jim McAllister just as he is pulling his Ford Fiesta out of the parking lot. The urgency? Ms. Flick wants Mr. M. to approve her nomination signatures. Mr. M. tells Tracy to put them in his box and he'll look at

Tracy Flick (Reese Witherspoon) eagerly anticipates gathering enough student signatures to place her on the ballot for student body president in the film *Election,* a dark comedy that exposes the promises and failures of American democracy. (Photofest)

them tomorrow, but Tracy insists. She wants him to approve them now, so she can start work on her campaign immediately. He quickly flips through them, says they look okay, and hands them back. Tracy is confused. Isn't he supposed to keep them, filing them away in order to ensure that the process has been followed correctly, in case any questions arise about the democratic nature of the upcoming campaign? Jim does hold on to the papers, but only to appease Tracy. In the next scene we see him throwing these papers out, alongside the fast food wrappers and other debris that has collected in the floor of his car.

In a way this is a minor scene, but it gives us some insight into both Tracy's and Mr. M.'s takes on democracy. For Tracy, it is as if the procedure serves as a cover for her true intentions. For all of her insistence regarding the demands for following the proper procedures of democracy, Tracy is really not all that enamored with the truer principles of democracy. To begin, Tracy sees herself as tapped by destiny to win the election. Sure, she gives lip service to the importance of the will of the voter and hard work, but when confronted with the real workings of democracy (two challengers, both of whom are potentially formidable) she bristles. When she spots Paul Metzler with his nomination papers in the cafeteria, the sighting is accompanied with a war cry—after all, how else to respond to what she sees as a threat to her rightful ascendancy to the throne of power. When she does confront Paul about his nomination efforts, her first question is: "Who put you up to this?!" Despite all her concerns regarding nomination papers and proper procedure, when it comes down to it, Ms. Flick is really not all that concerned with the substance of democracy—that is, whether the process of democracy somehow ensures a more democratic substance. She is the rightful heir of the presidency. Where does Paul get off challenging that? The procedure is in place in order to give all the trappings of a democracy. But in reality, Tracy is little concerned about democratic governance. After all, some are destined to rule. And, as Tracy points out in the opening scene of the movie, if you interfere with destiny, you will suffer.

The truth is, however, that someone *did* put Paul up to running against Tracy Flick, and she knows it. Paul's entry into the race was not a result of some desire swelling up in a member of the student body to actually make the election more democratic, not just in process but in substance. Far from it. In fact, when Paul is tapped to run against Tracy by Jim McAllister, Paul's immediate and initial response is: "Who, me? Nooo. I never. . . . I don't know anything about that stuff, Mr. M. Besides, that's Tracy Flick's thing. She's always working so hard and. . . ."

Paul's initial response is not discomfort due to the lack of competition in the election. This has not even crossed his mind. In fact, Paul is quite comfortable with the lack of competition, as is the rest of the student body. If Mr. M. had not tapped Paul to run against Tracy, it looks like all elections for the different positions in the student government association would have been noncompetitive races. The presidency is the only challenged seat, and this is due in large part to variables having nothing to do with concerns regarding competition. This is clearly the case when it comes to Paul's sister, Tammy Metzler (Jessica Campbell), who puts her hat into the proverbial ring for no other reason than to get back at her former lover, who is now dating Paul. The same holds true for Mr. M.'s motivations for encouraging Paul to run, which have much more to do with getting back at Tracy for the unacknowledged role she played in the firing of a fellow teacher (as well as her proclivity to appear in many of Mr. M.'s sexual fantasies) than a true concern for competitive elections. The standard operating procedure when it comes to the elections at Carver High, at least from the perspective of the student body, is that the election is not really necessary—those who are most interested in student governance are the ones already involved in the activity of governance and are, in many ways, rightful heirs to the leadership positions.

This perspective, illustrated by Tracy Flick and by Paul Metzler's reaction to being encouraged to join the race, is not far removed from the understanding of democracy offered by the democratic theory of pluralism. On the flip side, the perspective Jim McAllister pays lip service to is not far removed from the understanding of democracy offered by what is sometimes referred to as the developmental theory of democracy.[10]

One of the major concerns regarding democracy is what role the citizens are to play in governance. Democracy is generally defined as "popular sovereignty"—that is, a type of government in which supreme power is invested in the people. Very few hold that for a country to be considered democratic its citizens must be directly involved in the decision-making of the state, as in the kind of democracy found in ancient Athens. However, just how active citizens need to be in order for a democracy to be considered truly democratic has been and continues to be debated.

From the development perspective, for a nation to be truly democratic, one must see active, sustained, and energetic participation from large portions of the citizenry. The developmental perspective offers a very idealistic view of citizens—that is, not only do citizens have the desire and motivation to be actively involved in decision-making (whether this be through attending town hall meetings, voting, running for office, writing representatives regarding their concerns, etc.), but they also actually have the capacity to be knowledgeable, intelligent, rational actors. Furthermore, the more citizens actively engage in the process of democracy, the more they acquire what John Stuart Mill refers to as civic virtue—that is, the capacity "to look beyond their self-interest to the well-being of all society." Acquiring civic virtue serves as an additional check on an abuse of power, a real concern in any form of government where sovereignty rests with the people.[11]

The developmental theorists argue that as people are more actively involved in civic enterprises, they begin to not only learn the tools needed to be a vibrant democratic participant (compromise, willingness to respect rights of those in the minority, etc.) but also to realize that their own well-being is inextricably linked to that of the community. From this perspective, the more people participate in the democratic process, the stronger that democracy becomes. This is in line with the "habits of the heart" Alexis de Tocqueville discusses in his seminal text, *Democracy in America*. In that text, de Tocqueville addresses his concerns regarding the demise of democracy in America. One concern is that the individualism that is a key component of U.S. political culture will be our downfall. Not that individualism is the motive behind tyranny, but rather that if a despot were to rise up, radical individualism may make us blind to the rise, as our concerns are squarely placed with ourselves and our immediate families rather than seeing how our well-being is in large part connected to the community.

Another potential downfall to democracy in America is our concern with material acquisition. Again, this would be damaging to a democracy not because seeking wealth leads to abuse of power in and of itself, but because being single-minded in terms of improving one's own material standing would take the place of the more civically minded endeavors (voting, volunteering, etc.) that are necessary for the health and vibrancy of a democracy. What serves as a check on the natural instability of a democracy are these civic virtues and habits of the heart acquired through participation.

This is, in part, what makes up the core of the argument Jim McAllister presents to Paul Metzler as he persuades him to enter the presidential race, and it is also the rhetoric he employs in defense of Tammy Metzler's candidate speech at the student assembly. To Paul, Mr. M. not only argues the anti-democratic nature of the noncontested election, but more importantly encourages him to participate because he has a civic obligation to do so . . . not only in order to make the election more democratic, but also to "give something back" to the high school community.

> *Jim:* Paul, what's your favorite fruit?
> *Paul:* Huh? Oh. Uh . . . pears
> *Jim:* Okay, let's say . . .
> *Paul:* No, wait—apples. Apples.
> *Jim:* Let's say all you ever knew was apples. Apples, apples and more apples. You might think apples were pretty good, even if you occasionally got a rotten one. Then one day there's an orange. And now you can make a decision. Do you want an apple, or do you want an orange? That's democracy.
> *Paul:* I also like bananas.

Jim: Exactly. So what do you say? Maybe it's time to give a little
something back.

This scene fits well with the shattering of Paul's own individualistic pur-
suits—sports and popularity. He is searching for the meaning of life—and
perhaps he will find it through civic engagement.

We see the developmental perspective also come out in McAllister's
response to the school principal's desire (played delightfully by Phil Reeves)
to kick "that little bitch" Tammy out of the race after her "speak the truth"
campaign speech at the student assembly. States McAllister: "Walt, we can't
throw her out of the election just because we don't like her speech. That's not
what student government's about." From McAllister's perspective we must
persist with the exercise in democracy even if it in part raises some uncomfortable truths or even threatens to bring about the end of the democratic system
itself (which may happen, if Tammy wins the election, as she has promised to
disband the SGA), because it is through these challenging exercises in civic engagement that students acquire the virtues needed to maintain democracy.

Tracy Flick is a little less idealistic when it comes to notions of civic
virtue and participatory democracy. As noted above, Tracy Flick is all about
the trappings and appearance of the democratic process—the nomination
papers, the campaign signs and buttons, the well-organized campaign
speech (which in fact serves as a model of the well-written speech, not
that far removed from what one has heard on many a real-world campaign
stop). However, when it comes to the point where the process of democracy actually interferes with her destiny to rule, she is no longer a friend of
the process. She calls into question Paul's motivation to run; she questions
whether or not "burn-outs" are indeed "citizen-enough" to sign Tammy's
nomination papers. Likewise, when anger regarding the threat Paul is posing
to her campaign boils to the top, she responds with an egregious violation of
democratic process, ripping down his campaign signs to the sounds (again)
of the war cries, indicating that she adheres to the rules of the game not out
of long-held respect for these rules but rather because she needs the appearance of an untainted process as a cover for her true intention—seizing and
maintaining power. This becomes all the more clear when she lashes out at
Tammy for "confessing" to the crime that Flick herself in fact committed.
Tracy feigns deep harm and demand for retribution from Tammy, knowing
full well that she did not commit the "poster atrocity," because she needs the
process to remain untainted in order to achieve her goals.

How does this relate to the perspective on democracy offered by the pluralist viewpoint? Pluralism is in large part a response to the more idealistic understanding of the role of the citizen within a democracy as outlined above by the developmental model of democracy. While the developmental theorists argue that citizens have the capacity and will to engage in democratic participation frequently and meaningfully and that they should in fact actively engage in the political process, the pluralists argue that such an intense level of participation is neither necessary nor beneficial to the maintenance of democracy. From this perspective, participants in the democratic process are not always the most informed and rational actors.[12] Therefore, to encourage participation just for the sake of participation does not necessarily result in creating more civically minded citizens. On the contrary, participation that is motivated by passion and not reason can result, at best, in drastic and potentially destabilizing shifts in government, and at worst, the election of a demagogue or dictator. For the pluralist, decreased levels of participation in a democracy are not necessarily negative. Lack of participation could very well indicate voter satisfaction with the status quo, and some studies have indicated that even if nonvoters had voted, their participation would not have changed the outcome of the election. This is not to say that pluralism would actively discourage participation (only the harshest critics see pluralism as a cover for elitism, or worse). What is most important is that the electorate has the opportunity to join a political party and/or interest group and to vote. Whether or not the electorate actually takes advantage of this opportunity is much less of a concern to the pluralist.

It is here where we can locate the apparent conflict between Jim McAllister and Tracy Flick—the conflict between the developmental and pluralist theories of democracy. Opportunity for democratic participation alone is not enough for Mr. M.—he wants a more truly democratic process as the foundation for the school election. At the opposite end of the spectrum, opportunity is more than enough for Ms. Flick. Imagine the chaos that would ensue if the voice of the apathetic and disaffected was actually able to shape the policy of Carver High?

This "chaos," however, is in fact the actual result of the election for student body president at Carver High. Even though Tammy Metzler is disqualified due to her claimed responsibility for the torn down posters—a "crime" she did not commit—her name remains on the ballot. And when all the votes are tallied, she is the actual victor of the election—garnering 290 votes (that ultimately must be counted as "disregards") to Tracy's 257 and Paul's 256.

And it is here that we find entry into the irony that anchors all of Payne's films, as well as the irony that anchors much of politics in the United States. The only political message that actually resonates with the students is the message delivered by Tammy Metzler in the student assembly prior to her disqualification. It is really the only truthful political message that any of the candidates actually delivers during the course of the campaign, yet it is a message that neither the candidate is actually willing to make good on nor the institution is willing to tolerate (Tammy jumps at the opportunity to get kicked out of the election, as the ensuing expulsion will expedite her transfer to the all-girl Catholic school of her dreams).

Tammy's message of political truth is that this election really doesn't matter because no one's lives will substantially change as a result of the election. And in another delicious moment of irony, the only person who openly embraces her "radical message" is the very person willing to violate the most fundamental expression of democracy. It is our beloved civics teacher, Mr. M., the champion of competitive election and civic responsibility, that in the end cannot stomach the actual "will of the people," as he tampers with the outcome of the election, crumpling two of the ballots Tracy needs to win the squeaker of an election. Discontent with the outcome of the more substantial workings of democracy (the people ended up picking the rotten apple even though they could actually choose an orange!), Mr. McAllister takes matters into his own hands and robs Tracy of her electoral victory, her destiny.

An act of a true tyrant, indeed, but can you really fault dear Mr. M.? What is wrong with a little tyranny from time to time, as long as that tyrant is benevolent? And perhaps it is unfair to define Mr. M.'s vote tampering as a truly tyrannical act. One wonders whether the United States may be a more equitable and truly democratic place with less Tracy Flick's at the helm. Furthermore, is it not possible that the idealism that underpins the developmental theory of democracy is as equally dangerous as the tyranny expressed in Mr. M.'s vote tampering? The insistence that the will of an active electorate is the stalwart backbone of democracy is clearly much more dangerous than the action of the elite, particularly if the active electorate is uninformed, ill-educated, and unappreciative of the values needed for a functioning democracy (compromise, patience, tolerance of divergent points of view) and the elite is not.

Despite his insistence to the contrary, when it comes down to it, Mr. M. is in fact not much of an adherent to the principles outlined in the developmental theory of democracy. Like Ms. Flick, Mr. McAllister is much more comfortable configuring a democracy along the lines of pluralism—a battle between elites to define the policies of the government. Mr. McAllister has little interest letting the "people" decide who should lead them, particularly when the people make such a poor choice. And much like Tracy Flick, Mr. McAllister allows a role for destiny. Mr. M. sees interfering with Flick's ascendancy to power as just as much a part of his destiny as Flick considers her rise to power to be a part of her own destiny.

But in the end, it is not concerns regarding the substance of democracy that prevail, but the procedure. The vote tampering is revealed. The results of the election are corrected, and beloved Mr. M. is forced into resignation due to his tampering with the democratic process. Ms. Flick moves on to Georgetown and lands a prestigious job as an aide to a U.S. congresswoman (or she at least looks prestigious, cloaked in the ubiquitous blue suit of those in power). Mr. M. moves to New York and is a docent at the Natural History museum, living a life as equally pathetic (and equally unrecognized) as the one lived in beautiful Omaha. In the end, Ms. Flick was right: try to mess with destiny and you will suffer. (In the Tom Perrotta novel that the screenplay for *Election* is adapted from, Mr. M lives in obviously more sufferable conditions, remaining in Omaha working as a used car salesman). Yet, this determinist, defeatist lesson leaves quite a nasty aftertaste in the viewer's mouth. This very well may be Ms. Flick's destiny, but why her? Why is it always that the Tracy Flicks of the world seem to have an unchallengeable grasp on power?

Conclusions on Democracy: Reflection on the Realities and Pondering the Promises

One is left wondering what the moral of the story is. What is the lesson we are to learn about life and democracy from this little tale of a high school election gone awry? Perhaps we can find guidance through an observation made by Samuel Huntington about democracy: "Critics say America is a lie because its reality falls so short of its ideals. They are wrong. America is not a lie; it is a disappointment. But it is a disappointment only because it is also a hope."[13] Political life in a democracy is fraught with disappointment. We find ourselves a part of an electorate that is largely uninformed, at times apathetic, at other times mobilized by damaging passions that find little basis in reason. We are confronted with policymakers and other political leaders that seem to have little concern for the public good yet tremendous interest in power and self-aggrandizement. Campaigns for public office have become an endeavor without end and with little substance. A disappointing scene, indeed. Yet, as Huntington states, we experience American democracy in disappointing terms precisely because of the promises that are at the core of the founding principles of democracy. One can consider the Declaration of Independence as the document that outlines these promises, and we have spent nearly all of the last two and a half centuries trying to make good on these promises, with varying degrees of success. At times these promises are nearly realized. At other times we fall miserably short. And herein lies our capacity to experience profound disappointment and hope.

Notes

1. Paul Fischer, "Payne Goes Sideways and Smells the Wine," *Film Monthly,* October 22, 2004, http://filmmonthly.com (accessed June 12, 2007).

2. David Ansen, "And One for the Road," *Newsweek* (December 16, 2002), 64.

3. Agnes Repplier, as quoted in "Quotations for Use in Civic Education," printed by the Center for Civic Education, Calabasas, Calif., http://www.civiced.org/pdfs/QuotationsCivicEducation.pdf (accessed August 17, 2007).

4. Freedom House, Mission Statement, http://www.freedomhouse.org (accessed August 17, 2007).

5. Robert Dahl, *Democracy and Its Critics* (New Haven, Conn.: Yale Univ. Press, 1989), 177.

6. For just one example of low voter turnout in local primaries, see "Election, What Election?" editorial in the *Milwaukee Journal Sentinel,* February 27, 2006.

7. Statistics on federal voting come from the U.S. Census Bureau, and can be found online at http://www.census.gov/population/www/socdemo/voting.html (accessed March 4, 2008).

8. For a breakdown of voter turnout of specific demographic groups, see American National Elections Studies, found online at http://www.electionstudies.org/nesguide/2ndtable/t6a_2_2.htm (accessed June 6, 2007).

9. All quotes come from the screenplay for *Election,* written by Alexander Payne and Jim Taylor, found at http://www.script-o-rama.com/movie_scripts/e/election-script-screenplay.html (accessed June 6, 2007).

10. For a more complete discussion of these different models of democracy, see William Hudson, *American Democracy in Peril: Eight Challenges to America's Future* (Washington, D.C.: CQ Press, 2006).

11. Hudson, *American Democracy in Peril,* 11.

12. There is much research substantiating just how uninformed the American

electorate is. For a nice summary of recent research on the uniformed electorate, see Ilya Somin, "When Ignorance Isn't Bliss: How Political Ignorance Threatens Democracy," *Policy Analysis,* no. 525 (2004): 1–28.

13. Samuel Huntington, *American Politics: The Promise of Disharmony* (Cambridge, Mass.: Harvard Univ. Press, 1981), 262.

Afterword

POPULAR CULTURE, POLITICAL PUNDITRY, AND THE BIRTH OF THE PRESIDENTIAL COOL

Joseph J. Foy

There are numerous ways, as evidenced throughout this volume, that popular culture has become inextricably linked to politics and governance in the United States. Since the first edition of this book was published, the case for the importance of popular culture in helping us to understand politics has become even stronger. The 2008 elections, and the political atmosphere that followed, demonstrate just how pervasive and important popular culture has become in directing and shaping an understanding of institutions, actors, and events.

First, it is clear that popular culture is a means through which individuals can make connections between current events and an established frame of reference. Examples of this abound. In a September 17, 2008, column, *New York Times* correspondent Roger Cohen used the lyrics from Coldplay's megahit "Viva la Vida" to redefine perceptions of Wall Street and problems of private gain eclipsing the public good following the market implosion in the United States. Beginning with the lyrics: "I used to rule the world / Seas would rise when I gave the word / Now in the morning I sleep alone / Sweep the streets I used to own," Cohen describes the pervasive culture of power in top firms that led to unchecked risk taking ("I used to roll the dice / See the fear in my enemies' eyes"). However, the gamble was too much in the end, and everyone paid for it. Cohen sees this major market collapse as the death of the "me-culture" that can usher in a new era of progressive politics with an eye on the public good, and he issues a call to America to rediscover the public sphere—all summed up in a pop song: "Now the old king is dead! Long live the king!"

Popular music was not the only avenue for understanding and coming to terms with the financial crisis in the United States. In the twelfth episode of its twentieth season, *The Simpsons* also took on the lending and mortgage crisis. Entitled "No Loan Again, Naturally," which originally aired on March 8, 2009, this episode finds the Simpsons having their home foreclosed on after Homer takes out a home equity line of credit to pay for the family's extravagant annual Mardi Gras party (Homer even calls his house a "sucker" for getting stuck with the bill). The brilliance of this show lay in the ability of writer Jeff Westbrook to capture the multiplicity of factors behind the mortgage crisis. On one hand, Homer is clearly to blame for not understanding the implications of the balloon repayment schedule of his home loan, but, on the other, so is "Countryfine: The Lemonade and Mortgage Company" for misleading him and playing on his ignorance, knowingly giving him a loan that he couldn't repay. And where were the regulations, either internal or imposed by the government, to protect the consumer or prevent the lending agency from floating a loan to someone who would not likely have the financial means to pay it back? In the end, it is Ned Flanders who has to save the Simpsons from being turned out of their home—not government, not the banks, but a private citizen who bears the brunt of this multilayered crisis.

Apart from the financial collapse, popular culture has been used as the basis for helping people come to terms with other political realities. Perhaps most interesting is that popular culture provides the starting point for understanding its own role in the public sphere. For example, when it was released in 1957, Budd Schulberg and Elia Kazan's classic film *A Face in the Crowd* received high praise for Andy Griffith's energetic and uncharacteristic portrayal of Lonesome Rhodes—a guitar-playing drifter whose witty, down-home folkisms make him an instant celebrity. Broadly speaking, the film provides a cynical exposure of the power of media and celebrity to transform democracy into demagoguery. With scenes that have Rhodes coaching a U.S. senator on what the American people want ("Politics have entered a new stage: television. Instead of longwinded public debates, the people want slogans. 'Time for a change!' 'The mess in Washington!' 'More bang for a buck!' Punch lines and glamour!"), and one of Rhodes's handlers declaring "that in TV we have the greatest instrument for mass persuasion in the history of the world," *A Face in the Crowd* has become a classic look into the interplay of mass media and democratic politics.

Of course, the reviews at the time of the film's release were not without criticism. The primary critiques of the film were reserved for "the suggestion that popularity as an entertainer carries with it the capacity to influence public opinion," something that film critic Moira Walsh, who wrote those words in the June 15, 1957, edition of *America: The National Catholic Weekly Review,* went on to describe as a "dubious premise at best." Walsh's review joined *New York Times* film critic Bosley Crowther's assessment that Rhodes's style of demagoguery "would either have become harmless habit or the public would have been finished with him." Put simply, in 1957 it seemed almost unthinkable that folksy bromides expressed by a popular entertainer might somehow have the power to shape how the public thought about the political.

Fast-forward fifty years to 2007, a year the A. C. Nielsen Company estimates that 99 percent of American households have at least one television (with the average household possessing 2.24), and the average American watches an estimated four hours of television each day, for a total of 250 billion hours viewed by Americans annually. Certainly these numbers are staggering and on their own are enough to give us pause. However, the Pew Research Center released a study on July 30, 2006 that further examines these trends across a variety of media. The Pew studies revealed that while only 24 percent of people aged eighteen to twenty-nine "read a newspaper yesterday," 40 percent "watched a movie" and 28 percent "played a video game." Among the same age group, 49 percent "watched TV news yesterday," while 61 percent "watched non-news television," and although 62 percent "went online yesterday," only 24 percent reported "getting news online yesterday."[1]

It is within the context of these trends that David Haven Blake, whose work on democracy and fame in the television age led him to reexamine the film, writes in an article for TomPaine.com that *A Face in the Crowd* "was astonishingly prophetic in understanding the role that television would play in shaping political campaigns." Blake argues that if we are to look around us "we find [Rhodes's] DNA in the long tradition of media personalities who have tried to identify themselves with populist power—Pat Robertson, Jesse Ventura, Arnold Schwarzenegger, Rush Limbaugh and his 'ditto-heads' among them."[2] Far from being a dubious premise, *A Face in the Crowd* seems to have tapped into the awesome power of media and celebrity and popular culture wield over democracy.

What is notable about *A Face in the Crowd* is that scholars like Blake recommend using this movie as a means of understanding the role modern media personalities play in shaping the national dialogue and of evaluating the impact mass media and celebrity influence has on contemporary democratic discussion. We can understand this phenomenon best by having the story laid out for us in its entirety in a movie. For example, he references radio talk-show host Rush Limbaugh, a college dropout who began his career not as a political analyst but rather as a radio disc jockey and promoter for the Kansas City Royals and perhaps best epitomizes the "king-maker" power wielded by Lonesome Rhodes. Like Rhodes, Limbaugh is an entertainer, not a professional analyst or a politician. However, in 1994 he was awarded with an honorary position in the Republican Party's U.S. House of Representatives caucus for his role in helping usher in the "Republican Revolution."

Also, like Rhodes, Limbaugh has developed a considerable media empire that conveys an incredible amount of political power. According to results released by *Talkers Magazine* in 2007, *The Rush Limbaugh Show,* which runs for three hours a day Monday through Friday, is heard by at least 13.5 million listeners each week. The significant amount of influence Limbaugh wields over his primarily conservative listeners was revealed in 2009 when White House chief of staff Rahm Emanuel described Limbaugh as the voice representing the Republican Party and Republican National Committee chair Michael Steele was forced to call Limbaugh and apologize for dismissing his influence and criticizing his inflammatory entertainment as being "ugly," lest he face the continued ire of Limbaugh and his listeners. The notion that a popular talk show host could wield such a significant amount of political power may come as a surprise to some. For scholars like Blake, however, the Limbaugh's political power and his impact on American democracy should come as no surprise; his story was told through film by Schulberg and Kazan in 1957.

In the music of Coldplay, the satire of *The Simpsons,* and the social criticism of the film *A Face in the Crowd,* we see ways popular culture can help audiences interpret contemporary politics through an established frame of reference. Most important, though, the 2008 elections demonstrate how pop culture is shaping the way people—in particular youth voters—are presented with the core controversies and candidates being presented to them. By embracing entertainment talk shows and comedy programs, utilizing e-media like social networking sites and text messaging, transforming hip-hop music into direct political advocacy, and employing viral Internet messaging strategies, campaigns in 2008 helped drive an estimated 22 to 24 million young people to the polls, an increase of at least 2.2 million over 2004. Popular culture has become an effective tool of tapping into traditionally disinterested and disaffected audiences and reawakening them to the political.

Of course, 2008 is not the first election cycle in which we see popular culture playing a role in shaping how people understand campaigns and candidates. Marked by the four-second appearance of Richard Nixon on *Rowan & Martin's Laugh-In*, where he, seemingly confused by the premise, awkwardly uttered the phrase "sock it to me," modern campaign politics seems to be dominated by appearances of candidates and aspirant hopefuls on comedy programs and late night talk shows. In June 1992, while campaigning for the presidency, Bill Clinton made his famous guest appearance on *The Arsenio Hall Show,* wearing sunglasses and blowing strains of "Heartbreak Hotel" on his saxophone. After his famous "yowl" on the 2004 campaign trail, Howard Dean appeared on *Late Night with David Letterman* to perform a "Top Ten" list that included him "switching to decaf."

Following in this bourgeoning tradition of politicians making inroads with voters through entertainment programming, Sarah Palin, the Republican nominee for vice president, made an appearance on *Saturday Night Live* on October 18, 2008, that resulted in the show's highest ratings in fourteen years (more than 14 million viewers). Palin's appearance garnered over 2 million more viewers than the head of the Republican ticket, Senator John McCain, who appeared on *SNL* just before the election to joke about being a "true maverick—a Republican without any money." On the Democratic side, both Barack Obama and Hillary Clinton made appearances on *SNL* during their primary bids, and entertainment talk show hosts from Jay Leno and David Letterman to Jon Stewart and Stephen Colbert chatted with candidates from both parties all trying to reach out to the moderate and undecided voters who were no longer picking up daily newspapers or tuning in regularly to network television news.

Like entertainment media providing connections between voters and politicians, the way mass media and the tools of popular culture help reach audiences that are composed of the mainstream electorate also find roots much earlier than 2008. In 1952, addressing the power of television and the appropriation of popular entertainment for campaigns and elections, Adlai Stevenson famously mocked his rival, Dwight Eisenhower, by commenting on his use of TV ads, sloganeering, and jingles: "I think the American people will be shocked by such contempt for their intelligence. This isn't Ivory

Soap versus Palmolive." Never capturing the importance of these strategies as a tool to direct public opinion, Stevenson was summarily defeated by Eisenhower—he was only able to garner eighty-nine votes in the Electoral College. Likewise, in the 1960 presidential debate between John F. Kennedy and Richard Nixon, the power of campaigns that understand how to use mass media became readily apparent. Whereas Kennedy's team grasped the importance of image as it was being conveyed through television, thereby making sure that Kennedy wore makeup and spoke directly into the camera to make it seem as though he were talking directly to people in their living rooms, Nixon wore nothing but a five o'clock shadow, and his eyes darted across the studio audience, adding to the perceptions of viewers at home that he was "shifty" and not to be trusted. Stevenson's prediction that Americans would never be so easily persuaded by the use of television to convey catchy slogans and campaign songs quickly gave way to the far more accurate prediction by his aide, George Ball, who offered what was at the time meant to be a cynical slam on celebrity-style strategies: "Presidential campaigns will eventually have professional actors as candidates."[3]

What made the 2008 election such a definitive one for realizing the importance of the interplay between politics and popular culture was not, therefore, that popular culture and mass media influenced the way people were thinking about candidates and issues, but instead how utterly immersed the election became in popular culture. This is perhaps due to the fact that no other campaign team in American history has so effectively wielded the tools of popular culture as a means of making connections into the American voting public—especially among youth voters—than Barack Obama's in 2008. Utilizing social networking sites like Facebook and MySpace, buying advertising space in popular video games, employing e-mail and text messaging to communicate with supporters, playing basketball with the North Carolina Tar Heels during practice, and gaining endorsements from celebrity power brokers like Oprah Winfrey, George Clooney, Samuel L. Jackson, Chris Rock, Jennifer Aniston, and Scarlett Johansson, the Obama campaign tapped into popular culture so as to make in-roads with traditionally disinterested and disaffected voters. Moreover, popular culture seemed to take on a life of its own surrounding the Obama campaign. Hip-hop artist will.i.am of the Black Eyed Peas recorded two songs based on speeches delivered by Obama during the campaign, "Yes We Can" and "We Are the Ones," which went viral on Internet media forums like YouTube. Michelle Obama's fashion choices began being replicated and mimicked by mainstream designers to meet consumer demands for the "Michelle look," and people could have photos of themselves transformed into the iconic red, white, and blue image of Obama's "Hope" campaign posters on the website "Obamaicon.Me."

Obama's embracing of popular culture did not end with the conclusion of his campaign. Celebrity artists—including U2, Stevie Wonder, and Beyonce—gathered to begin the historic inauguration of America's first African American president, and *Ebony Magazine* recently named Obama among Jay-Z, Marvin Gaye, and Muhammad Ali as one of the "Top 25 Coolest Brothers of All Time." Obama seems to have embraced, and been embraced by, the image of what CNN.com called as "Presidential Cool," referring to the ubiquitous Obama t-shirts, posters, hats, and paraphernalia adorning so many Americans even after the election. Not only does his team continue to use social networking sites and e-mail and text and Twitter to communicate with people in the United States, he has engaged in pop diplomacy notably by, during his first diplomatic visit to England, giving Queen Elizabeth II an iPod filled with videos and music.

Although some may bristle at the degree to which America's forty-fourth president seems to be wrapped up in popular culture, his use of such tools helped him capture 52.9 percent of the vote, winning 365 votes in the Electoral College. His victory, propelled in part by minority and youth voter turnout, speaks to the success of Obama as a candidate but also to the degree he was able to utilize the tools of pop culture to increase engagement. Turnout among American youth aged eighteen to twenty-nine was up nearly 9 percent from 2004, with the number of voters under thirty in 2008 reaching 51 percent—the third highest turnout for young people in American history. Moreover, Barack Obama won 66 percent of the youth vote, as opposed to the 31 percent received by John McCain. Looking to the future, the democratic effect of effectively employing popular media is something that carries with it the promise and hope of revitalization of a more civically engaged America through the promotion of greater inroads with the American youth.[4]

For a democracy to successfully meet its purpose of providing the lion's share of governance power to the people, it is essential for the people to feel a sense of connectedness to politics, governmental actors and institutions, as well as political events. Popular culture not only serves as a basis for establishing those connections, it can be used to inspire mobilization and action. As scholars, students of politics, or those just interested in understanding the political forces that influence and direct so many aspects of our lives, it is critical that we continue to explore and examine the role popular culture plays in politics. Only by understanding the importance of entertainment and culture produced for consumption by the masses can we truly comprehend this government of, for, and by the people.

Notes

1. See "Nielsen Reports 1.1% Increase in U.S. Television Households for the 2006-2007 Season," *Nielsen Media Research* (August 23, 2006), http://en-us.nielsen.com/tab/industries/media# (accessed October 20, 2009). Norman Herr confirms that number reporting that approximately 99 percent of all households have at least one television set, and the average number of sets in the typical American household is 2.24. Herr, "Television and Health," *Sourcebook for Teaching Science* (May 20, 2007), http://www.csun.edu/science/health/docs/tv&health.html (accessed October 20, 2009)

2. David Haven Blake, "Prophetic Face in the Crowd," *TomPaine.com* (November 1, 2007), http://www.tompaine.com/articles/2007/11/01/prophetic_face_in_the_crowd.php (accessed October 20, 2009).

3. Museum of the Moving Image, "Eisenhower vs. Stevenson 1952," *The Living Room Candidate: Presidential Campaign Commercials from 1952-2008*, http://www.livingroomcandidate.org/commercials/1952 (accessed October 20, 2009).

4. George Pillsbury, Julian Johannesen, and Rachel Adams, *America Goes to the Polls: A Report on Voter Turnout in the 2008 Election*, Nonprofit Voter Engagement Network, http://www.nonprofitvote.org/voterturnout2008 (accessed October 20, 2009).

CONTRIBUTORS

GREG AHRENHOERSTER earned his M.A. and Ph.D. at the University of Wisconsin–Milwaukee, where his research focused on sports references in twentieth-century American fiction. Currently serving as an associate professor of English at the University of Wisconsin–Waukesha, Ahrenhoerster has published several chapters and articles focusing on sports and literature.

MANDI BATES BAILEY is assistant professor of political science at Valdosta State University. She received her Ph.D. from the University of Kentucky in 2007. Her dissertation, entitled *Race or Place? The Impact of News Depictions of Urban and Rural Poverty*, examines the news media's role in shaping attitudes toward welfare. Her research has appeared in the *American Review of Politics*.

J. MICHAEL BITZER is assistant professor and chair of the Department of History and Politics at Catawba College in Salisbury, N.C. Bitzer, who holds a doctorate in political science from the University of Georgia's School of Public and International Affairs, teaches courses in American politics, public administration and policy, and law. He also has taught the course "Society and *The Simpsons*" for Catawba's freshman seminar program, in which students are introduced to the role of satire as social commentary about American politics, religion, culture, and even donuts. Bitzer's research focuses on southern politics, U.S. campaigns and elections, and twentieth-century U.S. political and legal history.

CHRISTOPHER A. COOPER is assistant professor of political science and public affairs at Western Carolina University, where he teaches classes and conducts research on various aspects of American politics. He also serves as the department's Master of Public Affairs director and is a faculty fellow at the Center for Regional Development, where he works on applied research, surveys, and data analysis. He has had over a dozen articles published in a variety of journals, ranging from the *American Review of Politics* to *State Politics and Policy Quarterly*, and has contributed chapters to several edited volumes in political science.

TIMOTHY DUNN is assistant professor of philosophy at the University of Wisconsin–Waukesha. He is the author of "The Value of Solidarity" (*Southwestern Journal of Philosophy*, 2005) and coauthor of "Moral Musings on a Cigarette Smoking Man" in the edited collection *The Philosophy of* The X-Files (2007). He earned his Ph.D. from Rice University, and his research interests include ethics, egoism, and social/ political philosophy.

DICK FLANNERY is professor of political science at the University of Wisconsin Colleges. He received his B.A. at Syracuse University, and his M.A. and Ph.D. at the University of Wisconsin in Madison. He was most recently published in *The Philosophy of* The X-Files (2007) and is the coauthor of *The Good Life* (1990).

JOSEPH J. FOY is assistant professor of political science at the University of Wisconsin–Waukesha. Having earned his Ph.D. at the University of Notre Dame, Foy also served as a Manatt Fellow for Democracy Studies at the International Foundation for Election Systems. He is a contributing author to *The Philosophy of* The X-Files (2007), *The Executive Branch of State Government* (2006), and *Steven Spielberg and Philosophy*. His current research interests include the ethics and logic of power, democracy studies, and the politics of popular culture.

JOHN GRUMMEL is assistant professor of political science at Upper Iowa University. He is coauthor of several articles, including "Revisiting the Racial Threat Hypothesis—Voter Support for California's Proposition 209" (*State Politics and Policy Quarterly*, 2003) and "The Effects of Ballot Initiatives on Voter Turnout in the American States" (*American Politics Research*, 2001). Current research interests include voter participation, political communication, and political culture.

MARGARET HANKENSON is associate professor and department chair of political science at the University of Wisconsin Colleges, having received her Ph.D. at Purdue University. She has recently presented research on the reinvigoration of adversarial journalism post-Katrina, and her research interests include media and politics, postmodern political theory, and American political culture.

JENNIFER J. HORA is assistant professor of political science at Valparaiso University, where she teaches courses on American institutions. She obtained her Ph.D. at the University of North Carolina at Chapel Hill. She has published in *Presidential Studies Quarterly* and *The Executive Branch of State Government* (2006). Her research interests include executive politics and presidential persuasion. In particular she focuses on the interaction between the executive and legislative branches during the Johnson and Nixon presidencies.

CRAIG W. HURST is chair of the Music Department of the University of Wisconsin Colleges and professor of music at the University of Wisconsin–Waukesha. At UW-Waukesha, Dr. Hurst directs the symphonic band and jazz ensemble and teaches a variety of general education fine arts, ethnic studies, and interdisciplinary music courses. Hurst holds degrees from Boise State University (B.M.), North Texas State University (M.M.E.), and the University of North Texas (Ph.D.).

DEAN A. KOWALSKI is associate professor of philosophy at the University of Wisconsin–Waukesha. Dean has written a number of chapters exploring the philosophy of popular culture, from James Bond to *Goodfellas,* and is the editor of *The Philosophy of* The X-Files (2007). He also authored *Classic Questions and Contemporary Film: An Introduction to Philosophy* (2004) and a handful of articles on the freedom and foreknowledge problem, including "Some Friendly Molinist Amendments" (*Philosophy and Theology,* 2003) and "On Behalf of a Suarezian Middle Knowledge" (*Philosophia Christi,* 2003). His most recent research interests include exploring various meta-ethical relationships between ethics and religion.

KRISTI NELSON FOY earned her B.A., magna cum laude, at the University of Notre Dame in political science, and went on to receive her J.D. at Duke University School of Law. Since graduating, Kristi has entered the legal profession as a member of the Labor Relations and Employment Practice Group at the law firm of Michael Best and Friedrich in Milwaukee, Wisconsin, and is a member in good standing of the American Bar Association and the State Bar of Wisconsin. While practicing law, Kristi has authored a number of legal articles, including "When Is Unequal Pay Okay?" "New Minimums for Minimum Wage Laws: Recent City, State and Federal Challenges to $5.15/hour," "Religious Expression at Work: Careful Compromise," and "Hesitate Before You Terminate: Simple Steps to Help Ensure that a Temporary Employee Does Not Become a Long Term Liability."

BRETT S. SHARP is associate professor of political science and director of leadership studies at the University of Central Oklahoma. He has published in several scholarly journals, such as *American Review of Public Administration* and *Review of Public Personnel Administration.* He recently received the Faculty Member of the Year Award from his college, as well as numerous other awards for teaching and scholarship. He teaches the innovative course *Music in American Politics* and has presented at numerous professional conferences in such areas as "Teaching with the iPod" and "Music as a Pedagogical Tool for Teaching American Politics."

NATHAN ZOOK is assistant professor of political science at Montgomery College in Rockville, Maryland. He received his doctorate in political science at Indiana University for his research on domestic groups in the foreign policy realm. He enjoys lecturing on taboo subjects such as religion and politics and developed a course on terrorism prior to September 11. His most recent research involves analysis of faith-based nongovernmental organizations seeking to influence U.S.-Israeli policy.

INDEX

Page numbers in italics refer to illustrations and captions.

Kinsley, Michael, 181
Klein, Chris, 234
Kool and the Gang, 210
Koppel, Ted, 50
Korematsu v. United States (1944), 100
Krauthammer, Charles, 175–76, 181, 183
Kurtz, Howard, 138

Lampell, Millard, 226
Langella, Frank, 152
Larby, Ahmed Ben, 189
Late Show with David Letterman, 5, 137, 146
Lauper, Cyndi, 210
Law and Order, 97–98, *101*, 102, 106, 108, 113
law of nature, 22, 29
Leary, Denis, 157
Ledbetter, Huddie "Leadbelly," 226
Lee, Harper, 104,
Lee, Spike, 1
legislative branch, 5, 35, 42, 63–64, 66, 67, 77, 92
   benefits, 120
   See also Congress
Lennon, John, 202–3
Leno, Jay, 5, 137, 142, 146
Leviathan, The (Hobbes), 21
Lewinsky, Monica, 92
Lewis, Huey, 210
liberal arts education, 9, 13
liberalism, in American politics, 50, 161, 213
libertarianism, 117–18, 123, 130, 195
liberty. *See* freedom
Library of Congress, 220, 226
Lieberman, Joseph, 138
Lightfoot, Gordon, 209
Lilith Fair, 231
Limbaugh, Rush, 161, 171
Lincoln, Abraham, 70

Lindh, John Walker, 218
Lippmann, Walter, 43
Lipset, Seymour Martin, 44, 54
"Little Red Songbook" (*The IWW Songs*), 221
Live Aid, 210
Live Earth, 208, 211
Live 8, 210
Lloyd, David, 19, 21, 37n1, 38n11, 39n18
lobbying, 63–65, 74, 77, 120–22, 124
Locke, John, 4, 19–20, 29–32, 34–36, 38–39nn15–18, 40n27, 130
Loggins, Kenny, 210
Lomax, Alan, 219, 225–27
Lomax, Bess, 226
Lomax, John, 225
Louiso, Todd, 121
Louzecky, Dave, 159
low culture. *See* popular culture
Lowe, Rob, 82, 122
Luban, David, 183, 184n13

Macbeth (Shakespeare), 10
Madison, James, 118–19, 127, 130, 155–56
Maines, Natalie, 207
Mamet, David, 157
Man of the Year (2006), 129
Manson, Charles, 118
manufacturing uncertainty, 124
Marsan, Eddie, 24
Marshall, Jerilyn, 12
Matrix, The (1999), 19
Mauer, Marc, 112
Mayer, Jane, 172
Mayer, John, 207
McBride, Allan, 44
McCain, John, 138, 143–44, 180
McCarn, Dave, 223
McCarthy, James, 125